FOLKLORE OF AN ISLAND
MALTESE THRESHOLD CUSTOMS

TARCISIO ZARB

FOLKLORE OF AN ISLAND
MALTESE THRESHOLD CUSTOMS

Publishers Enterprises Group (PEG) Ltd

Published by
Publishers Enterprises Group (PEG) Ltd
PEG Building, UB7 Industrial Estate,
San Gwann SGN 09, Malta

First published 1998

ISBN: 99909-0-097-3

Printed in Malta by P.E.G. Ltd, San Gwann

*To our forefathers,
with gratitude and affection.*

CONTENTS

PREFACE

This book attempts to explain the structure of certain threshold customs of taboo character which the Maltese have built in the past and which they are still developing through the never-ending contacts and interactions with other peoples and life itself. I have tried to avoid extremes as much as possible that is uncritical credulity on the one hand and absolute scepticism, equally unconnected with evidence, on the other.

Some people may regard such a subject as a tangled mass of trivialities. Personally I regard it as a vital part of the human experience and an important sector of the study of man. All the information gathered tells us something about men who, consciously or unconsciously, have some 'magical ideas' embedded in their minds.

Throughout my research work I have tried to educe the reasons behind what may at first sight appear as trivialities because, idiotic as they may appear, they are certainly not random and senseless but the product of experience and the social interaction of people.

I have tried to avoid building up an encyclopaedia of behavioural patterns, without giving the relevant information and advancing hypotheses about these behavioural patterns. However, in order to substantiate the relevant anthropological data by the information gathered, I have had to reproduce full quotations from the interviews I conducted with elderly people. I have also attempted to give a critical evaluation of the information obtained. This, I hope, could lead to further research on the subject from other angles, or to an expansion of it.[1]

In the faithful rendering into English of these extracts from my interviews, I adopted the method used by Mr J. Cassar Pullicino and Prof. J. Aquilina in their various folkloristic and linguistic works.[2] In their translations these authors, while being literal, tried to reproduce the intrinsic semantic connotations.

Research conducted in the field of taboo offers a great challenge to the research worker. The reasons are varied and different. The author's own taboos tend to restrict his fieldwork. Apart from this, he himself might not be conscious of certain taboo issues present in his social and cultural environments because of his limited vision, owing to lack of objectivity in his selection process. Perhaps this is the greatest hindrance a fieldworker has to face in collecting material for a book on taboos.

On the other hand, fieldwork needs informants, who are

---

1. Most of the tape-recorded interviews, which include the majority of the quotations in this book, are to be found in the archives of the Public Broadcasting Services.
2. See, for example, J. Cassar Pullicino, *Studies in Maltese Folklore*. See also J. Aquilina, *A Comparative Dictionary*.

often themselves carriers of the taboos to be investigated. These informants, on their part, tend to be so greatly attached to their beliefs, and consequently so 'taboo-minded', that they are most reluctant to give information. Questions put to them on such issues tend to be embarrasing for various reasons. They are concerned with certain attitudes and behavioural patterns which are socially disapproved of, or which belong to the private world of the individual. Sometimes such questions would require an answer of 'low prestige' and the investigator must keep in mind that his informants may be rather sensitive in these matters.

The informants who helped the author with the necessary case material for this thesis ranged from old men and women to young boys and girls. The author used the direct method for getting the information, as already hinted at earlier on in this preface. This was later on transcribed verbatim and carefully analysed. At the same time the author was constantly on the lookout for behavioural patterns which fall under this field of study in the social and cultural environments in which he found himself. Daily newspapers, magazines, periodicals, and detailed studies on the subject (although these are almost non-existent as far as the taboo aspect is concerned) also helped a great deal in the building up of this book.

In order to get as much material as possible from 'taboo-minded' informants, the social investigator must first establish a good relationship with his informant. Only then can the investigator proceed to ask the difficult questions, on account of the delicacy of the subject in question. The best way to reach such a point in the discussion is to begin by talking on some thing in general without trying to go straight to the subject. In spite of this some informants tend to be most adamant in their taboos. These informants must be disregarded, although their very unwillingness to impart any knowledge whatsoever might help to provide indirect information about taboos, which might be of great help. The presence of young children, and sometimes even of third parties, might hinder the interview considerably. A guarantee of anonymity will help a great deal.

Middle-aged people tend to be the best informants with regard to the taboos of the past. Their answers usually take the form of a contrast between the mentality prevalent in their young days on the one hand and their present mode of thinking on the other – which in turn still holds a little back from general modern trends which they call 'civilization'. The information given by elderly informants, however, is of greater interest from the 'folkloristic' point of view as regards the exposition of facts, manners of speech, narrative style, and innuendos. On the other hand, children, together with young people and intimate friends, give any information they may have with 'pleasure'.

Most of my informants are representative of a whole cross-section of Malta's different social classes, with the majority of them coming from the humble classes and from rural communities. By and large, the informants on whose information this book is based are over 70. Strictly speaking, therefore, this book, rather than being a mirror of our present generation, reflects more correctly past modes of behaviour which are still lingering on in the minds of our elderly generation. I have also made use of information given *en passant* during informal questioning of students whose ages vary from 12 to 15. This questioning was made during classroom lessons, in a private and a government secondary school.

I have classified the results of fieldwork spread over a period of three years according to the principal crises of man's life, namely, birth, puberty, marriage, and death, which are the main transitional periods of human existence. A separate chapter deals with the various taboos connected with various days of the year and unusual happenings.

Finally I would like to acknowledge the help of Mr J. Pace, B.A.(Hons.), M.A. and Mr Louis J. Scerri, B.A.(Hons.), M.A., for diligently reading the bulk of the text and also for making most helpful comments; Mr Tony Terribile, Miss D. Ellul and P.E.G. Ltd for the photographs; Mr Philip Xuereb, B.A.(Hons.) for his help and support when he was a producer with the Rediffusion Group of Companies; Mr J. Cassar Pullicino, the leading folklorist on the island, for his encouragement and inspiration; and all those informants, and other helpers, who are many, without whose help this book would have been impossible.

TARCISIO ZARB
Hal Kirkop, Malta
15.05.97

INTRODUCTION

Dealing with taboo involves taking many problems into consideration. The word *'taboo'* is open to different interpretations depending on the sociological context in which it is used. The passage of the word 'taboo' from Polynesia to Europe means the passage of this verbal item from one specific context to another which is totally different. Change in meaning is, therefore, sure to happen.

Various scholars have given different interpretations to the word because they have studied taboo from different angles. The taboo theories of Freud, Levy-Bruhl, Frazer, and others offer various interpretations of taboo, some of which prove to be very useful. Still, there is much controversy about the word and no clear definition has as yet been agreed upon.

Taboo in Polynesia

The word *'taboo'* comes from the Polynesian archipelago. It was introduced into Europe by Captain Cook who first met the word in 1777 at Tonga. During his visits to the islands of the Pacific Ocean, Cook found that the word 'tabu', sometimes spelt 'tapu' or 'kapu' according to the locality visited, was in common use. He gave a clear and consistent account of the notion involved, stating that *tabu* has 'a very comprehensive meaning, but in general signifies that a thing is forbidden, being applied to all cases where things are not to be touched'.[1] He also emphasized its 'mysterious significance' and duly noted 'the mixture of religion in a certain ceremony concerning which we seldom got any other answer to our inquiries but taboo'.[2] His observations, written during his brief visits to the islands, are the 'classic' passages which made the word known to Europeans.

Captain James King, who in 1779 took over after Cook's death and continued the narrative of the voyage, also makes reference to taboo among the Sandwich islanders. He states that this word could be applied to both persons and things and that it was also used to denote anything 'sacred, or eminent, or devoted'.[3] King was impressed by the 'most implicit and scrupulous obedience'[4] of the natives with regard to the prohibitions laid upon them, but he could not decide whether this was on any principle of religion or merely in deference to the civil authority of their chiefs. Elsewhere, however, he describes taboo as a kind of 'religious interdiction'.

In its social aspects taboo refers to this system of prohibitions as observed in certain customs and sometimes

---

1. *Encyclopaedia of Religion and Ethics*, Vol. 12.
2. Ibid.
3. Ibid.
4. Ibid.

developing, as in the case of the natives of the Polynesian Archipelago and other peoples, into an institution. Objects forbidden are as numerous and varied as human experience, for any person, thing, act, situation, and so on may be considered so dangerous that meddling with it recoils upon the person concerned. Caution is required in dealing with such objects because the danger with which they are invested is such that it can never be explained. It is always assumed. Hence in Polynesia what was *tabu* must be handled with care; what was *noa* (the opposite of taboo, which means 'the profane, the familiar, the everyday' – a word which failed to enter our vocabulary) could be handled with impunity.[5]

The word 'taboo' gained currency in European languages in the nineteenth century. At that time it was understood to rise from an inferior mentality and that it was characteristic of 'primitive' tribes who were in ignorance of the environment surrounding them.

Definition of Taboo

It is not easy to find an all-inclusive definition bearing the manifold and often divergent manifestations of taboo. Franz Steiner has warned against looking for such a definition and he merely suggested that taboo 'is an element of all those situations in which attitudes to values are expressed in terms of danger behaviour'[6] and proceeds to say that 'we cannot see all this in terms of a single problem, whether we solve it or leave it unsolved'. This happens because 'several quite

5. Ibid.
6. F. Steiner, *Taboo*, 21

different things have been and still are being discussed under the heading taboo'.[7] Therefore, although attempts have been made to narrow the definition of taboo, no such definition exists because of the very nature of taboo itself.

Steiner's statement regarding the complexity of taboo can be immediately corroborated by any research worker who carries out scientific work in this field.

The vast anthropological literature dealing with belief systems of various tribal communities shows that the ritual behaviour which characterizes various crises points in their lives has its counterpart in our society. However, the corresponding beliefs in non-literate societies are taken far more seriously and are socially of much greater significance.

The term 'taboo', when applied to the customs of non-literate peoples, may be defined as 'prohibition against certain kinds of behaviour, violation of which is believed to be punished automatically or by supernatural means'. The condemnation by a divinity of disapproved behaviour is still to be found in certain behavioural patterns of our own society.

The term is also largely connected with the sanctity and ritual interdictions connected with things, sacred or unclean, but the term is also sometimes used to include anything forbidden or improper. The influence of religious or quasi-religious beliefs is far stronger in 'primitive' than in 'civilized' societies although some idea equivalent to taboo is universal.

This book attempts to record those behavioural patterns, which, although they do have the social significance they had in past years, are still to be found with varying degrees of power among various people. On the other hand, I have

---

7. Ibid., 20.

tried to couple this information with behavioural patterns which still carry a social meaning and have a social role in our Maltese context, although not to the same extent of, say, a decade ago. I have tried to avoid dealing with the more complicated level of taboos, which, although they are basically taboos, are too important and intrinsic a part of our religion and social structure.

In other words, my definition of taboo is related to those beliefs that have to do with pollution, avoidance, and danger and which have no foundation in either Canon Law and Civil Law. This has allowed me to examine a whole range of modes of behaviour that are apparently not rational and not explicable in terms of law. Here, however, we find behaviour that figures as it were in popular law, since the transition from what people believe to what is established by law is sometimes very gradual.

Such a thesis might be conducted along various lines, as the following quotation shows:

An inquiry of this sort might be conducted along various lines: ethnographically, by an effort to trace the diffusion of taboos; or historically, by a search for the contacts between peoples which may explain this diffusion; or psychologically, by the attempt to formulate ideas underlying the system of taboo in its many ramifications. I have not wholly neglected these various approaches to this subject, but my concern has been to show or try to show how important a place taboos held in the cultural evolution of mankind.[8]

In this book I have not set out to add any ideas whatsoever to the literature of taboo when approached along any of these lines; my aim was rather to gather and analyse those

---

8. H. Webster, *Taboo – A Sociological Study*, 5.

behavioural patterns which have taboo significance in the Maltese context.

The following definitions have, in one way or another, helped me to form my own understanding of 'taboo' in the context of this book:

A negative sanction, that is, a prohibition against certain acts whose infringement is believed to result in an automatic penalty usually sickness or death, without human mediation. Sanctions of this kind requiring ceremonies of purification and of confession are to be distinguished from customs, conventions, social rules, or restrictions based upon fear of social pressures or of the consequences of ill luck.[9]

A prohibition instituted for the protection of a cultural group or as a safeguard against supernatural reprisal.[10]

A system of religious and social interdiction and prohibition, the most famous and fundamental of the social institutions of Polynesia. The concept and observance, however, are common among most primitive peoples. Tabu sets apart a person, thing, place, name (sometimes even the distinctive syllable of a name), or an action as untouchable, unmentionable, unsayable, or not to be done for a number of reasons: a) because of its sacredness or holiness; b) because it possesses some inherent mysterious power; c) because it has become 'infected with the supernatural' (as priests, kings, chiefs, strangers, pregnant women, etc.) and therefore has acquired this mysterious power; d) because it is unclean (as certain foods, sick persons, criminals, corpses, etc.) or because it is highly dangerous (as corpses, the names of the dead, names of gods, etc.), e) or to effect an end (as tabus against interference with birth, marriage, sexual functions, etc.); f) or to insure protection from theft, trespass, damage (as tilled fields, personal belongings, etc.).[11]

---

9. *New Catholic Encyclopaedia*.
10. *Webster's Dictionary*.
11. *Funk and Wagnall's Standard Dictionary of Folklore, Mythology and Legend*.

The terms refers to prohibition on conduct which if enacted would endanger some or all of the relationships constituting the universe in which men live.[12]

Tabù may be defined as a negative sanction, a prohibition whose infringement results in an automatic penalty without human or supernatural mediation.[13]

In social psychology, the term taboo is applied to certain usually unofficial but highly regarded norms in a group or society. It is applied in particular to social prohibitions of an irrational nature when punishment is threatened when they are violated.[14]

Taboo is an element of all those situations in which attitudes to values are expressed in terms of danger behaviour. This can further be specified by three characteristics. First, that element is expressed in the form of a prohibition; taboo is a negative rule of social behaviour. Second - for not all prohibitions are taboos - its binding force is directly related to ultimate grounds such as tradition, divinity, or tradition endorsed by divinity; (In this context, 'divinity' stands for all suprahuman powers which are thought to control man and his world. I avoid the sofar inconclusive discussions as to whether taboo is always associated with the sacred and is automatic in the infliction of sanctions.) The reasons why tradition, or divinity, or both, should impose the observation of this or that taboo are not apparent. Third, the sanction attached to the transgression of taboo is out of proportion with the importance of the action prohibited; unless order is restored by appropriate ritual, this sanction is inevitably in one way or another inflicted on the transgressors.[15]

These definitions, because they highlight certain characteristics, are somewhat incomplete and do not offer a complete definition of the word 'taboo'. However, in the light

---

12. *A Dictionary of Sociology.*
13. *Encyclopaedia of Social Sciences.*
14. *Encyclopaedia of Psychology.*
15. M.R. Bascom, 'Folklore and Anthroplogy' in *The Study of Folklore*, 26.

of these definitions and other definitions given by authoritative scholars of the subject such as S. Freud, J.G. Frazer, E. Crawley, R.R. Marrett, and others, I have succeeded in understanding what the word 'taboo' stands for, and in placing it in the Maltese context.

It is not easy to classify this book under any one branch of the humanities, say folklore or cultural anthropology. However, it can be easily classified according to the following quotation taken from an essay by W.R. Bascom, one of the leading anthropological folklorists.

After stating that the dual affiliations of folklore with the humanities on the one hand, and with social science on the other was well recognized, he sets out to 'bridge the gap by presenting the anthropological approach to folklore', as he sees it:

Of the four branches of anthropology, cultural anthropology, which is also referred to as social anthropology, ethnology, or ethnography, is most closely associated with folklore. Neither physical anthropology nor prehistory archeology have any direct relationship to folklore, although the latter may occasionally provide information regarding past developments and population movements which is useful to the folklorist. Linguistics is somewhat more closely related, both because the style of verbal expression of a tale or proverb is influenced by vocabulary and grammatical structure, and because linguists have found folktales and myths convenient devices for collecting linguistic texts, with the result that some of the most carefully recorded and translated American Indian tales have been published by linguists. Folklore, however, falls squarely within the fourth field, cultural anthropology, which is concerned with the study of the customs, traditions, and institutions of living peoples.[16]

---

16. Ibid.

Literature and Taboo

Some literature on taboo in the old anthropological sense is to be found under the title of customs and beliefs. In 1772 Count G.A. Ciantar[17] was the first to give a full description of Maltese birth, marriage, and funeral customs. This in its turn proved the ultimate source of local customs described by later writers such as St. Priest (1791),[18] d'Avalos (1818), Miege (1840), and Lacroix (1848). G.P. Badger,[19] in his *Description of Malta and Gozo* (1838), also devoted a section to the study of the customs of Malta. In 1865 P.P. Castagna[20] included 45 popular beliefs and superstitions in his *Storja ta' Malta*. V. Busuttil[21] added and improved on what had already been written by his predecessors in his *Holiday Customs of the Maltese* (1894). Joseph Cassar Pullicino[22] has published a systematic account of what he himself heard from the lips of a representative cross-section of the people and traced in manuscripts or printed sources about the observances and beliefs connected with conception, pregnancy, and childbirth.

17. G.A. Ciantar, *Malta Illustrata* – 'Breve notizie d'alcune usanze dei Maltesi'.
18. Chev. St. Priest, *Malte par un voyageur françoios*, 31-6.
19. G.P. Badger, *Description of Malta and Gozo*.
20. P.P. Castagna, *L-Istorja ta' Malta bil-Gżejjer Tagħha*, 2nd ed., 97-118.
21. V. Busuttil, *Holiday Customs in Malta*, 164-89.
22. J. Cassar Pullicino, *Studies in Maltese Folklore*, passim.

TRANSITIONS OF
MAN'S LIFE

From time immemorial the transitional periods of life –
birth, puberty, marriage, and death – have always been most
critical moments in man's life. The strong importance
traditionally attached to them still prevails today. The non-
literate man, animated almost entirely by immediate,
personal conderations, felt intuitively that his own life and
the lives of the members of his clan and tribe depended
directly upon three decisive moments: birth, marriage, and
death.

From the remotest periods of his existence, man, rising
above mere animal intuition and habit to the first, vague
processes of reasoning, thought, and purposive action, faced
the problem of self-maintenance. He began to understand
that he could not face the problems of his existence by
himself. Later he realized the value of group organization
in conserving and increasing his physical resources. The clan
and the family became the first units of human existence and

social organization. The problems of safeguarding the life of every individual of the clan and of the family became the primary problems of every man.[1]

In these remote times the human mind, which had not yet evolved the concept of God, vaguely sensed some powerful force beyond the immediate, visible world. This gave rise to the belief in spirits most of which were especially active at the moments of birth, puberty, marriage, and death. This led to various rituals, 'superstitions', and taboos, many of which are still to be found in our 'modern' societies. A comparative analysis of these practices shows that they follow a consistent pattern, and are meant to ensure the effective completion of the change-over.[2]

A. van Gennep, a Flemish anthropologist, introduced the term *rites de passage* into anthropological terminology in order to refer to these practices in the crises of man's life. This term is used to refer to the ceremonies and rituals which centre about the individual life. The term 'rites of intensification' refers to those rituals and ceremonies which mark occasions or crises in the life of the community as a whole.

At a time when people sometimes failed to behave predictably, and as a result the rhythm of daily activity was disturbed, they had to develop certain patterns of behaviour designed to guard, by one means or another, against the unexpected, and better to control man's relationship with the universe in which he lives. Rites of passage, then, mark

---

1. J. Morgenstein, *Rites of Birth, Marriage, Death and Kindred Occasions among the Semites*, 5.
2. Ibid.

the important events in the life of an individual. Van Gennep insists that these social changes are more important than biological ones. Social maturity only rarely coincides with physiological puberty; more often it precedes or follows puberty by a significant number of years. He believes that the crises rites facilitate change, helping the individual to pass through the difficulties of transition and the shifting of roles. Rituals of this nature are composed of the following three elements: separation, transition, and reintegration. The element of separation disengages the individual from his former status; that of transition gradually removes the barriers to the new status; and that of reintegration marks his acceptance into everyday life in his newly-acquired status.

In Malta there are not the intricate ceremonies characteristic of non-literate societies. These transitions, however, are marked by religious ceremonies such as baptism, confirmation, and marriage, which can be seen as reflections of their anthropological prototypes. This does not mean that these crises in Malta are not accompanied by taboos and 'superstitions' which, although not having the sanction of the Church, still remain strong among the people. Hence these crises are accompanied by various taboos and superstitions which govern the change-over and help in the separation of the past from the future and symbolize renewal and re-birth. Most of these practices result from lack of knowledge and outmoded patterns of behaviour which were the general rule during the past when institutionalized education was almost non-existent.

The social revolution of the past fifty years or so has done a good deal to modify pressures in our lives, with the result that many of these taboos and superstitions characteristic of these transitional periods are being disregarded. The Second World War was decisive in the changes brought about in patterns of behaviour and the conception of life in general.

In the following chapters I have tried to bring together various taboos which are to be found in Malta in connection with these main crises of man's life, analysing them in the light of relevant anthropological literature. I have tried to consider rites practised in Malta through the full span of human life, from birth to death, in the form of present-day remnants of past taboos. Various sections of the following chapters, although they do not fall directly under one scientific definition of taboo, are in themselves the result of a taboo mentality and also generators of other taboos. Supplementary information helps in shedding light on the social aspect of these taboos.

BIRTH

The concern with the processes of human reproduction and with the propagation of the species can be seen in the very first works of art which emerge from the mists of prehistory, authentic examples of which are to be found in Malta. The squat, female figurines excavated from various archaeological sites in Malta help us to infer that fertility has always been a basic human concern.

This concern in turn led to various precautions and prohibitions, spells and incantations, things to be done and things to be avoided at all costs. Most of these precautions are of a taboo character.

Among non-literate people, a pregnant woman was usually separated from her family and tribe, especially with the approach of delivery. The reason for this seclusion lies in the belief that such a woman could endanger not only herself but also others who might come into contact with her because a woman in childbirth is ritually unclean. People in non-literate societies hold that contact with such a woman is even worse than contact with death and the dead.

Anthropologists hold that the real source of this pollution was, of course, the copious flow of blood – always and in all situations a source of the deepest impurity. Anything the mother touched, or anyone who touched her, would become similarly impure by contagion: hence her isolation. Otherwise the religious and social life of the group could not proceed. Such prohibitions are to be found among many non-literate societies. In the light of this information, the following beliefs found in the Maltese contexts can be better understood.

The Visual Taboo

Many old beliefs and customs linger on, a legacy of the time when birth was a dangerous mystery; among these, the belief that the foetus, trembling in its mother's womb, is vulnerable to external influences figures predominantly. Whatsoever the mother sees transmits itself through nerve cells which will influence the shape and the shaping of the embryo. This belief, based on the principles of sympathetic magic, subjects pregnant women to taboos.[1]

Women avoid looking at ugly objects, monstrosities, deformed persons, animals, and all sorts of unpleasant things fearing the possibility of the birth of similar offspring. Miscarriage is also feared. To ward off the evil influence, they

---

1. Sir J.G. Frazer states that sympathetic magic is made up of positive and negative precepts. Whereas the positive percepts are charms, the negative percepts are taboos. He continues to say that the whole doctrine of taboo would seem to be only a special application of sympathetic magic, with its two great laws of similarity and contact. Frazer, *The Golden Bough,* 19.

make the sign of the cross with the thumb of the right hand on their bulging bellies.[2] The evil influence could be warded off by looking in a basin of water and washing in the same basin.[3] Looking at beautiful objects will have positive effects on the embryo. The principles of sympathetic magic are at work here, just as in the case of the negative effects.

This belief is widespread among pregnant women in Malta, especially those for whom birth still offers that great sense of mystery owing to lack of knowledge about birth. The following information provided by middle-aged and elderly informants confirms this statement:

MISTOQSIJA: X'jigri meta mara tqila tħares lejn xi ħaġa kerha?

QUESTION: What happens when a pregnant woman looks at something ugly?

TWEĠIBA: SAVERJA: Jitwieled għageb ... Le ... Dik ma nemminx biha għax ...

ANSWER: SAVERJA: The child would be a monstrosity ... No ... I do not believe that because ...

T: ĊETTA: Eh ... ħares temmen għax dik ... Ganġija kellha wieħed għageb.

A: ĊETTA: Oh ... you should believe because Ganġija had such a monster ... She gave

---

2. An expression heard in every-day speech says: *Trid tagħmel seba' mitt salib fuq żaqqek daqs kemm hu ikrah: Alla jista' kollox.* 'He is so ugly that you have to make the sign of the cross for seven hundred times on your belly: God knows how ugly he is.' The contextual referent of this expression, heard at Ħas-Sajjied, Birkirkara, was *Is-Slawt,* a dark-complexioned individual who in the Malta context is considered most ugly. For further information about this habit, see Cassar, *Medical History,* 429. See also Cachia, in *Maltese Folklore Review,* 429, 233.

3. Cassar Pullicino, *Studies in Maltese Folklore,* 209

Għamlet nâni. Għadu ħaj sal-lum. Għax marret tara ċirklu u stagħġbet minnu. Marret tara l-kummiedja u rat wieħed nâni u għamlet wieħed bħalu. Għadu ħaj sal-lum. Ħaditha. Mela m'hawnx. Nafu jien ta. U xiħ dan. Għandu ż-żmiem dan in-nâni.

T: SAVERJA: Imma jien naħseb ... bejn iwa u bejn le. Għax hawn wieħed. Ommu stagħġbet fuq xi mogħża. Għandu wiċċu proprju ta' mogħża, bil-widnejn b'kollox. (Bid-daħk) Iwa mhux weqfin bħal tagħha imma ...

birth to a dwarf. He is still alive. Because she went to the circus, she saw a dwarf and was astounded. And she gave birth to one like him. He is still alive. She's had it. Of course we do find such things. I know him myself. Today he is quite old, this dwarf.[4]

A: SAVERJA: But I am only half-convinced. I know a certain man whose mother was amazed on seeing a goat. His face resembles that of a goat, even his ears. (Laughing) Of course they aren't as erect as the goat's but ...[5]

4. The person referred to in this quotation is called *il-Gangi* after his mother's nickname and lives at Zabbar. This story is quite widespread. Anna Smith, an 80-year-old informant from Valletta, confirmed the story. She said that this dwarf had a very big head and a very small body and he was never taken outside the house. Pawla Attard, a 90-year-old informant from Kirkop, referred to a similar deformed person but in this case the child was born without hands and feet. This deformity came about as a result of the mother's looking at such a man.

5. S. Borg and C. Vassallo, a 50-year-old and a 70-year-old informants respectively from Zabbar, during an interview by the author in Vassallo's household in May 1974.

The informants added that during pregnancy a woman is not supposed to look at passing funerals or to pay visits to relatives who are in mourning because of the negative effects this might have on the foetus. She might give birth to a dead boy or girl. Television and films must not be watched by the pregnant woman or 'the child will have a tendency to cry excessively'.[6]

The negative aspects of the detrimental results of looking at ugly images is emphasized more than the positive aspect of looking at beautiful objects.

Ġanna Borġ from Birkirkara said that her daughter gave birth to a son resembling Baby Jesus because during Christmas time she used to gaze at the image of Jesus in the manger. Others speak of having children resembling saintly images kept in their bedrooms. Sacred images and statues in the churches and chapels of the village or town used to attract the mothers' attention, especially during the long hours they spent praying before them. Many a time this led to the custom of naming the child after the saint who has granted special favours. In Birkirkara children are still called by names such as *it-tifel ta' Sant'Antnin*, the child of Saint Anthony, *San Speditu*, Saint Espedito.[7]

The *ex-votos* to be found especially at *Tal-Ħlas* Sanctuary

---

6. Cassar Pullicino, *Studies in Maltese Folklore*, 213.
7. In these two expressions, heard by the author in the locality of Ħas-Sajjied, the mother saying these expressions was referring to the Baby Jesus Saint Anthony is holding in his hands – a statue to be found in the Chapel of Saint Anthony found at the beginning of this locality. The child is referred to as Saint Espedito, because Espedito is sculpted as a round-faced almost hairless young man with a head resembling that of a baby.

Tal-Ħlas Sanctuary – a centre of devotion and ex-votos

on the outskirts of Qormi; *Tal-Ħerba*, Birkirkara; *Tal-Grazzja*, Żabbar; and other sanctuaries in Malta and Gozo show the devotion of the Maltese towards sacred beings, to whom they attribute the birth of a healthy child. [8]

The Touch Taboo

Certain children are born with some part of their skin bearing a different shade of colour from the rest of their body. Most of these 'stock marks' or 'birth marks' as such stains are called, disappear altogether after the first months of the child's life, but some persist for life. Often these appear near

---

8. For more information, see Cassar Pullicino, *Studies in Maltese Folklore*, 219-20. See also Attard.

the eyes stretching to the cheeks, although they can be found in any part of the body. It is held that the mark appears in the location of the body that the pregnant mother first touched.

It is commonly believed that such stains (M. *xewqa*, 'wish') are caused by an unfulfilled wish. Pregnant women must have all their wishes granted, otherwise the result will be either a miscarriage or a child with a stock mark shaped like the thing that had excited the unsatisfied appetite of the mother. All the necessary precautions must be taken to satisfy the mother's wishes to avert or neutralize any danger.

This belief is of wide prevalence and still firmly rooted among the Maltese who treat it as one of the Church's precepts. The pregnant woman together with her relatives and neighbours follow the rule; otherwise they feel they have commited an outrageous act. Even unwitting infringements of the rule are not justifiable.

Ghalik jinqasam tas-sultan, 'For your sake the king's property would be shared with you', is an expression referring to this custom which shows the strength of this belief, which has, however, no medical support. (Medically speaking, the birth mark is a result of a little defect in the formation of the baby in the womb.)

This 'superstitious' belief is extensively and staunchly supported by informants, who speak of stains bearing the shapes of broad beans, paste, peas, grapes, wine, sausages, liver, and so on. It is interesting to note that the characteristic of such birth marks is their lack of a defined shape – *Qrolla* – *dabra bhas-shab ... kif tohrog*, 'A red mark – cloud-like patch'.

In the following quotation, Raffaele Corso tries to give an explanation to support the validity of this belief. Still, however it must be kept in mind that the writer was speaking about a Sicilian context:

Desiderare ardentemente significa aver ricevuto una forte impressione; significa aver viva l'immagine d'un oggetto. Mentre la donna – scriveva Avicenna – desidera ardentemente alcuna cosa, sempre rivolge nel pensiero l'immagine della cosa desiderata; per lo che viene a formarsi negli spiriti animali una idea di quella; i quali spiriti, poi mescolandosi col sangue, imprimono in lui la detta immagine. E perchè questo sangue è destinato dalla natura a nutrire il corpo, mentre la donna tocca con la mano una parte del suo corpo, tira quel sangue così segnato per particolar nutrimento della parte toccata, e quello venendovi segnato dall'immagine della cosa desiderata, la imprime anche nella parte nutritiva.[9]

All those concerned with the birth situation must see that they take all possible measures to ensure that the birth of the child will be safe. This regulation of a precautionary character (sympathetic prohibition) must be followed to the letter. It is an obligation:

Darba waħda kien hemm waħda li kellha xi tgħid ma' waħda u din kien se jkollha u ma tathiex minn dak li kienet qiegħda tiekol. X'ħin marret tqerr, il-qassis ma riedx jagħtiha assuluzzjoni.

Once there was a woman who had quarreled with another woman who was pregnant, and she did not offer her some of the food she was eating. When she went to confession, the priest would not grant her absolution.[10]

---

9. Corso, 23. For further comparative material about the subject, see Pitrè, Vol. II, 126-7. See also Cassar Pullicino, *Studies in Maltese Folklore*, 212-3.

10. M. Axiaq, an 85-year-old informant from Żebbuġ, Gozo, residing in St Julians, in an interview with the author in September 1974.

This shows that one is duty-bound to abide by this rule even if he is not on speaking terms with the mother in question.

This feeling of obligation can be seen from the following quotation in which a blood-pudding vendor, while selling in the streets, on being faced by a pregnant woman, describes what he should do. The way he describes his behaviour is almost ritualistic in character:

This inner, almost instinctive, demand to safeguard the

Jien kont inbigħ il-mazzit. Fejn kont nilmaħ mara tqila kont naqta' biċċa mazzita u ngħidilha: Ħa ... kulha. Tgħidli: Grazzi. Ngħidilha: Le, mhux grazzi. Ħa ħu, għax dik mhux inti se teħodha. Ħaddiehor se jeħodha. U ħaddiehor m'għandux ibati minħabba l-mistħija tiegħek. – Fhimtni? It-tarbija.

I used to sell blood pudding. Whenever I met a pregnant woman, I used to cut a piece of blood pudding, and tell her: Here ... eat it. She tells me: Thank you. I answer: No. It's not a question of thanking me. Take it, because that is not for you. It is someone else who is going to eat it. This someone else must not be the victim of your shyness. Do you understand me? It is the baby.[11]

---

11. M. Axiaq, an 80-year-old informant from Għaxaq, during an interview with the author in March 1975. During the interview Żaren, the informant, in order to emphasize the effects of food taken by pregnant women on their babies, spoke of the seed of *Buqixrem*. He said that this seed when eaten by pregnant animals leads to abortion. In the old days it was taken by women to procure an abortion. He added that this is prohibited by the Church and absolution of this sin can only be granted by the bishop.

life of the child growing in the womb allows no half-measures. A young woman from Ħas-Sajjied in Birkirkara used to stop persons going by with their shopping and ask them to give her a little of what they were carrying. She did this even with persons she did not know. This was the case especially on Sunday mornings when housewives used to pass by with their baked dishes fresh from the village oven. Passers-by used to stop and give a potato or two to the expectant mother.

Another inhabitant of this locality recalls the days when her neighbour used to hand down by means of a basket, hanging from a rope, a portion of *minestra*, 'vegetable soup'. In Birkirkara pregnant women carry a roasted carob with them, just in case they crave for something and cannot have it.[12]

More Texts

Fiż-żmien kien hawn dixx, misjub bl-isem ta' bubaqra. Dan id-dixx kien jingħalaq biċ-ċavetta. Il-wiċċ tad-dixx kien kollu mtaqqab u għalhekk ir-riħa kienet toħroġ. U kien hemm raġel għaddej bl-ikel ġo waħda minn dawn. U kien hemm mara u ħassha ħażin. Marru jiġru għand dan ir-raġel u qalulu: Baqagħlek minn dak il-laħam li kellek fil-bubaqra?

In the past we used to have a dish known as *bubaqra*. This could be closed by a key. However, the surface of the dish was full of holes and one could easily smell what was inside. Once a man passed by carrying such a dish. And a certain woman fainted. Quickly people went to this man and asked him: Have you any of that meat left which you had in the

---

12. H. Gauci, a 45-year-old informant from Birkirkara, during informal questioning by the author in August 1974.

Qallhom: Le. Ftit għadam fadal. Qalulu: Mela darb'oħra għaddi bih maqful. U talbuh ftit mill-għadam li kien fadal. *bubaqra?* He answered: No. There are only a few bones left. They told him: Next time please do close the dish when passing by. And they asked him to give them some of the remaining bones.[13]

This story shows once again the strength of this taboo. The informant added that certain women feel ill when they smell food which they are not able to taste.

Cases of miscarriage as a result of an unfulfilled wish are not often mentioned although this might be the case in the following account:

Kien hemm mara li kien digà kellha żewġ kurramenti. Bil-ħsieb li kollox jimxi sewwa r-raġel daħħlilha seftura, iżda t-tarbija li kellha twieldet b'ħalqha miftuh u mejta. Il-majjistra qaltilha li kienet mietet b'xewqa. There was a woman who already had had two miscarriages. In order to prevent any further ones, her husband employed a maid to help her. But her baby was born with its mouth wide open and dead. The midwife told her that the baby's death was due to a wish.[14]

The following quotations speak of the various effects of unconsumated wishes:

13. M. Axiaq.
14. Ibid.

Kien hemm mara li rat lil raġel jiekol l-għeneb u stħat tgħidlu biex jagħtiha l-għeneb. Misset ħdejn widnejha u t-tarbija li kellha twieldet b'żewġ tebgħat żgħar f'dik il-parti li misset b'idejha meta kienet għadha tqila.

Meta mara tkun tqila, b'mod speċjali meta tkun waslet fl-aħħar, jekk ikollha kelb, u tkun tħobbu ħafna, hija għandha tneħħih minn ħdejha għax jista' jkollha tarbija b'wiċċ ta' kelb. Hawn min twieled u kellu biċċa fenek ... hawn min jixtieq biċċa fwied ... titlagħlu f'idu skond fejn tmiss ... hawn min jixtieq l-inbid u t-tarbija jitlagħlha wiċċha kollu aħmar. Jgħidulek: Dik xewqa. Ma tiġix. Hekk tibqa'.

There was a woman who saw a man eating grapes and was shy to ask him for some. She then touched her ear and gave birth to a baby bearing two small stains exactly in the place she had touched with her hands when she was pregnant.[15]

When a woman is pregnant, especially towards the end of her time, if she has a dog, of which she is very fond, she must get rid of it or she could easily have a child with a face resembling a dog's. Children have been born with rabbit marks ... a certain woman had a mark on her face resembling piece of rabbit... Some crave for liver ... and give birth to children bearing a stain resembling liver on the part they touch. Some have a craving for wine and the baby will have a red stain all over its face. They tell you: That is a wish: it will not go ... it will remain so for ever.[16]

15. A. Smith, an 80-year old informant from Valletta during an interview by the author in February 1974.
16. Ibid.

In these prohibitions based on sympathetic magic one notices that anything which for the 'primitive' mind seems potentially dangerous leads to avoidance, and subsequently to prohibitions. Hence these prohibitions are utilitarian in character and are in accordance with experience. Therefore, they are not irrational. In fact, although they appear unreasonable for us, they were originally based on reason.

Food and Drink

During pregnancy women avoid eating certain things which might prove detrimental to their well-being. In certain societies such avoidances are the products of taboos. This cannot be said of the situation in Malta, as far as the material gathered shows. Informants say that pregnant women used to stop eating vegetables pickled in brine, a traditional favourite with the Maltese. Based on the law of similarities as explained by Frazer, however, the custom of eating poultry after the delivery of babies was most common among the Maltese because it was believed that it helped the offspring to hold their necks straight within a short time. This, however, cannot be taken to be based on taboo, although women used to resort to extreme ends to make sure that they abided by the custom.

Sexual Intercourse

During this period,[17] abstinence and restrictions were the rule.

_____

17. It is interesting to note that traditionally the Maltese thought that if a woman passes urine following sexual intercourse she will not become pregnant and that if sexual intercorse takes place in a standing-up position the sperm will not enter.

Sexual intercourse during the entire pregnancy or toward the latter part of it would result in sickness, deformity, or even death for the child; the mother would produce no milk or sour milk; the father would be unsuccessful in hunting and fishing.[18]

In the light of this quotation, how much truth is there in the incident brought to the notice of the author by an informant from Birkirkara who spoke of a baby born blind because of continued intercourse during the last months of pregnancy?[19]

Intercourse must not take place before forty days after birth. This restriction is clearly expressed in this expression: *Għal erbgħin ġurnata l-mara jkollha l-qabar miftuħ*, 'The woman's grave remains open up to the fortieth day.' During these forty days the woman is not under the obligation of following the Church's precept of attending mass on Sundays and Feasts of Obligation.[20] *Jekk tqiegħed sulfarina tara kollox miftuħ*, 'If you place a match [in front of the mother's womb] you will see everything open.'[21] This can further be seen from the following information:

Mara tkun suġġetta għall-mewt – ikollha l-qabar miftuħ sa erbgħin ġurnata. Din minħabba f'żewġha – biex żewġha kemm jista' ma	A woman would be subject to death – up to the fortieth day. Her husband should not approach her. If he does so he will have a rash and she

18. Douglas, 52.
19. The information was specifically referring to *Tal-fulu*, 'Of the bean', an inhabitant of Birkirkara. She referred to the father as being *Annimal*, ' An animal'.
20. M. Axiaq.
21. Ibid.

jersaqx lejha. Jekk jersaq jimtela msiemer u hi taqbadha emoragija – timtela bid-demm u tmut. Għalhekk bil-qabar miftuħ.

will die of a haemorrhage. That is why we say that the woman's grave remains open.[22]

Apart from sexual restrictions there are other ceremonies and customs to be followed during these forty days. These customs seem to be trivial in nature but since they are respected they must be deeply ingrained in the Maltese psyche. People in Malta unconsciously regard the forty days following birth as a phase of transition of the utmost importance. Today, however, these customs seem to have acquired a rational explanation. Thus the nails of a new-born child should not be cut before forty days or else the baby would have a whitlow *(M. dieħes)*. When a female baby is forty days old her godmother takes her to a midwife or some one else for her ears to be pierced for ear-rings *(M. ħoloq)*.[23] Whoever does the washing of the baby's cap after the Christening should be considered a godparent for a period of forty days. (The water used in the washing was used to water plants and not thrown away with as usual because it might contain some holy water.)

During this period the mother was said to be *imniefes* or *bl-infasa* 'puerperal'. De Soldanis records in his dictionary that 'our women believe that if a woman after confinement calls on another woman in a similar condition during these forty days, *imniefes lil imniefsa* ... before the said forty days have passed one of them would die. It is not known how this

22. Ż. Axisa
23. J. Cassar Pullicino, *Studies in Maltese Folklore*, 236.

belief originated, nor have I been able to discover any basis for it.' The belief survived up to the twentieth century in a slightly mitigated form given by Busuttil: 'If two women who have been confined on the same day meet before the forty days are over, one of them will suffer some misfortune, either in her own person or in that of her child. According to an informant from Balzan, the danger may also extend to the godparents; should these happen to be an engaged couple, they are advised not to marry before the period of forty days.[24]

In Malta the woman is not supposed to leave her house before her offspring is baptized and presented in church. Certain people did not even leave their new-born without a baby's cap *(M. skufja)* before it was baptized. The child is said to be a Turk, that is a heathen, because he is still unbaptized. Procrastination in baptizing the child is most risky because the child in the meantime is under the power of the devil. This means that the baby will take a long time in passing from the state of taboo into the state of normal, daily existence, like the rest of the community. Those who take a long time in baptizing their children are held in very low esteem among the rest of the community. The unmistakable original character of baptism as a rite for the expulsion of evil spirits, the removal of taboo, and the admission into a state of normal existence is at the basis of these taboos.

The pollution resulting from sexual intercourse is intensified when it takes place outside the bonds of matrimony. Extra-marital sex, it is quite widely believed,

---

24. Ibid, 234. It might be added here that the author, in 1978 in the locality of Has-Sajjied, Birkirkara, heard a young mother saying that she was not going to visit her sister who has had another child during the same period, lest dire consequences take place.

In Malta the woman is not supposed to leave her house before her offspring is baptized and presented in church

contaminates the guilty parties and may also bring disaster to those with whom they come into contact or even to the entire social group. Such ideas cannot have been without influence in evoking a negative ethical attitude towards illicit sexual relations.[25]

---

25. Douglas, 139

This attitude is responsible for the custom which prohibits visits to mothers during confinement from a woman who is living immorally.

It is considered a 'sin' to sleep with a baby before he is one year old. Mgr. Pietro Duzina who, in 1575, was sent to Malta by the Vatican to report on the religious state of the Maltese islands, ordered parish priests to instruct parents to avoid sleeping in the same beds as their children so as not to smother them.[26] Maria Axiaq, a Gozitan informant, stated that she did not sleep with her children before they were one year old. She recalled the Old Testament story of King Solomon and the two women who asked for his advice after one of them had accidentally smothered her baby while he was sleeping in her bed.

Why forty days?

No specific reason can be given to the number forty in the Maltese context. However, the following quotation may shed some light upon its origin:

Ceremonies upon the fortieth day are not very frequent but quite significant. The classic instance of such a ceremony is based on the ancient Israelite provision, recorded in *Leviticus*, 12, that a woman was ritually unclean during the first forty days after the birth of a daughter. During this period she apparently remained closely attached to her home; at least, she was strictly forbidden to contact the sanctuary or to touch anything sacred. At the end of this period, she visited the sanctuary in order to offer there her sacrifice of purification. With this act she was restored to her normal state of existence. Today in non-Israeli sections

---

26. Cassar Pullicino, *Studies in Maltese Folklore*, 39.

of Palestine, a child is wrapped in swaddling clothes for the first forty days after birth.[27]

This seems to be linked with the notion, prevalent among many ancient peoples, that human pregnancy lasted 280 days (seven times forty) and that forty-day phases were of particular importance in the development of embryos, young animals, and even plants.

Among the Semites baptism was fixed, as a rule, for the fortieth day after birth because, according to Semitic belief, the fortieth day marked the close of the second stage of the power of evil spirits; for this reason it was the right time for the performance of ceremonies for their expulsion. Accordingly, Adam is represented as fasting and standing immersed to his neck in the waters of the Jordan River for forty days, in order that the evil of his former acts might be washed away from him. And for the same reason, undoubtedly, the New Testament represents the period of temptation of Jesus as lasting for forty days, implying thereby that after the fortieth day the power of the devil ceased automatically.[28]

The notion that the first forty days of pregnancy were critical was developed by the Greeks. According to Aristotle (384–322 BC), the fortieth day was the day on which the male child was believed to stir in the womb for the first time; this was already an ancient belief in Aristotle's day. The followers of Pythagoras (6th century BC) had developed a theory about the forty-day phases of pregnancy. The belief that women

---

27. Morgenstern, *Rites of Birth, Marriage, Death and Kindred Occasions anomg the Semites*, 28.
28. Ibid, 82.

are unclean for forty days after childbirth is found in many parts of the world today.[29]

In its particular connection with pregnancy and childbirth, the forty-day period took on a general significance for health and hygiene.

Apart from this the number forty has been sacred and mysterious to peoples as far apart in time and place as the ancient Babylonians and the modern Eskimos. The Babylonians attached a special significance to forty, calling it *kissatum* meaning 'the excellent quality', which they understood as an expression of fullness, and the universe conceived as a totality. This number was sacred to Ea, the god of sweet waters. It was the number of offerings to the gods at important festivals in Babylon; in Nineveh it was the regular period for mourning and fasting. The fury of the evil spirits was thought to last for forty days.

Under the influence of Babylon, other ancient Semitic peoples regarded forty as a sacred number; it is acually the most frequently-mentioned sacred number in the Old and New Testaments and in the Talmud, after the number seven.[30]

The Moon

The calendar is one of the most important social institutions evolved by Man. The conception of the passage of time is obviously seen in the alternations of night and day. A longer cycle was naturally suggested by the lunar phenomena which among non-literate communities is held to be the measure

---

29. Webster, *Taboo. A Sociological Study*, 130.
30. Ibid, 141.

of time. The period of lunation seems to have been generally estimated as 30 days, although 29 is also used. Evidence from non-literate people attests the importance attached to the changes of the moon. The four lunar phases provide an obvious means of calculating the passage of time. All this shows the importance attached to the moon – an importance which is almost universal.

In astrology, the sun is the masculine symbol of fatherhood, while the moon the female symbol of fertility. Indeed, for centuries the moon was thought as 'the Great Midwife' because it was thought to rule woman's generative functions.[31]

The belief that the moon governs the hidden processes of nature gave rise to various patterns of behaviour which regulate the lives of the Maltese, especially when they have to face such phases as menstruation, sexual intercourse, and birth. Epilepsy is also regarded as being closely related to the changing forms of the moon. The occult power with which this mysterious celestial body is invested made the Maltese almost slaves of its movements for long ages. They are governed by a strong taboo-fear in their behaviour, lest they do not conform to the moon's movements. The need to observe the moon, apart from religious or taboo reasons, was no doubt mainly connected with economic reasons. The phases of the moon served as a convenient basis of reckoning to anticipate the right moments which supply the best food. Animals must be brought in the world at seasons most favourable to their health and maintenance.

For the Babylonians, the greatest astronomers of antiquity, the moon was the queen of the night and the

---

31. Ibid, 150.

ancestor of the sun whom she exceeded in power, while the earth was its child over whom its rays had great power. It was believed that the moon had a magical power because it drew to itself the hidden potencies of the stars and constellations. These radiant emanations from the other celestial bodies were said to pour upon the earth.[32]

Lunar calendars still exist among the Arabs for instance and in various religious festivals, including some Christian celebrations. Local beliefs surrounding the moon are of a universal character. Hence Maltese beliefs have their parallels all over the world, for instance in Sicily, England, Spain, and among the non-literate.

Man is greatly influenced by the moon's periodicity, showing never-ending change. It starts like a slender crescent, goes through a period of development until it reaches a state of fullness, and then declines:

That the moon has certain effects on moist substances; that they are apparently subject to her influences; that, for instance, increase and decrease in ebb and flow, develop periodically and parallel with the moon's phases, all this is well known to the inhabitants of seashores and seafaring people. Likewise physicians are well aware that she affects the *humore* of sick people, and that the fever-days revolve parallel with the moon's course. Physical scholars know that the life of animals and plants depends upon the moon, and experimentalists know that she influences marrow and brain, eggs and the sediments of wine in casks and jugs, that she excites the minds of people who sleep in full moonlight, and that she affects (?) linen clothes which are exposed to it. Peasants know that the moon acts upon fields of cucumbers, melons, cotton, etc., and even make the times for the various kinds of sowing, planting, and grafting, and for the covering of the cattle depend upon the course of the moon. Lastly astronomers know that meteorologic occurrences

---

32. Ibid, 50.

Peasants know that the moon acts upon fields of cucumbers, melons, cotton, etc.

depend upon the various phases through which the moon passes in her revolutions.[33]

There prevails an almost universal belief that the menstrual cycle of women is linked to the lunar cycle. Biological evidence confirms that the cycle of human ovulation approximates the lunar month, a fact which is preserved in the term 'menstruation' which signifies 'monthly', i.e. occuring every lunar month. This has led to the belief that the lunar changes cause menstruation and have the power of impregnation and hence it is associated with childbirth.

J. Cassar Pullicino explains the relevant Maltese beliefs and proverbs about the moon:

The moon is regarded with awe, complimented, and appeased; otherwise

---

33. Ibid, 125.

The threshing floor

Typical Maltese cart

the mother will be afflicted with disease and maybe more frequent pregnancies. *Qamar*, 'Moon' in Maltese is of masculine gender and, as Aquilina suggests, people attribute to it the power of impregnation in some proverbs. Thus the Maltese saying warns: *Ħares lejn il-qamar bil-ħajra, għax għalik ikollu l-għira*, 'Look at the moon with longing, because it will be jealous of you.' Also *Meta tiżżewweġ, il-qamar bik ibewweġ*, 'When you marry, the moon runs away with you i.e. you will soon become pregnant. The best thing for a married woman is not to worry about her menses: *Tgħoddx il-ġranet tal-qamar, għax ma jħallikx tistabar*, 'Don't count the lunar days, or you'll be restless.' Above all: *Tisħetx il-qamar fl-art, għax itik niket u mard*, 'Don't curse the moon on earth, lest you be affected with grief and disease.'[34]

Other proverbs which shed light on the idea that the moon stimulates female responsiveness and thus increases a woman's fertility are the following: *Jekk fil-qamar thuf, issaħħan il-ġuf*, 'If you wander about in the moonlight, the womb will get warm'; *Il-qamar jekk tfittxu, ifittxek, u jekk ma tfittxux, ma jfittxikx*, 'If you seek the moon he will do so too; if you don't, he will not look for you.'[35]

The moon is also said to have a profound influence on all living things. The waxing moon sends powerful impulses of 'growth' energy to the Earth and this affects all things that grow, causing them to increase in size and strength. As the moon wanes or declines in size, growing things similarly decrease in energy. This belief can be found among all peoples, primitive and advanced, all over the world. On the basis of this theory, plants are said to grow best if sown two days before the full moon so that they can gather strength as the moon waxes. Farmers still sow by the moon. Many people

34. Cassar Pullicino, *Studies in Maltese Folklore*, 206.
35. Ibid, 208.

believe that seeds sown at the time of the waning moon will not prosper. The fact that experiments do not always support these beliefs in no way diminishes faith in them.

The various species of the animal kingdom are likewise affected by the moon. The mating urge of large animals also seems to be heightened during the waxing of the moon; hence the proverb, *Meta l-baqra tilgħaq tintha, il-qamar ikun kwinta*, 'When the cow licks her behind, it is full moon.'[36] The moon has also influence on a brooding hen:

Kien hawn raġel minn hawn jismu Petest. Kienu jgħidulu: Jiswa bajd tal-qroqqa? Kien jgħidilhom: Bil-qamar, barra minn fuq kulħadd.

There was once a man named Petest and people used to ask him: Can we eat eggs from under a brooding hen? And he used to tell them: There is the influence of the moon, God help us.[37]

Men too respond to the fluctuations of the moon. The peculiar effect of the moon on the minds of men and women has been noted since ancient times. The fuller the moon, the more turbulent, excitable, and impressionable the mind becomes. It is a common observation among those who have to deal with groups of people that there occurs a noticeable increase in unusual, eccentric behaviour during the time of the full moon. Indeed, there has always been a widespread belief in a direct connection between the moon and lunacy;

---

36. Ibid.
37. K. Schembri, an 80-year-old informant from Birkirkara, in an interview with the author in September 1974.

the notion of 'moon madness' has in some cases been privately subscribed to even by psychiatrists. The moon is popularly held to have a definitely disturbing effect on the minds of the insane and all those who are afflicted with nervous disorders. The word 'lunatic' itself is derived from the Latin *luna*, moon, thus preserving the basis of the age-old theory. These notions have also found a place in Maltese traditions. According to one proverb: *Dak li ġġib fil-qamar fl-ebda kwart ma jkollu sabar*, 'Whom you conceive in moonlight will find no rest during any quarter of the moon.' Also the offspring of a lunatic will be hot-blooded: *Raġel miġnun jgħammar shun*. Another common superstition states that a disturbance takes place in the distribution of the bodily fluids if a person sleeps without covering in the direct light of the moon.

Texts

Kienu jgħidu: Tfittixx il-qamar – fl-antik – speċjalment min ikun marid. Għax mhux l-ewwel darba li t-tabib jgħidlek: Mal-qamar imut. Tfittixx il-qamar għax il-qamar ifittxek. Voldieri jekk inti toqgħod spiss tiffitta fih tiġi forsi disgrazzja u aħna konna nwaħħlu fil-qamar. Tassew, ibatu b'ħass ħażin, jinxteħtu ma' l-art, toħroġ ħafna ragħwa minn ħalqhom. Hawn min jomgħod ilsienu, jagħmlulu bħal

In olden days they used to say: Do not try to get the moon, for the moon will get you. This is especially the case with sickness. For it was not unusual for the doctor to say that with the next moon the patient will die. This means that if you gaze too much at the moon some ailment will befall you. We always used to blame the moon. It seems as if this were true. Of course it is true. They also used to speak

muftieħ f'ħalqu biex ma jilħaqx ilsienu. L-iżjed li jagħmel meta jkun kwinta. F'dak iż-żmien ikun hemm influenza kbira fuq dawn l-affarijiet. U hawn min ifittxu f'ċertu mottivi fl-ewwel kwart. Il-qamar barra minn hekk jgħidu: Meta jitfaċċa fl-ewwel kwart, ħares lejh, jekk ikun wiċċu 'l fuq, jgħidu l-baħrin imqajmin, jekk ikun wiċċu 'l isfel, il-baħrin reqdin, voldieri kalma. Ċertu nisa jgħidu li mal-qamar kollox isir. M'hemmx bżonn nifhmu ċertu dak... tifhmu x'inhuma dawn. Anke t-trabi. Hawn ħafna min jgħidlek li meta jkun daqsxejn qamar ħażin, ma tantx ikun tajjeb il-qamar, jistgħu jitwieldu trabi jbatu b'tal-qamar. U kien hawn ħafna dari ... u jbatu per eżempju bil-ballu san vitu. Jgħidu mill-qamar ġej kollox. Għalhekk meta telgħu fil-qamar l-ewwel darba kienu żammewhom kwarantina, għax qalu li l-qamar mimli mard. Kienu żammewhom kwarantina,

about people who were under the influence of the moon. They really feel sick, fall to the ground, and they foam at the mouth. They used to put a key in their mouths so that they would not swallow their tongues. This takes place mostly when the moon is full. During this time there is great influence on such things. Certain people try to attribute to the moon certain motives in its first quarter. One belief says that when the moon appears in its first phase, and it is facing upwards, then they say that the sailors are awake, whilst if the moon faces downwards, it means that the sailors are asleep, that is the sea is calm. Certain women say that everything takes place with the moon. There is no need to expand on this issue ... you understand what we mean. Even new-born babies are influenced by the moon. Under a certain malefic moon, children might be born epileptic. And

tmint'ijiem ħa jaraw ġabux magħhom xi mard. Ċertu annimali min-naħa l-oħra għandhom ċerta influenza mill-qamar bħan-nisa tagħna l-istess. Allura kulħadd kien ifittxu l-qamar. Il-qroqqa f'Marzu nagħmluha ma' ċertu qamar. Fit-2 ta' Frar meta jkun qamar sħiħ ngħidu nitilqu l-kanali basta jkun tal-qamar. F'Marzu nagħmlu l-qrajjaq għax *come di fatti* anke jgħidulek Frar u t-tfal tiegħu, voldieri l-flieles, għax il-flieles ta' Marzu jkunu tajbin għax joħorġu b'saħħithom. Il-qamar kellu influenza fuq bnedmin u annimali b'mod speċjali annimali li jkunu qishom in-natura tal-mara bħall-baqar, bħall-mogħoż.

in my days there were many who suffered from this sort of ailment, others suffered from St Vitus' Dance. They say that the moon influences every-thing. That's why when man first stepped on the moon, the astronauts were kept in quarantine; they said that the moon was full of ailments. They kept them for eight days to be sure that they hadn't brought any disease. Certain animals, on the other hand, are influenced by the moon in the same way that women are. Hence everyone tries to follow the phases of the moon. We place the brooding hen over the eggs in March under a certain moon; on 2 February, if the moon is a favourable one, we mate the canaries. As they say February and its children, meaning the chickens of March, are the best. The moon influences man and animals, especially female animals, like the cow and the goat.[38]

38. Smith.

Jgħidu min jorqod għad-dawl ta' qamar kwinta jista' jistordih u mbagħad kultant żmien jibda jtih tal-qamar. Jgħidu għax jistordik. Jixroblok il-menti. Jien ngħid għalija, kien jagħmilli rasi tugagħni meta kien ikun kwinta. Ma kontx nista' nħares lejh – hekk b'għajnejja naturali. Hawn ħafna jorqdu għad-dawl ta' qamar fuq il-bjut u tant ikunu taħt l-influenza tiegħu li jista' jiffjakkalhom il-menti jew jagħtihom tal-qamar.

It is said that he who sleeps in the light of the full moon may feel dizzy and he will suffer from periodical epilepsy. Bacause, according to tradition, the moon makes you dizzy and sucks up your brain. Speaking for myself, the full moon used to give me a headache. I could not gaze at it with my naked eyes. Those who sleep in the moonlight might be influenced by it, it might weaken their minds or they may have epileptic fits.[39]

Others believe that meat left in the open air in the moon's rays will turn green. An informant told the author that she had once left some sausages in a place where the rays of the moon could reach them and the very next morning they were completely worm-infested.

Ritual impurity and evil spirits

The ritual impurity of the parturient mother and her child exposed them to unusual danger especially during the first few days after birth. The belief in a changeling, in Maltese *mibdul,* show one of the dangers. Some women think that the children affected with kalaazar, a spleen disease known

---

39. Ibid.

as *marda tal-bicċa*, are in reality changelings and they also look on a baby suffering from *huttafa*, a wasting disease, as a *mibdul*.[40] St Julian was invoked in the diseases of children such as rickets, pertussis, and kalaazar or leishmaniasis. The sick child was taken to St Julians Bay, where a statue of the Saint still stands, and given a sand-bath. A pit was dug, the little patient placed in it and covered with sand for varying periods of time ranging from two to thirty minutes. After copious perspiration was induced by this means, a cordial was administered to the child.[41] A similar procedure was also recommended for sick adults, whence the saying *Mur indifen San Ġiljan*, 'Bury yourself at St Julians.'[42] Analogous customs were connected with the ruined church of St Cyrus near Zurrieq and with the crypt at St Corrado in the church at Qala in Gozo.[43]

Bath

The state in which the child comes into the world necessitates the giving of a bath. Anthropologists hold that the *raison d'etre* of such baths is not primarily sanitary. The physical care given to the child depends mostly on superstitions and taboos. Hence it was the custom to put a ring and some money, for example a crown or half-a-crown, in the bath for good luck:

40. Cassar Pullicino, *Studies in Maltese Folklore*, 53. See also 248-9.
41. Hennen, 541.
42. T. Zammit, 'Tas-Sliema u San Ġiljan', 12.
43. L. Zammit, 'Remains of St. Cyrus Church', 10.

Meta konna naħslu tarbija fil-banju konna nagħmlu ċurkett u flus – per eżempju ħames xelini. Kemm tkun tista' tixħet ġol-banju ixħet biex ikollok ir-riżq. It-tarbija tkun xortiha tajba. Kien hemm raġel miżżewweġ li dam ħafna ma kellu tfal, meta kellu tarbija minflok ġix-xelini jew tmintax irbiegħi tefa' ħames liri tad-deheb.

When we used to bathe the baby we used to put a ring and some money in the bath – say a crown. The more you put the better for this brings good luck to the baby. Once there was a married man who had to wait a long time before having a child. When the baby was finally born, the father, instead of putting two shillings or half-a-crown in the bath, put in five gold sovereigns.[44]

The Evil Eye

The ritual impurity of the mother and child makes them most susceptible to the influence of the evil eye. It is not only anger, jealousy, and feelings of enmity, but also praise, admiration, and well-wishing which can injure the child by arousing the malice of envious spirits. It is, therefore, considered unlucky to express any admiration for a baby without saying the special formula: *Ikun imbierek Alla*, 'God be praised'. This custom is to be found among various peoples, depending upon the nationality of the people and their respective religious faiths. In the Near East, for example, for anyone to praise a child's beauty is 'most

---

44. S. Borg.

dangerous and worse than an insult'.[45] In Greece, where susceptibility to the evil eye was greatly believed in, during childbirth all mirrors were removed from the room, since it was considered possible to cast the evil eye on oneself.

In Morocco, when the look of a person is accompanied with words of praise, the danger is considered so great that it is always necessary to add, as a precaution, the phrase *tbark allah*, 'May God be blessed' (Fez); or, *Gul tbark llah, llah ya tek la'ma fi l-a'ainin*, 'Say "May God be blessed, may God make your eyes blind" '(Ulad Bu'aziz). There may even be danger in being praised without being looked at, as when somebody speaks of another person's children in their absence. One reason why words of praise or admiration are considered so dangerous is no doubt that they are often connected with envy; but this cannot be the only reason, since evil effects are expressly attributed to them even in cases where the person who speaks is entirely free from any such feeling. In accordance with one of the laws of the association of ideas, which generally play such an important part in many magical beliefs, namely the law of association by contrast, the praise or admiration of something good readily recalls its opposite – the more so as the future is always uncertain and future is not to be relied upon.[46]

The supernatural notion in the attitudes to fate and the future of the child can also be seen in the avoidance of weighing the child, which is again based on the fear of the evil eye. Young mothers in Malta often used to avoid going around the streets with their young babies, lest they became the victims of the evil eye.[47] Avoidance of exposure was considered the safest precaution.

45. For further information, see Cassar Pullicino, *Studies In Maltese Folklore*, 246.
46. Westermarck, Vol. II, 418.
47. A. Zarb, a 54-year-old informant from Birkirkara, in an interview with the author in August 1974.

The full breasts of the mother giving milk to her child can also be the victims of the evil eye. Żaren Borġ from Dingli spoke of his wife as having possessed shrivelled breasts for four whole years as a consequence of the evil eye. Il-*Bukaċċina*, from Nadur, however, when asked whether she used to breast-feed her children in front of others, remarked rather ironically: *Se jgħinulek il-beżżula?* 'Are they going to cast the evil eye on your nipple?' Żaren Axisa from Għaxaq was of the opinion that breast-feeding in public was the habit of shameless women. Breast-feeding was a widespread custom, producing a sense of guilt if not practised. Mr Axisa is of the opinion that those mothers who do not breast-feed their children run the risk of tubercolosis, because the breasts do not purify themselves.[48] The general idea was that whilst a woman is breast-feeding she cannot become pregnant.

Various anecdotes, narrated by individuals, speak of the influence of the evil eye, to which they attribute most of the ailments visiting their children. They 'tend to explain and interpret all natural phenomena either by the intervention of saints if the effect is good, or by some magico-supernatural power, such as the evil-eye, if the results are harmful'.[49]

The evil eye is considered to have a most devastating effect on piglets and, especially, young rabbits. This explains the use of horns which are said to serve in order that a

---

48. The same informant also referred to the well-known custom of hiring women to breast-feed children of well-to-do families although such a woman had to be a person of good habits. They were afraid lest the bad habits of the wet-nurse would pass to their baby with the milk.
49. G. Zammit-Maempel, 'The Evil Eye and Protective Cattle Horns in Malta', 4.

**Horns serve in order that a stranger's eye will strike the horn
either at the tip or at the centre of the set.**

stranger's eye will strike the horn either at the tip or at the
centre of the set. Such movement of the eye is considered to
be quite sufficient to destroy the 'electro-magnetic influence'
of the evil-eyed person.

The following are various examples about the meaning
of the evil eye itself and its baneful influence, not solely on
the young, but also on grown-ups:

Kelli tifla li kellha xi seba',
tmien xhur. U tinqala' waħda
u qalet: Ara Lonza, x'tifla
għandha. Ħadithieli ġol-
ħanut, u meta ġabitha t-tifla
kienet qisha mgħaxxa.
Baqgħet ... baqgħet sakemm

I had a child of about seven
months. And a woman said of
her: Just look at Lonza's
child. She took it with her to
the shop, and when she
brought her back, she
already looked weak. And

xeħtithieli taħt it-trab … xorbithieli. L-għajn tnixxiflek qalbek. L-għajn tidħol. Mhux minn kulħadd. Imma forsi minn wieħed minn kull elf. Jiena ġrali każ li nammetti. Ikolli żewġ żrameġ, fenka u fenek, u tiġi waħda għandi minn dawn ta' barra. Missierha kont xtrajtu mingħand Ġanni ta' Kalċi. Kienet xtratu x-xiħa mingħand sinjur. Tliet wiżniet kien fih. U ġiet biex tibgħat xi ħaġa t-tifla, dil-mara. Kienet sejra Karmni tiegħi l-Istralja, u dawn iż-żrameġ qegħdin iħarsu lejna – lejn il-mejda, qegħdin jieklu biċċa ħobż. Allura x'għamlet? Qegħdin jieklu b'widnejhom weqfin … l-għada tiġi l-mara ta' Karmnu tiegħi u tmur tmisshom bl-ixkupa. Ma ċċaqalqux. Baqgħu kif kienu – widnejhom weqfin bil-biċċa tal-ħobż ġo ħalqhom. Dan li

that was the beginning of the end … she was the death of her. The evil eye dries up your heart.[50]

The evil eye exists, although only one in a thousand is endowed with its power. I admit that it once happened to me. I had a couple of rabbits we had bought from Ġanni ta' Kalċi. And a stranger came to my house. It was the time when my Karmni was going to Australia and these two rabbits stood gazing at us – we were at table – they were munching some bread. What did she do? They were eating with their ears uplifted with a piece of bread in their mouth. The following day my Karmu's wife paid me a visit and she touched them with the broom. They did not move. They remained with their ears uplifted with the piece of bread in their

---

50. S. Borg, the informant also added that the faith in the evil eye in her is very strong, 'Mulej Alla aħfirli', 'Lord my God forgive me'.

qed ngħidilkom veru. U qaltilhom: Ħallihom għax ix-xiħ ma jemmenx dak. Għax meta jgħidli xi ħaġa – Hawn tfal tant sbieħ ta' l-Ingliżi, ma jgħajnuhomx, se jgħajnu tiegħek? Għax hekk kien id-diskors. U ħallewhom kif kienu. Insomma din għaddiet u ġagħlitni nemmen.

mouth. What I'm telling you is true. And she said to them: Let them be because he [the informant] does not believe. Because he used to tell me. Out of so many lovely English children, why should they cast the evil eye on your child. Because that was what I used to tell her. And they left them as they were. This incident made me believe in the evil eye.[51]

Ikolli tarbija darbtejn ... ta' l-ewwel tiġi waħda. (Taf li n-nisa dari jużaw is-sidrija?) Qaltilha: Daħħal sidrek għax qed joħroġ il-ħalib. Minn dak il-ħin, wara kwarta, il-ħalib ma baqax joħrog minn hawn (il-beżżula) imma minn taħt abtha. Damet erba' snin, u ma kellhiex tfal u l-ħalib għadu ħiereġ minn taħt abtha.

Well, I had two children. When I had the first one a woman came to me and told me: Cover your breast because it is oozing milk. (You know that before women used to wear waistcoats.) As from that moment the milk did not come out from the nipple but from her armpit. This went on for four years and in the meantime she had no children.

Jerga' jkolli tifla oħra u kellha disa' xhur u taf li l-

My wife used to leave the house at five in the morning

51. Ż. Mifsud.

mara tieghi kienet tohroġ mill-hamsa ta' filghodu u tidhol fil-hamsa ta' filghaxija, dejjem tiġri biż-żiemel, tinnegozja ... u qabdet dit-tifla u kellha bżonn tmur ir-Rabat. Marret ir-Rabat, dahlet f'hanut u qabdithielha sid il-hanut. Ara mbierek Alla, u tiġri dejjem minn bil-lejl sa bil-lejl, x'tarbija għandha kemm hi gustuża. Kemm hi qawwija. – Tiġi d-dar, u taghtiha accessjoni u tmutli sa l-ghada fil-ghodu.

L-għajn hija perikoluża. Tiġi wahda u tkun tghir ghalik. Tarak tghix bi kwietek, filwaqt li hi ma tkunx tista' tiehu ruh. U ghalhekk tghir ghalik. U li jkollok tgharraqulek. Anke qsari minn fuq il-hajt jaqghu wkoll. Anke familja timradlek.

and return at five in the afternoon, always travelling on horseback doing all kinds of business. When I had the second child, she was than nine months old, my wife had to go to Rabat and took the child with her. When she was at Rabat she entered a shop and the shop owner took the child in her arms and said: Praise be to God, look what a lovely child she has, how plumpy she is, and you are always on the move day and night. When she returned home the child had a fit and died the next morning.[52]

The evil eye is dangerous. It is cast by someone who is envious of you. You live in peace minding your own business whereas she can never find peace. And she will ruin everything you have. She can cause pots to slip from a wall. She can make a whole family ill.[53]

52. Ibid.
53. Ż. Axisa.

66

Il-bniedem mingħajr ma jrid jimtela bik. Jieħu ħsiebek, mingħajr ma jkollu għalfejn – bejnu u bejn ruħu. Darba kien hemm raġel li qal lil wieħed qassis li huwa ma kienx sejjer jara l-guva tal-kanali li kellu, għax kien jibza' minn xi diċerija, minħabba li kien jgħajjen. Iżda l-qassis qallu: U le ... dawk ħmerijiet. Imur jarahom u l-għada jsibhom kollha mejtin. Ħwejjeg li ma jitwemmnux. L-għajn u l-magħmul, l-iktar ħaġa kerha. Il-magħmul m'hemm xejn għalih.

Mort għand proxxmu u kif dħalt fuq il-pożaombrelli rajtilha luviera b'bajda ġo fiha. Għidtilha: Dik x'tissinjifika? Qaltli: Dik biex min jidħol hawn, l-ewwel għajn ... l-ewwel ma tmur tkun fuq il-bajda. Allura ma

The person [with the evil eye], without wanting to, thinks about you all the time. You're always in his mind for no special reason, deep in his mind. Once there was a man who told a priest that he wasn't going to see his canaries which he [the priest] had because he was afraid of evil tongues because he had the evil eye. But the priest said to him: This is just nonsense. He went to see them and on the following day [the priest] found them all dead. It is unbelievable. There is nothing worse than the evil eye and spells. Spells are even worse because they are too powerful.[54]

I visited an acquaintance and as I entered I saw an egg-cup on the umbrella rack with an egg in it. I asked her: What does this signify? She told me: It is there to attract the evil eye and to stop its gaze from being directed on

---

54. Ibid.

tistax titfa' għajn fuq ħwejjeg oħra. Din saret tal-Pietà. U hawn ħafna min jagħmilha.

Iż-żebbuġ tat-tbaħħir konna nqegħduh fuq platt. Imbagħad inqabbdu sufarin u nduru bih. Konna nagħmlu fuq sagħtra wkoll għax inkella ż-żebbuġa waħedha ma tixgħelx. U konna ngħidu seba' kredijiet u seba' avemarijiet.

Jaħarqu ż-żebbuġ. Jitfgħu fuq pala jew għuda. Tbaħħar meta jkollok l-oġġett ma tantx aħna: Kemm għandha tifla sbejħa Marija. Bdiet tħokk għajnha u l-għada tagħwret. Kellna baqra prima. Kellna nagħġa prima. It-tnejn tgħajnu. Il-baqra ħabtet għal xi ħadd u n-nagħġa nixfet mill-ħalib. Hawnhekk iż-Żebbiegh stess. Jekk jiġi bniedem indaħħluh ġewwa imma jekk jiġi bniedem ieħor ma

anything else. This happened at Pietà. And it is a common usage.[55]

We used to place the olives for fumigation on a plate. Then we used to set it aflame and we used to take it all around the place. We used to add a wild thyme or else it wouldn't burn. And we used to say seven Creeds and seven Hail Marys.[56]

They burnt olives. And they used to place it on a spade or a piece of wood. And you fumigate someone or something which has some ailment: What a lovely girl Marija has. She began to rub her eye and on the following day her eyesight weakened. We had a first-class cow. We had a first-class sheep. Both of them fell under the malign influence of the evil eye. The cow charged someone and the sheep did not give any

---

55. A. Smith.

56. K. Camilleri, 75-year-old informant from Mġarr, in an interview with the author in September 1975.

ndaħħluhx biex jarax il-bhejjem. Ikollu lsienu. L-oġġett ifraħ bih imma turix li inti fraħt ħafna għax li ma kien ġralu qatt, jiġrilu mbagħad. Biex ma jgħajnuniex konna ngħidu r-Rużarju. Il-qarn kienu jagħmluh biex juru li għandu l-għoġol jew għandu l-baqra. Xi ħadd ikollu l-għoġol biex n-nies jieħdu l-baqra ħdejh. Żeppu Naħħola r-Rabat kien jagħmel qarn fuq il-bieb u Pietru tal-Kapton il-Biżbeżija kellu l-għoġol ukoll.

more milk. This happened here in Żebbiegħ. We let certain people in but others we don't, not to let them look at the animals. The tongue is at the back of all this. Don't be over enthusiastic about any object or else something unexpected might happen to it. We used to say the Rosary not to fall victims of the evil eye. The horn was used to indicate possession of a calf or a cow – They used to place a calf so as people might take the cow to him. Żeppi Naħħola from Rabat used to place a horn on the door and Pietru tal-Kapton from Biżbeżija also had the calf.[57]

The Churching of Women

Originally the function of the churching of women was one of purification and reintegration into the worshipping community because of the belief that the woman was unclean. Today this ceremony is rarely performed but in the old days it was considered very importan and served to render thanks to God.

---

57. T. Muscat, an 82-year-old informant from Mġarr, during an interview with the author in October 1975.

Ġużeppa Borġ from Selmun, who had eight children 'presented to Our Lady of Mellieħa', describes this ceremony in these words:

Jingħataw żewġ xelini għaċ-ċerimonja. Il-qassis jiltaqa ma' l-omm u t-tarbija ħdejn il-bieb ta' barra tal-knisja. Jagħmel l-istola fuq l-omm u t-tarbija fl-istess ħin. Wara dan, iċ-ċelebrant, flimkien ma' binha u ommha, imorru lejn l-altar filwaqt li l-omm iġġorr ix-xemgħa f'idejha u l-qassis jaqra t-talb taċ-ċerimonja. Kif jaslu ħdejn l-artal jinżlu għarkubbtejhom u jgħidu l-litanija tal-Madonna.

Two shillings are donated for the whole ceremony. The priest meets the woman and her baby near the entrance door of the church. He puts a stole over the mother and the child simultaneously. Following this, the celebrant, together with the child and the mother, proceed to the altar whilst the woman carries a candle in her hands and the priest reads the prayers relevant to the ceremony. On reaching the altar they kneel and say the litany of Our Lady.[58]

Usually this ceremony took place in a sanctuary dedicated to Our Lady, such as Tal-Ħerba at Birkirkara, Tal-Grazzja at Żabbar, Tal-Mirakli at Lija, or in Gozo at Ta' Pinu.[59]

In this manner both mother and child are reintegrated within the community after the rites of baptism and the

---

58. Ġ. Borġ, a 75-year-old informant from Selmun, during an interview with the author in April 1974.
59. For further information, see Cassar Pullicino, *Studies in Maltese Folklore*, 234.

churching of women, which are intended to remove the taboo incident to birth, are performed.

The concept underlying the taboo in this situation is that all things created by or emanating from a supernatural being are his, or at least are in his power. He defends jealously the newly-born and relinquishes it only when he receives a sacrifice as a substitute for the tabooed person.

Such rites take place during other crises of many life-span. They are twofold in character – partly magical and partly religious. Such rites as the churching of women are obviously purificatory and magical in character, although at the same time they acquired a religious dimension.

The Way Out of a Question

Sex is an integral part of human life, one of man's basic biological needs, and the means to propagate the species. Naturally it figures prominently in most 'primitive' rituals, customs and plastic art. This can be seen from the pregnant neolithic mother goddess, where the pregnant woman is literally the apotheosis of the power of feminity, the divine symbol of fertile Mother Earth. In folk consciousness elaborate *rites de passage* surround birth and other life crises. The primitive thought idiom invests the sexual act with magical powers.

Pregnant women used to take all possible measures to make sure that no information is given about this phenomenon, which might generate dirty thoughts, unnatural feelings, and morbid curiosity, especially among the young. Women, who were pregnant for the first time, usually were somewhat ashamed of being pregnant. These undertones of shame often made communication about the subject difficult. Speaking on this subject was limited to the female sex. Their culturally-inherited knowledge was transmitted through whispered advice. The close relation between mother and daughter also helped in the propagation of information.[60]

During pregnancy, especially when the woman's physical appearance provides visible proof that she is with child, seclusion is important, as the proverb states: *Mara b'tarbija ma tesagħhiex ta' Brija*, 'A woman with a child does not find Ta' Brija road big enought for her.' [61]

The traditional faldetta, a spacious black satin headgear, helped a lot in keeping pregnancy hidden by concealing the figure of the pregnant woman. This is proved by the proverbs: *Mara bl-għonnella qatt ma taf x'għamlet u x'kellha*, 'You can never tell what a woman wearing a faldetta has done or has had.' This is better illustrated in this quotation:

Dari kulħadd kien jilbes onest. Anqas tikkom-prendi li bniedma tkun se ssir omm. Kien ikollna bħal dbielet b'ħafna ġmigħ jew xi bluża mitluqa quddiem. Meta tkun bl-għonnella dik il-ħabta kont mistura ħafna. L-għonnella kienet satra. U dari anke kienu jmorru jixtru minn ħanut. Mhux

In my days everyone used to be honestly dressed. You couldn't say whether a woman was pregnant or not. We used to wear a full skirt or a wide smock. The faldetta itself covers you modestly. Moreover, in my time, on leaving their homes to run some errand, they used to put on long clothes with an

---

60. For more information about the subject, see J. Boissevain, *Ħal Farruġ – A Village in Malta,* 17-8.

61. J. Aquilina, *A Comparative Dictionary,* 196, no. 62

bħal-lum. Ilbiesi twal, anke fardal quddiemhom. Jaqbdu t-tarf tagħha attaparsi qed tilgħab bih biex tkun onesta u ma tidhirx x'tagħmel. Dari ma tafx l-antiki kollox dnub. Dak skandlu ... u dak sebaħ u dak dalam. U għalhekk kienu jżommu kollox mistur.

apron in front. In order to make sure that her figure did not show she just used to play with the loose end of this kind of apron. Don't you see? In the past, everything was considered to be a sin, a scandal, and all this sort of thing. Hence they used to keep everything secret.[62]

'The faldetta itself covers you modestly.'

---

62. A. Smith in an interview in January 1973.

73

Such a quotation illustrates the normative ideal behaviour patterns which surround the birth-situation, as expanded in the foregoing information. The code of honesty bound all. The clothes were intended to conceal completely the figure of the pregnant woman.

In contrast with all these observances and secrecy, with which pregnancy was attended, Shidyaq's 'al-Wasitah fi Ma'rifat Ahwal Malitah said:

> When a Maltese woman is pregnant, she struts and thrusts her abdomen that all the passers-by may notice her.[63]

Although Shidyaq's account seems to be prejudiced, to say the least, proverbs and sayings show that the Maltese woman is very proud of her procreative power, hence such behaviour as referred to by Shidyaq's cannot be altogether discounted. This can be further corroborated from the following information, in which the informant explains somewhat ironically the great change which has taken place in the way pregnant women used to dress in his days and the present:

Mara tilbes id-dubblett – biċċa ħwejjeġ madwar qaddha, imdawra romblu – biex l-omm ma turix. Mhux bħal-lum – trajbu tal-bizzilla

A [pregnant] woman puts on a long skirt – she also puts on a piece of cloth wound many times round her waist, so that she will not be conspicuous.

---

63. P. Cachia, 'An Arabic's view of XIX c. Malta Shidyaq's "Al-Wastah Fi Ma'rifat Ahwal Malitah" ' in *Maltese Folklore Review*, Vol. 1, no. 5.

qasir, għax jgħidulek, min ma jafx irid jitgħallem.

Today, the opposite is happening. Pregnant women nowadays wear short skirts, because, according to their beliefs, those who are ignorant of these things must learn about them.[64]

The extremities resorted to in order to hide the physical changes taking place in the woman can also be seen from the following proverb: *Id-dbielet twal ikarkru t-trab, imma id-dbielet qosra jkarkru l-erwieħ*, 'Long skirts carry dust, but short skirts carry away souls [to hell].'[65]

Expectant mothers used to prepare the *għież*, 'the baby's trousseau', long before the arrival of the baby. Usually the baby's trousseau used to be ready at least four months before delivery. This usually consisted of a *fustana*, a *franella*, a *twittija*, a *ħarqa*, a *qlejba*, and two *qmejsiet*.[66] These clothes used to be hidden somewhere out of reach so that the other children of the family would not see them and ask embarrassing questions. Women having their first baby used to buy their pushchairs long after they were married, otherwise the neighbours would begin scandal-mongering.

The inquisitive nature of children, the What-is-it? reflex – the urge towards learning – as it is called by Pavlov, many

---

64. Ż. Axisa.
65. J. Aquilina, *Comparative Dictionary*, Chap. XIV, no. 9.
66. For further information see, Cassar Pullicino, *Il-Folklore Malti*, 43-44. See also idem *Studies in Maltese Folklore*.

a time makes them ask their mothers embarrasing questions. Where do babies come from? Why has a certain woman grown fat? How are babies born? The precautions taken to avoid such questions in the old days usually worked. Old people state that their children did not ask such questions. Today's younger mothers, however, state that the children have become more 'cunning' and ask more questions. In such situations mothers had their evasive answers and untrue statements ready to stop what they regarded as morbid curiosity; otherwise they simply dodged the questions.

The answers given to children are fantastic – the product of transmission from one generation to another: the 'explanation' that *It-tfal jiġu bil-vapur,* 'Children are brought by ships' falls under this category of fantastic ready-made answers to be given in the context. Other answers are of individual coinage. Certain communities have their own pat answers drawn from their own physical environment: *It-tfal jiġu mill-Maqluba,* 'Children are brought from il-Maqluba', is an answer which has no meaning to children outside Qrendi, near where Il-Maqluba – a karstic depression – is to be found. Usually these evasive answers are the products of past ages and certain topical references have passed out of popular usages. Thus 'cradles', in which boys used to be found, are no longer in use today. Other answers show that they are of recent coinage. *Daħal il-konvoj,* 'The convoy has entered harbour', as the inclusion of English word denotes, is also of recent origin.

The most widespread answer given to children who ask their mothers where babies come from is that they are brought by ships. Idiosyncratic ways of putting the answer differentiates one answer from another but only in minor details. Ships in the child's mentality surely stand for

It-tfal jiġu bil-vapur, 'Children are brought by ships.'

mysterious powers, bringing with them unknown things from abroad. Such answers are surely effective in reaching their required end, namely that of satisfying the insatiable curiosity of the child without at the same time giving him the right information.

The ship which brought a 12-year-old from Qrendi came from Africa and had various glass compartments behind which babies were placed to be seen by their mothers who wanted to buy one of them. The ship which brought another boy from Mosta carried various bags, surrounded by flowers and blue or pink butterflies, depending on the sex of the baby. The explanation given to children at Selmun runs thus: *Daħlet skuna u mar missierek għażel waħda,* 'A trawler entered harbour and your father chose a baby girl'.[67] Children from Qormi are told that they are brought to Malta on board Turkish ships. A friend of mine told me that when he was 13 years of age he still used to go near the shore at Marsascala watching out for some ship which might be carrying babies.

At the back of all these evasions and half-truths there lurks the fear of imparting the knowledge, as the following quotation shows:

Missierek mar fuq il-vapur. Kien hemm kaxxa, fetaħha, u minflok waħda sab tnejn. Hekk ngħidlu lit-tifel li għandu 13-il sena. Issa jemmen u ma jemminx ma	Your father went on board the ship. There he found a box, opened it, and instead of finding one boy he found two. This is the answer I give to our 13-year-old.

67. Ġ. Borġ, informant from Selmun.

nafx. Imma ma nagħtihx sodisfazzjon ta' kif u x'fatta, għax m'għandix dak il-wiċċ.

Now I don't know whether he believes or not. But I am not going to give him any real information as regards birth because I would be ashamed.[68]

Babies are to be found among thistles and thorns. This answer, according to information gathered from Għaxaq, often led young children to search for babies in the fields.[69] If the parents behave themselves, there comes the Holy Spirit and brings a baby swaddled in clothes which he places near the window. At Birgu a lotto draw will put in your possession a baby or two. Another Way-out-of-a-question runs thus:

Jitfgħuhulna mis-saqaf. Kellna nagħmlu kurtinaġġ biex nilqgħuh għax inkella jweġġa' siequ – l-omm tgħidilhom: Waqajt u weġġajt riġli. – Mhux ħafna skandli. Ħadd ma jaf xejn. – Waqajt għax mort niġri biex inġib lit-tarbija u weġġajt riġli. – Illum mhux hekk.

They threw the baby down through the ceiling. We had to make that decorated cradle to catch him, otherwise he would have hurt himself. – No improper information. Everybody used to be ignorant of such things – I stumbled while running to fetch the baby and hurt my feet. – That's what I would tell them. Today it's different.[70]

68. K. Galea, an 80-year-old informant from Mġarr, Malta, during an interview with the author in her residence, September 1975.
69. L.J. Borġ, A 12-year-old informant from Qormi, January 1976.
70. A. Smith.

The following answer is an easy one when compared with the preceding one, which is somewhat complicated:

Missierek mar ir-raħal għax in-nanna kien jgħidilha biex iġġibilna t-tfal – jew tifel jew tifla. Ara ġiet in-nanna bih Tumosu.	Your father went to the village because he had been asking your granny to bring him a child, either a boy or a girl. Look she has brought Tumosu with her.[71]

A rocket brought to Earth a young boy from Birżebbuġa, while another boy from Tarxien reached Earth by means of a parachute. An aeroplane driven by Christ brought a young boy to his mother. A stork brought another child.

The following information is somewhat poetic and is used quite often:

Jiena kelli tifel jaf jitkellem. U kien ikolli t-trabi wara xulxin. U darba minhom dat-tifel staqsieni: Ma ... dan minn fejn ġie? Għidtlu: Għax jiena nkun rieqda u jgħaddi anġlu u jagħtina tarbija mill-qoffa u jpoġġihielna ħdejna. Għidtlu: Imbagħad jien malli nqum insib din it-tarbija tant	I had a boy who was already able to talk. And I used to have children, one after the other. Once upon a time my son asked me: Mummy ... where did you get that boy from? I would tell him: Whilst I am sleeping an angel comes along and gives me a baby from his basket. I told

71. K. Camilleri, an informant from Mġarr – 75 years old, during an interview by the author at her residence at Mġarr in September 1975.

hi ħelwa. Qalli: Imma kif tagħrfuh – tifel jew tifla? Għidtlu: għaliex hemmhekk għandna inkwatru fil-kamra tas-sodda – Ġesù bit-tfal. Għidtlu: Tifel ikun liebes ħwejjeġ ħomor u tifla tkun liebsa ħwejjeġ bojod.

him: When I wake up I find this nice baby. He asked him: But how do you recognize a boy from a girl? I told him: Because there we have a picture – Jesus with the children. We had such a picture in the bedroom. I told him: A boy would be dressed in red clothes and a girl would be wearing a white dress.[72]

Similar to the above is the following:

Meta ommi kien ikun se jkollha tarbija, ibiegħdu lit-tfal mid-dar: Il-Bambin bgħatilna lil din it-tarbija. Il-biċċa l-kbira l-antiki kien ikollhom Kurċifiss bl-anġli madwaru. Kien iwaddab-ilhom wieħed minn dawn l-anġli. Dan il-Kurċifiss bl-anġli kien ikun f'inkwatru: Waqgħu mis-sema. Għax ma kienx hawn dak il-ħażen bħalma hawn illum, x'waħda

When my mother was about to have a baby, brothers and sisters were kept away from home: Baby Jesus sent us this baby. Usually, most of the elderly used to have a Crucifix surrounded with angels. The babies were thrown by one of these angels. This Crucifix with angels used to be in a picture-frame. They dropped down from heaven. Because in

72. Ġ. Grech, an informant from Rabat, 70 years old, during an interview with the author in June 1974.

din. Fl-istess ħin kien jiġri li those days people weren't as mhux dejjem kienu jkunu bad as today's. At the same jafu dak li kellhom ikunu time, consequently, many jafu. Għalhekk il-bniedem didn't know what they ought f'certi mumenti jiġi fiex jiġi to know. That is why things għax ma jkunx imgħallem. happened at certain moments, because they weren't taught.[73]

Certain individuals refer to various localities, villages, or buildings as the places where children are brought from. Sometimes these buildings are the hospitals or their surroundings. A boy from Mqabba was told that he was found by his mother near *Tal-Ħniena* Chapel, near *Il-Maqluba*, in a cradle hanging between two trees. A boy from Santa Venera was found near a stream. Children from Qormi sometimes are found at the *Infetti*, 'The Contagious Diseases Cemetery', whilst children from Victoria, Gozo were told that they were brought from Saint George, where there is a hospital. *Il-majjistra ġabet lit-tarbija*, 'The midwife brought the baby', is a most common way-out-of-a-question.

Il-Bambin tana tarbija, 'Baby Jesus has given us a baby', is the most acceptable answer given by the Maltese, because it is nearest to Catholic beliefs, and also a most effective answer with children.

The following quotation gets its power from a half-truth.

Kont ngħidilha: Minn fejn I used to ask her: From ġibtu dak it-tifel li għandek where did you get the boy

---

73. S. Borġ.

Il-Bambin tana tarbija, 'Baby
Jesus has given us a baby'.

hemm? – Għax il-Bambin għamilli wieħed taħt it-taraġ ġol-bagalja u mort ġibtu minn hemm. Kont nagħmillha: Allura kif issa lixxa u qabel ... Kienet tagħmilli: Għax kelli żaqqi tuġagħni bil-gass u t-tabib tani u neħħejt il-gass ... allura niżlet. Imma jiena kont ngħidilha: Imma għaliex meta titkellem man-nies tagħmlilhom is-sinjali? Darba qlajt daqqa ta' ħarta ġo snieni għax kienet qed tagħmel is-sinjali lil oħra. Kienet qed tagħmlilha erbgħa b'idha. Għidtilha: Ma ... dawk x'jiġifieri? Qaltli: Di ... pumm ... Illum it-tfal kollha jgħidulhom. Kollha jafu.

you have over there? Baby Jesus put one for me under the staircase in a box and I took it with me. I used to press on with more questions: How is it then that now you are slim while ... She used to answer: Because lately I have been suffering from wind and now I am cured, therefore my belly has become as usual. Still, I had more questions to put forward: Why do you make signs while speaking with other people? Once I was slapped in the face when she was making signs while speaking to another woman. She was gesturing with four fingers. I asked her: Mum, what does that mean? She answered by slapping me on my face. Today children are given all the information.[74]

This answer brings out the great secrecy with which this phenomenon is surrounded by certain individuals who succeed in keeping their physical changes secret, even to the

---

74. Ibid.

members of their own nuclear family who are always at home. Such a behavioural pattern is the result of a deep aversion towards giving the least information about this matter. This is further on seen from the following quotation:

Jiena ma kont ngħidilhom xejn ruħi. Xejn ma kont ngħidilhom. Jiena, l-aħħar tifla li kelli, kulħadd kien kbir, kulħadd kien kbir, għax iż-żgħira kellha 11-il sena. Anqas ħadd kien jaf li kien se jkollna 'baby' ieħor. Marru l-iskola ... min mar għax-xogħol ... u kif ġew raw it-tarbija. Għidtilhom: Dik tagħna.

I didn't give them any information, my lad. Nothing at all. When my last daughter was born, her brothers and sisters were already grown up because the youngest was 11 years old. No one knew that I was going to have another baby. They went to work or to school and on coming back they saw the baby. I told them: That's ours.[75]

The traditional form of giving the message that a baby new born was: *Qaltlek ommi ejjew oqogħdu*, 'My mother told you that you may come to visit her.'[76] The birth is not directly referred to.[77]

The taboo put on information regarding sex surely does not help in the educational process or the personality

75. G. Borġ.
76. Cassar Pullicino, *Studies in Maltese Folklore*, 227.
77. It is interesting to add that an informant from Qormi told the author that she was so shy of such things – delivery – that she did not even tell her husband when her time was nigh. She used to let him go to work and give birth without his knowing beforehand.

formation of the child. The pathogenetic danger concommitant upon some of these concepts becomes evident when it is remembered that the infantile concepts are generally not corrected through knowledge acquired later, but are merely covered up by it, as many informants confim by their behaviour.

In Maltese society this lack of information in the informal education process and to some extent even in the formal educational process has led to great ignorance about the basic rules and attitudes connected with these matters. An informant confirms this:

Tmienja u għoxrin kelli meta żżewwiġt. U ma kontx naf kif jiġu t-tfal.	I was twenty-eight years of age when I got married. And I had no idea at all about the way children are born.[78]

78. K. Camilleri.

THE INCULCATION OF 'PROPER BEHAVIOUR'

People must learn their culture and adapt to it. Individuals must learn skills to make a living and the expected behaviour to carry on the social life of the group. Certain types of individual behaviour and personalities are rewarded. Others are discouraged.

Human beings do not learn cultures in the abstract but their own particular cultures. This education, in the wider process of society, forms one's personality. In this way man learns to adjust himself to living as a member of society.

The family exercises almost exclusive control over the infant child especially during his earliest formative years; friends, associates, and age mates together with the mass media also have their say in the confirming of the attitudes, opinions, and value systems of the individual.

In a society like Malta's, the individual learns both from participation and from precept. The formation of the personality of the child and socialization are the result of many factors. These include the closeness with which the parents and other carriers of socialization adhere to culturally prescribed routines.

As the infant grows into the child, his increasing interest in and exploration of the environment may be encouraged, hampered, or largely ignored, depending on the culture into which he is born. Some restraints will also be placed on his activities. The child will be kept from seizing harmful objects, going to perilous places, drinking something harmful, or violating religiously-sanctioned rules. However, the treatment of children is not unrelated to the requirements of the adult culture. Various mechanisms of education are used in the inculcation of basic attitudes, standards, and values during childhood. In the matter of discipline, supernatural powers may be resorted to. The child is told that certain transgressions are punished by various supernatural beings. Sometimes these are impersonated. In other words, coercive means are used to inculcate proper behaviour in children. This was especially the case with the traditional extended family which was a stable social institution and which evolved into a sort of co-operative system, serving for the emotional support and stability of its members and having educational, social, and economic functions.

However, there existed and there still exists a culture amongst groups of young children which is made up of games, songs often of a robustly profane nature, rhymes, and riddles. Children, urban and rural, have a wide knowledge of this folklore of childhood which is clearly transmitted to them by other children rather than by their parents, many of whom would have considered much of it vulgar. There seems to be an underground culture of childhood, located in peer groups of pre-school and primary school children, into which Maltese children are socialized despite family, school, and the media.

This chapter will treat the coercive means used by the family and other social institutions, especially religious ones, for the inculcation of proper behaviour in children. This emerges clearly from the various conventional expressions, used by parents, which carry with them the basic attitudes, standards, and values of the adult world. Most of them bear the characteristics of taboo.

This does not imply that either the culture as a whole or the education process specifically reduces all individuals in a given society to one or another of a prescribed series of personality types, each characteristic of the age group, status, or role to which the individual belongs. Neither does it imply that the individual undergoes no change after early life. As psychologists have shown, adult socialization depends greatly on the foundation laid in childhood.

The socializing process is not the same for boys and girls. However, both sexes are taught along the same lines, although not with the same intensity.

What characterizes most of the conventional expressions (to be given later on in the following chapter) which form part of our linguistic heritage and the conceptualization of the world around us?

In these expressions there is the use of imperatives (must) and operatives (shoulds) to ensure that the desired behaviour takes place: going to sleep when ordered to do so; staying at home; saying prayers; speaking decently; showing respect towards sacred objects; doing things in their right and appropriate time, and so on.

A close analysis of these conventional expressions shows

that most of them derive their power and effect from supernatural beings such as God, the devil, and the supernatural area of hell, fire, and mysterious and dark places. Death and night, together with the concept of black in general, also help in the inculcation of ideal cultural patterns during childhood. Animals and people with unusual characteristics also have their share in this area of human behaviour. In this way the infant acquires, from the wide range of behavioural potentialities that are open to him at birth, those behaviour patterns that are customary and acceptable according to the standards of his family and social group. All this shows the role of the family in Malta, which is not solely the basic unit of Maltese society but also that of the Catholic Church.

This mode of implanting the ideal patterns of the particular culture usually leads to a total avoidance of doing certain things, lest the worse were to ensue in the adult world. In the behavioural patterns of the adult world there is an echo of the modes of behaviour inculcated during childhood. In fact, all the taboo-fears associated with supernatural beings, places, and situations such as God, the devil, spirits, heaven, hell, 'black', 'red', death, and other behavioural patterns in the adult world, know their origin to childhood.

Hence the various subdivisions of this chapter relative to the formative childhood days are going to be treated more extensively with regard to the adult world, where there is a replica of the child's world.

God and the Devil

The view of hell and fiery heat helped parents to make their children behave: Hence *Il-Bambin iġiblek in-nar*, 'God will bring you fire.' This is often said to children who misbehave. This is sometimes specified, as in the saying: *Jekk ma toqghodx kwiet, il-Bambin jibghatlek ġamra nar*, 'If you do not behave properly, God will send you a flame of fire.' The specification of the referent in this context is surely to be more effective on the child's mind because it brings the picture nearer to reality.

Black, which is the hue of death and which is linked with night and darkness, mourning and sorrow, and with evil, the Devil, and the 'powers of darkness' gives power to the following sayings: *Jekk ma toqghodx kwiet issir iswed*, 'If you do not stay quiet you'll become black'; *Jekk ma toqghodx kwiet, minflok helwa intik fahma*, 'If you do not stay quite, instead of a sweet, I'll give you a coal'; *Jekk tohroġ barra, jghaddi r-raġel l-iswed*, 'If you go out, you will meet the black man': *Jiġi tal-kantina ghalik*, 'The cellar man will come for you'; *Jekk ma toqghodx kwiet, mis-senduq johroġ ir-raġel l-iswed*, 'If you do not stay quiet, the black man will come out of the wooden chest.'[1]

The linking of black with evil, in the light of the dichotomy in the view of both Catholic and Muslim as emblems of goodness on one hand and evil on the other, can de seen from the following: *Jekk ma toqghodx kwiet, kemm inhabbat tliet tahbitiet u t-Torok jiġu ghalik*, 'If you misbehave, all I do is just to knock three times and the Turks will come for you'; *Tohroġx fl-intrata ghax hemm it-Torok fl-intrata*, 'Do not go in the hall because there are Turks there'; *Oqghod*

---

1. The ideal girl should not be too dark, because such 'Turkish' girls are regarded as dangerous and passionate, Boissevain, *Hal-Farruġ – a village in Malta*, 28. The proverb *il-mara sewda r-raġel taghmlu ghuda*, 'The dark-skinned woman makes her husband [as thin as] wood' confirms this idea.

attent ghax jiehdok it-Tork tal-habs, 'Be careful or the Prison Turk will take you'; *Attent ghax jiehdok it-Tork ta' taht id-dwieli,* 'Be careful, because the Turk who lives under the vines will carry you away.'

Turkish traditions in Malta are also to be found in the adult-world. These traditions can be classified under three headings: (i) Pious legends in connexion with churches, saints, shrines, crosses, and so on; (ii) topographical legends with folk-etymology as the predominating element; and (iii) ballads, including children's rhymes, and other survivals in everyday expressions.[2] In all this folk material, there is evidence of the deep hatred between the Christians and the Turks.

Apart from this, Turks figure predominantly in many ghost stories, where the Turk is usually short in stature and wears the traditional Turkish costume.[3]

However, in this category of deterrents, the devil, with the characteristics which he has gathered through the ages, rates most high in the adults' imagination, for whom he is a formidable reality and, as a consequence of which, a most 'useful' deterrent: *Jigi x-xitan ghalik,* 'The devil will appear to you', where the devil is mentioned directly, and not with any of its euphemisitc appellations. This is surley intended to exert great influence on the behaviour of children. *Jidhirlek ta' l-infern, (ta' denbu twil),* 'he who lives in hell (the long-tailed one) will appear to you' is a deterrent which makes use of a specific characteristic of the devil. The same can be

---

2. Cassar Pullicino, 'Pirates and Turks in Matese Traditions' in *Scientia,* Vol. xiv.
3. Diacono; 'Dehriet u Apparizzjonijiet', see also P. P. Borg, 'Haqq it-Torok Tal-Habs' in *l-Orizzont* – 3.3.76

said of the deterrent, *Ġiġi tal-Qrun għalik*, 'The horned one will come for you', which is accompanied by the symbol of horns with the fingers, for the better depiction of the devil's image.

A common picture, which used to be hung in many Maltese households, in which the horned devil carries the bad person away with him to hell, used to serve as a useful deterrent. Hence: *Jekk ma toqgħodx kwiet, jiġi x-xitan u jieħdok bis-sodda b'kollox*, 'If you misbehave, the devil will come and carry you away together with your bed'. Foul speaking is deterred by the expression, *Jekk tgħid pastażata x-xitan jaħraqlek ilsienek*, 'If you say foul words, the devil will burn your tongue.'

The mirror, with its supposed association with the devil, gave rise to the deterrent in the expression: *Jekk ma toqgħodx kwiet nurik il-mera*, 'If you do not stay quiet, I'll show you the mirror'.

Carnival, known as *Il-Festa tax-Xitan*, 'The feast of the devil', gave rise to the expression, *Tilbisx il-maskra fil-għaxija għax jidhirlek ix-xitan*, 'Do not put on the mask during the night or else the devil will appear to you.' Other sayings state that if you wear a mask on any other day except during Carnival, it will remain stuck to your face for the whole year. The same is said of a Carnival costume. This costume would remain stuck to you for the whole year if it is left on after midnight on Carnival Tuesday.

Death

The fear of death, although not conceived by the child in his play-age, is another deterrent for the young. The need to visualize its appearance has led to death being depicted as a fearful beast, a terrible angel, or an animated skeleton. Since

93

the first millenium BC death has been personified in various ways. The mythologies of ancient Egypt and Mesopotamia provide the earliest written evidence of this personification.

The personification of death is found in the expression: *Jekk tohroġ barra tara l-mewt ġejja*, 'If you leave the house you will see Death coming'. This provides for a boundary line between the outside world and the home itself.

The dead themselves also serve as a deterrent: *Jekk tohroġ barra, jgħaddi Lazzru*, 'If you leave the house, Lazarus will pass by.' Lazarus was the man who was raised from the dead by Jesus Christ. The story as narrated in the gospel makes a powerful impression on children, since it is heard quite often in the various religious institutions.

The notion that the mention of the name would summon the person himself is to be found in the deterrent: *Jekk issemmi lil xi ħadd mejjet, jidhirlek bil-lejl*, 'If you mention a dead person, he will appear to you during the night.' More strength is given to this saying by the association of death with night. Night, in conjunction with death, is associated with the alien realm of strange happenings. The fear of the dark is a universal human terror. Night is darkness, and darkness is linked with death.

Worse may follow for *Jekk ma tgħidx seba' Ave Marijiet meta tkun semmejt lil xi ħadd mejjet fil-batal, jiġu l-mejtin bl-għadma f'idejhom*, 'If you do not say seven Hail Marys after you take the name of some dead person in vain, the dead will come for you with the bone in their hands.' This saying, based on the above-mentioned notion, calls for atonement. The number seven, on the other hand, has a reputation for mysterious and uncanny power. It appears frequently in the Bible. As the number of a significant period of time, seven means completeness. It is connected with the inner rhythms of the universe and is powerful in magic. It frequently appears in spells and charms, as perhaps in this instance where the seven Hail Marys charm away the dead.

In the past the funerals of those who did not observe the rules of the Church took place during the night. This was especially the case with people in immoral cohabitation or of those who had not changed the Communion Card, i.e. did not fulfil their Easter obligation. In this case there is a distinction between what can be described as normal deaths, and those which are said to carry a certain wrong and dangerous connotation. No pity is felt for those people who had made a *mewta ħażina*, 'bad death'. They must be taken away as quickly as possible, lest the living be contaminated by their presence. This gave rise to the expression: *Jekk tmut jidfnuk barra*, 'If you die, you will be buried in the open'. This recalls the custom of burying non-practising Catholics in a place called *il-miżbla*, 'unconsecrated ground' literally a 'rubbish heap', outside the consecrated section of the cemetery – a most disgraceful burial, especially in a closed-group community like Malta.

Unusual Personalities

Effective deterrents are also to be found in the naming of unusual personalities, real or unreal, who are taken from the environment, and who carry a certain stigma with them. Unusual behaviour on the part of these personalities is sure to catch the imagination of the young.

Tiġi Mananni l-ħotbija; jekk ma toqgħodx kwiet nibagħtek għandha, taħbik ġol-ħotba u ma tarax aktar, 'Mananni the hunchback will come; if you misbehave, I will send you to her, and she will hide you in her hunched back and you will see no more', is surely an effective deterrent for instilling the proper attitude towards ready obedience to authority. The darkness of the hunched back which is associated with blindness is a powerful deterrent.

Scrooge, the protagonist of *A Christmas Carol* by Charles Dickens, catches the imagination of both young and old, the latter making use of it in such an expression as: *Jiġi Scrooge għalik u jieħdok miegħu*, 'Scrooge will come and take you with him'. *Jekk toqgħod thares taht l-imħadda jiġi ta' l-għajn għalik*, 'If you keep looking under your pillow, the man of the Evil Eye will come for you', an expression which refers to the very common belief in the Evil Eye, a belief which is surely not conceptualized by a child in his play-age. *Jgħaddi Gadawdu/ Dawdu*, 'There goes Gadawdu/Dawdu', is an onomatopoeic word used by parents at Żabbar and other parts of the island. *Harufu*, 'the small lamb', the nickname of a tramp from Floriana and *Il-pulizija tad-daqna*, 'the bearded policeman', together with *Ta' l-ixkora*, 'The man with the sack', and *Il-Gani* also have their share in instilling immediate obedience towards authority.

Sin

The concept of sin, which besides being a distinction between good and evil, is essentially a religious concept based on man's relationship with a transcendent reality, is also made use of to instil good behaviour on the part of the young. However, what the mother really means to say is not 'sinning' but 'wrong-doing'. This shows that a person who does not perform a role correctly may be liable not only to the pressure of parental authority but also to the penance imposed by the Church and to spiritual punishment after death.

Jekk tiekol il-figolla ta' l-Ghid qabel ma tkun tbierket, taghmel dnub, 'If you eat the Easter pastry before it is blessed, you will commit a sin.' This is said by mothers to their young so that they would not eat the pastry on Good Friday and Holy Saturday, especially when one considers that during these days rigorous fasting was expected. Treating bread carelessly results in transformation into a monkey, as the saying holds: *Jekk ticcajta bil-hobz, issir xadina*, 'If you treat bread irreverently, you will become a monkey.' This punishment derives its strength from the association of bread with the Holy Eucharist. Bulls, being equated with strength and infidelity in the adult world, give a special meaning to the following saying: *Jekk ma tghidx ir-ruzarju, tohlom bil-barrin*, 'If you do not recite the rosary, you will dream of bulls.' Dreaming of bulls is associated with bad luck in the popular explanation of dreams. *Jekk tigdeb, ilsienek l-ewwel ma jikolulek id-dud*, 'Your tongue will be the first thing to be eaten up by worms if you lie.' Lying, which is considered to be a 'sin', is punished by fires which consume the very tongues that committed the sin. An outward sign of disgrace, because it exposes the liar to others, is a cross which appears on the liar's forehead, as the saying has it: *Jekk tigdeb, jidhirlek salib fuq mohhok*, 'If you lie, a cross will appear on your forehead.'

The *Ave Maria*

Church bells are rung at sunset, popularly known as *Ave Marija*, to mark the end of the working day. This is one of the bells rung during the day, by which the people in Malta used to regulate their periodic religious activities before the coming of industrialization. In the past the bell used to be rung nine times, symbolizing the nine months Jesus spent in his mother's womb. *The Paternoster*, which is rung early in the morning, is followed by the ringing of the bells from the belfry of the church to announce the first Mass, *ta' l-ewwel*, and subsequent masses. At eight in the morning, at noon, and at sunset, the Angelus Bell is rung so that the people say the relevant prayers to the Holy Virgin. *Ta' Siegħa Lejl* is heard after sunset while *Ta' l-Imwiet*, 'The All Souls' Bell' is the final bell of the day.

The transition from day work to night is marked with special customs and restrictions. In the old days it was the custom to ring *l-Ave Marija ta' l-Għaġin*, 'The *Ave Maria* of the Pasta', thirty minutes before the *Ave Maria* proper. This *Ave Maria* took its name from the custom of eating *minestra* 'pasta' at this hour, one of the most common dishes on the traditional Maltese menu. Following the ringing of *Ta' l-Imwiet*, 'The All Souls' Bell', outside activities had to be reduced to the minimum. The last activity used to be that of people sitting in clusters near their houses, courtyards, and open doorways reciting the rosary before going to bed. Women going about after this hour were women of loose habits. *Id-dawran ta' bil-lejl qatt ma jġib ġid*, 'No good comes of [girls] gadding about at night' and the variant *Mara bil-lejl dellha tqil*, 'Heavy is the shadow of a woman who wanders about at night'.

The following quotation from an interview with an elderly woman from Nadur in Gozo shows the prejudice against girls who stay out at night after *Ta' l-Imwiet*:

Ma' ta' l-Imwiet ninġabru d-dar. Ngħidu r-rużarju u naħdmu l-bizzila biex ngħixu. Il-ġiri ma jiswiex. Dawk li jiġru jkunu dwieb tal-	With the ringing of *Ta' l-Imwiet*, 'The All Souls' Bell' we used to gather in our homes, recite the rosary, and make lace to earn a living. Running

magħżula. U konna tfal ma konna mmorru mkien. Dari ma kienx hawn kroroz. Jekk ma tkunx tifla sewwa jkun jaf kulħadd.

about is wrong. Those who go about in the night are mares (girls of loose habits). And when we were young, we never went any-where. In those days there were no cars. A girl of loose habits would be known to everyone.[4]

The following two quatrains emphasize again the association of this time of the day with loose sexual behaviour:

Ejja 'l hawn, biċċa minn qalbi, La darba kont minn xortija Issa ma nistax inkellmek Għax daqqet l-Ave Marija.

Come here, my own heart, Since you were part of my fate Now I cannot speak with you Because the *Ave Maria* has rung

L-Ave Marija daqqet U ħanini għadu ma ġiex,

The *Ave Maria* has rung And my dear one has not yet come,

Qbadt l-għonnella u ħrigt infittxu Insibu f'ħoġor it-tfajliet.

I put on the faldetta and went out in search of him And I found him in the lap of the girls.

Fear of staying out after this hour of the night gave rise to various beliefs which are of taboo character in the minds of our forefathers. Most of the beliefs surrounding the devil and the spirits are concerned with this time and with the

---

4. Il-Bukaċċina.

'dark' night. Apart from their specific interest, such supernatural beings served the utilitarian end of preserving the social scale.

Tas-Setta, 'Members of the Devil's Sect'

Tas-Setta provide parents with powerful bogeymen because of their supposed deviant and often revolting practices. Accusing a person of witchcraft is tantamount to charging him with foul crimes; this action throws into sharper relief the moral precepts of the society to which that person belongs.

The fact that the witch is used for making children more circumspect about their conduct is no doubt related to the tendency in many societies for belief in witchcraft to provide plausible points of backward reference in the explanation of misfortune. If someone falls ill or has an accident, both he and his fellow men can usually find some incident in his prior social interaction which will explain why someone had reason to have a grudge against him and why he should now be the victim of witchcraft. He may have quarrelled with someone of dubious reputation, or he may have failed to discharge an obligation towards someone who, though in a superior moral position, is now believed to have restored to an immoral form of retribution.[5]

The following are various anecdotes narrated by various informants which show how people practising witchcraft were used by parents to inculcate the behaviour patterns needed for the children to live according to the norms of their society. Otherwise, such a subject needs a wider historical perspective and more intensive research work.[6]

5. Maple, 101.
6. Research work about this subject has been conducted by Bonnici, 'Superstitions in Malta', *Melita Historica*, Vol. IV, no. 3 and idem. *Malta u l-Inkisizzjoni*.

It suffices to say here that the belief in witches, in other words women who are possessed by the devil, is a belief which developed in the Middle Ages, especially in the north of Europe, continued during the Renaissance, and survived even in our modern age. The sixteenth century, which is regarded as a century full of contrasting behaviour is the century which is mostly associated with witchcraft.[7]

However it has to be kept in mind that these are usually associated with Freemasons. It seems that the past generation of Maltese associated these 'Members of the Sect', *Tas-Setta*, with Freemasons, who, for them, were unbelievers.[8] This is perhaps the result of the secrecy which characterizes both Freemasons and the *Tas-Setta*. In fact Freemasonry began in the Middle Ages as an early trade union for builders. Its openness to all who accept a Supreme Being as the Great Architect of the world and its enticing air of mystery have made it the most popular of all secret societies. Most of the members join the society through some friend who is already an adept. Another connection between *Tas-Setta* and Freemasons is to be found in the practice of rituals that include secret words and signs.

Jien kont nisimgħu jgħid – missieri – li darba kien hemm mara u raġel tal-familja. U hi kienet tqum, x'ħin kienu jitilgħu jorqdu – meta tara li għadda ftit tal-ħin, tarah

I used to hear my father say that once there were a husband and a wife. And she used to wake up some time after having gone to bed, making sure that he was fast

7. Ferraironi, *Le Streghe e l'Inquisizione, Superstizione e realtà*, 3.
8. Ganado, *Rajt Malta Tinbidel*, Vol. 1, 34.

raqad sewwa – hi tqum, kellha l-fliexken – tindilek u ttir mit-tieqa. U darba mar warajha biex jara fejn marret. U daħlet ġo għar. U kien hemm sħabha hemm, jiżfnu u jogħlew. U hu biex juriha li żgur kien hemm, qatagħlha biċċa mill-għonnella. U reġa' mar id-dar fejn kien. U x'ħin ġiet u dan qallha: Fejn kont? Qaltlu: U mort s'hawnhekk u smajt quddiesa. Qallha: Iwa? Qallha: Ma kontx fit-tali għar? Qaltlu: Mhux veru ... mhux veru. Qallha: Mur ġib l-għonnella. Qallha: Ħalli tara qtajtlekx biċċa minnha. U marret ġiebet l-għonnella u sabet il-biċċa naqqosa. Ma stennietx x'għamlilha. Imma s-sinjal kien hemm. Imbagħad kissrilha dawk il-fliexken u taha taħna.

asleep. She wakes up – she had some bottles – she used to anoint herself and fly out of the window. And once he followed her to see where she was going. And she went into a cave. And there were her friends, dancing and jumping around. In order to show her that he had been in the cave, he cut off a piece of her faldetta. And he returned home. And when she came back, he asked her: Where have you been? And she told him: I went just round the corner to hear Mass. He told her: Sure? Weren't you in that cave? She told him: It is not true. It is not true. He told her: Go and bring the faldetta! So that we'll see the part which I cut off from it. And she went and brought the faldetta and she found a missing part. She had never expected such a thing to happen. But the sign was there. Then he broke all her bottles and gave her a sound beating.

MISTOQSIJA: Il-għala kienu jgħidulhom tas-Setta?
TWEĠIBA: Għax kienu jkunu miktubin, għandu jkun ma' ta' l-Infern. Jien ma nafx eh! Imma insomma, darba jien stess kont qiegħda fuq il-qiegħa – konna nidirsu fuq il-qiegħa, u bil-lejl kien ikun hemm ħafna qamħ taħt it-tiben, u konna mmorru norqdu hemm, għax missieri ma kienx ikun hemm, u konna mmorru aħna x-xebbiet norqdu fuqha. U bil-lejl ... jien m'nejn ġej ma nafx. Imma jien ħafna daqq bil-lejl smajt. U twaħħaxt. U trekkent tajjeb. U daħħalt idi ġot-tiben fuq il-qiegħa. U mbagħad fil-għodu, x'ħin għidt 'l ommi, ma ħallitniex immorru iżjed fuq il-qiegħa. Qaltli: Min irid jieħu, ħa jieħu. Min ma jridx jieħu, joqgħod. Qalet: Imma intom hemm ma tmorrux iżjed ... għax anqas ħaqq il-biża' li tibżgħu. – U ma morniex.

QUESTION: Why they were called *Tas-Setta*?
ANSWER: Because they used to be enrolled with the devil, maybe. I don't know. But, anyhow, once I myself was on the threshing floor – we used to winnow wheat on the threshing floor, and at night there used to be a lot of corn under the hay, and we used to go to sleep there, because my father did not stay there, and so we maidens used to go and sleep on the threshing floor. And at night ... I don't know where it was coming from, but I heard music that night. And I was terrified. And I huddled myself up as much as possible. And I put my hands into the hay on the threshing floor. And then in the morning, when I told my mother, she did not allow us to go on the threshing floor anymore. She told me: Let them take the risk, those who want to! But you won't go there anymore, because it isn't worth the fear you will be exposed to. And we did not go.

103

XI ĦSIBTUHOM?

Aħna, billi konna nisim-għuhom jitkellmu b'*Tas-Setta*, għidna: Eh ... għaddejjin tas-Setta minn hawn. – Issa aħna ma rajna xejn, għax aħna anqas stajna naraw daqskemm tkebbibna tajjeb u għaddasna rasna ġot-tiben.

JGĦIDU JGĦADDU FL-AJRU...

Jgħidu ... imbagħad x'ħin idoqq il-Pater Noster, jekk jinqabdu jkollhom isiru annimali ... isiru li jridu ... u missieri kien jgħid li darba kien jaħrat u kien hemm gremxula. Kien hemm gremxula u beda jagħtiha l-frak tal-ħobż meta kienet qed tiekol. Itiha...itiha l-biċċiet tal-ħobż. U hi tiekol. Imbagħad darba kien il-belt (kont nisimgħu jgħid lil missieri. Issa jien kont nisimgħu jgħid. Kont tfal). U tah jiekol, kien ġo ħanut. Beda jtih. Qallu: Għax...U x'ħin mar iħallas, qallu: Le. Qallu: Ma rrid xejn ... għax

WHAT DID YOU THINK THEY WERE?

Since we were accustomed to hear about *Tas-Setta*, we said: Eh ... *Tas-Setta* are passing by. Mind you, we never saw anything, because we couldn't see anything, we were so huddled up hiding our heads into the hay.

THEY SAY THAT THEY FLY IN THE AIR ...

They say so ... then after *Pater Noster*, if they are caught, they turn them-seleves into animals ... they can become anything they want to...and my father used to say that once whilst he was ploughing he saw a lizard. He was ploughing the fields that is ... he saw a lizard and he began to give it crumbs of bread and it began to eat the bread ... he gives it more ... he gives it crumbs of bread and it eats. And once he was in Valletta. (I used to hear my father say. Now, mind you I used to hear him say this when I was a little child.)

il-pjaċir li għamiltli int ma għamiluli ħadd. Qallu: Jien fejn rajtek b'għajnejja? Qallu: Ma kontx taħrat it-tali banda u bdejt tagħtini l-biċċiet tal-ħobż? Qallu: Dak kont jien. Qallu: X'ħin daqq il-Pater Noster kont ma' Tas-Setta. U kelli nsir annimal. (Issa kif jgħidu eh. Issa jien ma nafx.)

There was a man who gave him food. He was in a bar. He gave him more food. After having finished eating, my father went to pay him and the owner told him: No. He told him: I don't want anything, because you did me a favour, no one had done to me. But I have never seen you before. He told him: Weren't you ploughing in such and such a place and you gave me crumbs of bread? He added: I was that lizard. When the *Pater Noster* rang, I was with *Tas-Setta* and I had to become an animal. (This is what they say. I don't know anyhow.)

XI KWALITÀ TA' ANNIMALI JSIRU?
Li jridu. Anke jekk ikunu jridu jsiru qattus jew ... Bissibli minnu? Issa jien ma nafx. Fi żmienna dan ma kienx. Imbagħad jgħidu dawn l-affarijiet ma baqgħux isiru minn meta ħarget il-Via Sacra.

WHAT SORT OF ANIMALS DO THEY BECOME?
Whatever they want to ... They can become whatever they want to ... a cat or anything. But can this be true? I don't really know. This never happened in our days. And then they say that these things did not happen any more after the introduction of the Way of the Cross.

MINN FEJN KIENU JĠIBU L-ISPIRTU?

Jgħidu kienu jagħtuhom-lhom in-nies ħżiena, dawk l-affarijiet li kien ikollhom biex jindilku. Jgħidu li mbagħad dawk ma jistgħux jerġgħu lura għax meta jinkitbu kienu jeħdulhom id-demm u jagħmluh ġo flixkun. U meta inti tibda taħseb biex tikkonverti ruħek, dik it-taqtira demm li kienu jeħdulhom kienet tibda taqbeż ġol-flixkun. Huma jisparaw għall-flixkun u joqtlu lilek. (Issa la naf hekk u lanqas mhux.) Ma jgħidux li jagħmlu seħer? Jagħmlulek magħmul?

WHERE DID THEY GET THE OILS FROM?

They say that the evil people used to give them to them. I am referring to those things with which they rubbed themselves. They say that after the initiation they could not back out, because when they were enrolled they used to take some blood from them and put it in a bottle. And then when you think of turning over a new leaf, that drop of blood which they took from them used to bubble up in the bottle. They shot at the bottle and killed you. (Now, I don't know whether this is true or not.) And do they not say that they can bewitch you? Yes, they could.[9]

TAF XI STORJA DWAR TAS-SETTA?

Ara din smajtha m'għand kuġin tiegħi – m'għand Ċikku ta' Bellini – ix-xiħ li

ANY STORY ABOUT TAS-SETTA?

Look, I heard the following from my cousin, Ċikku ta' Bellini, an old man who lived

---

9. Ġ. Borġ.

kien il-Kappuċċini, Santa Liberata. U kienu jgħaddu dak iż-żmien jgħidu – ċerti ħinijiet, bejn id-daqq ta' l-ewwel u ta' l-aħħar, jgħaddu fl-ajru u kienu jkunu mhux spirti iżda bnedmin bħalna, biss kienu jkunu kumplikati magħhom u waqt li jkunu għaddejjin minn fuq il-Kappuċċini f'Santa Liberata, jew bir-riħ jew ma nafx, kif daqqet il-qanpiena, din il-persuna li kienet għaddejja waqgħet ġol-bitħa, żvirgunjata. U l-patrijiet ikkonfondew. Kien hemm ajk, li kien jaf xi ħaġa minn dawn l-affarijiet tad-dinja, u ma ddejjaq xejn. Ħa sikkina talponta u dawwarha dawra tond ma' dil-persuna. U malli l-ponta messet ma' l-ewwel darba taret. Jgħidu li l-gajjijiet ta' dawn, tas-Setta, kienu jintefgħu lejn iċ-Ċirkewwa.

with the Capuchins of Saint Liberata [at Kalkara]. They used to say at that time that these beings were wont to pass through the air at certain times, between the ringing of the First and Last Bells. They weren't spirits but human beings like us. But they were the accomplices of such spirits. When they used to pass over the Capuchins' Church at Santa Liberata perhaps because of the wind, I don't know – as soon as the bell rang, this person who was flying in the air, fell into the yard full of shame. And the monks were worried. There was a brother who knew something about such worldly matters and he wasn't at a loss at all. He took a pointed knife and with it drew a circle round this person. When the circle was completed, it flew away. It is said that hordes of such beings – *Tas-Setta* – used to meet at Ċirkewwa.

XI JKUNU TAS-SETTA?

Dik mażunerija. Mażunerija max-xitan għandha x'taqsam. Dawn mas-shahar ukoll għandhom x'jaqsmu. Kollha ma' xulxin imdaħħlin. Però dawk ikunu kkundannati li għal seba' snin ma jistgħux jersqu lejn iz-zuntier. Xejn. Ħaddiehor irid jitlob għalih. Però t-talb tiegħu ma jiswa xejn. Wara seba' snin, l-Isqof tal-post jagħmel li jista'. Jibgħat Ruma u l-kumplament. Ma jistax jidħol il-knisja għall-ebda funzjoni, anqas biex jara l-bini. Darba waħda, tgħid ommi, waqt li kienet fuq il-bejt, fis-Sajf, għaddew minn din il-klikka, u fost l-oħrajn waħda minnhom waqgħet-ilha ż-żarbuna fuq il-bejt, u r-raġel li kien hemm refagħha diż-żarbuna. Dan ir-raġel kien skarpan. Qal: 'Din iż-żarbuna minn tiegħi ... jien għamiltha.' Min kienet kien jaf imma ma qalx.

WHO WERE THESE *TAS-SETTA* PEOPLE?

That's Freemasonry. Freemasonry is connected with devils and witchcraft. They are all mixed up together. They were prohibited from approaching the Church porch for seven years. Someone else would have to pray for him. But all his prayers were in vain! After the seven years, the local bishop would do his best [to save him]. He would communicate with Rome and so on! The man wouldn't be allowed to enter the Church for any function – not even to look at the building. Once, as my mother used to say, while she was on the roof in summer, she saw a horde of them passing by. All of a sudden one of them dropped a shoe on to the roof and there was a man who picked it up. This man happened to be a cobbler. He said: 'This is one of my own shoes; I made it!' He knew whom it belonged to, but he wouldn't say!

A cobbler

QNIEPEN U SPIRTI ...

Meta jagħmlu xita u sajjetti qawwijin kienu jdoqqu l-qniepen. Imbagħad daqqa nisimgħu taż-Żejtun, oħra ta' Bormla, oħra ta' San Ġwann. Hemm qed idoqq. Hemm qed idoqq. U jdoqq kullimkien. U x-xita u s-sajjetti ma jimbarkawx. U n-nies kulħadd jiġri lejn il-knisja. Anke bil-lejl ġieli ġejna bi xkora fuq daharna.

BELLS AND SPIRITS ...

The bells used to be rung in heavy rains and thunderstorms. Then we would either hear the church bells of Żejtun, or Bormla, or San Ġwann. They're ringing here, there and everywhere but the rain and the thunderclaps still go on. And then everyone would run to the church. Even at night we used to go, with a sack

Għax il-qniepen huma l-vuci t'Alla, nismagħhom jgħidu jien. Il-qanpiena meta ddoqq, saħħa kbira għandha. Fuq kollox. Fiż-żmien ngħidu aħna, kien ikun hawn ħafna minn dawn l-ispirti ħżiena jiġru mas-saqajn, speċjalment minn x'ħin tispiċċa l-qanpiena ta' l-ewwel, ħafna jgħidulha ta' l-aħħar, sakemm idoqq il-Pater Noster, sakemm jibdew il-qniepen. Dawk il-ħinijiet kienu jaraw ħafna straġi minn din il-kwalità. Meta jindaqqu l-qniepen jispiċċa kollox. U din tneħħiet għax jew Papa Leone jew San Piju X kien għamel l-Ave Marija wara l-quddiesa u ordna xi talba 'l San Mikiel. Imbagħad tneħħew għal kollox. U għadna sal-lum ħadd ma jsemmihom.

X'TIFHEM BI SPIRTI ĦŻIENA?

Ikunu spirti, li aħna ma narawhomx, però għand-hom setgħa fuqna. U speċjalment aħna l-insara,

thrown over our backs. I used to hear people say that bells are God's voice. When the bell rings, it has great power over everything. At certain times there used to be many of these evil spirits roaming about, especially after the First Bell – many would call it the Last Bell – up till the *Pater Noster*, till the chimes begin. In that interval people used to see many such-like witches. Then after the chimes of the bells, everything comes to an end. But this has stopped. It was either Pope Leo or Saint Pius X who ordered the ringing of the Ave Marija after Mass and some prayers to St Michael. Afterwards they were stopped completely. And to this day no one mentions them any more.

WHAT DO YOU UNDER-STAND BY EVIL SPIRITS?

They are invisible spirits which have power over us, especially us Christians. Most probably, we'd have to have

probabbli jrid ikollna xi ħaġa tad-devozzjoni, biex ma jkollhomx qawwa fuqna, bħal ngħidu aħna, werqa żebbuġ imbierka, f'Ħadd il-Palm. Dawk l-ispirti ma jistgħux għalihom. L-ispirti kif jgħidu – l-anġli kienu fi tliet partiti. Il-partit ta' San Mikiel, il-partit ta' Luċifru, u l-partit tan-Nofs. L-ewwel tnejn qegħdin f'posthom, u l-oħrajn nismagħhom jgħidu qegħdin jiġru mad-dinja. U jien nisma' 'l ommi tgħid u xi nisa u xi rġiel oħra, li għandhom iż-żmien, li waqt li jkun ir-riħ qawwi ma kenitx tħallina ngħidu: Għaddi riħ għax kienet tgħidilna: Int taf min għaddej mar-riħ? U ssuċċieda anke xi spirti u kif tgħid ommi ssuċċieda spirti li daħlu fuq persuna u li ma kellhiex il-Kurcifiss min jaf x'kien jagħmlilha. Imma hu kien iżomm il-Kurċifiss u b'hekk ma sar xejn. L-ispirtu jgħidu jkun figura ta' bniedem imma ma jkunx figura tagħna għax inti bniedem tmissu imma l-

some holy thing on our person so that they won't have any power over us, like for example, an olive branch blessed on Palm Sunday. The spirits have no power over such things. As they say, the angels were divided into three parties – St Michael's party, Lucifer's party, and a middle party. The first two have their appointed place, but I have heard that the others still roam the earth. I used to hear my mother say, as well as other old men and women, that during a strong wind, we should never say: Pass away wind ..., because as she used to say: You never know who can pass by with the wind! – And it also happened, as my mother used to say, that some spirits entered a person, and if he did not happen to have a Crucifix, God knows what they would have done to him. But he always carried a Crucifix and so nothing happened. It is said that these spirits have a human

ispirtu ma tmissux. Ġieli dehru figuri ta' annimal. U annimali li m'għandniex fl-art tagħna, jgħidu.

form, but not exactly like ours, because a human being can be touched but not so a spirit. Sometimes they appeared in the form of an animal; but, they say, animals that do not live here on earth.[10]

IL-BELLIEGĦA

Bellie'a è il nome di un mostro immaginario che si dà ad intendere ai bambini abiti nei pozzi e ciò per impedire che si sporgano sulla bocca dei pozzi stessi: e l'espressione per distoglierli da questo è; *il-bellie'a tibilek* = *bellie'a*, del resto, viene dal verbo *bela'* = inghiottire e vale 'voragine'.[11]

This information about *il-belliegħa*, an imaginary monster, was used by parents to frighten children. They used to tell them that if they looked down into wells it would pull them down.

The following quotation sheds further light on the topic:

Meta kont xebba jien, mera d-dar ma kellniex, għax ommi kienet tgħidilna: Jekk tħarsu gol-mera, taraw id-dimonju. U jiena kont xebba bħal ħaddieħor. Meta kont nagħmel xagħri, kont inkun

When I was a girl we did not have a mirror at home because my mother used to tell us: If you look into a mirror, you will see the devil. Like all other girls when I used to comb my hair, I

---

10. P. Spiteri, a 63-year-old informant from Tarxien, during an interview with the author in September 1975.
11. Bonelli, 10.

irrid nara kif gejt. Kont immur inħares fil-ħerża tal-bir biex nara naqra x'imxatt u x'ma mxattx. Jekk ikun imċaqlaq l-ilma, dak ma tara xejn, għax l-ilma jkun qiegħed. U jekk ma dakx tara sewwa. U x'ħin ikun imċaqlaq l-ilma kienu jgħidu: Dik il-belliegħa. U jien lit-tfal kont nbeżżagħhom. Għax dari meta kienu għadhom żgħar it-tfal tiegħi, kien kulħadd bil-beritta għax ... Ih ... miskin mank xtrajtlu beritta? U kienu jgħidu: Jekk tmur tittawwal, il-belliegħa tgħolli sieqha u teħodlok il-beritta. Konna ngħidulhom: Għandha sieq b'ħafna swaba' mhux bħal tagħna u taħtafilkom il-beritta. Meta jkun jitħarrek l-ilma, għax fl-istess ħin fil-bir kien ikollna s-sallura biex tiekol dak id-dud irqiq għax dari mit-toroq u minn hekk kien jimtela l-bir. U t-toroq ma kinux ikunu ndaf bħal-lum tal-qatran. Kienu jkunu trab, imma mbagħad joqgħod u jiċċara l-ilma. Dak konna

would want to know how it looked, so I used to go and look down into the well to see my hairstyle. When the water wasnt't still. I could not see anything. But when it was still, I could see properly. If the water was moving, people used to say: That's the *belliegħa*. And I used to frighten my own children [with it!]. In the past, when my children were still young, everyone used to wear a cap because otherwise people would say: Poor boy! Why didn't you buy him a cap? And then they would say: If you look down into the well the *belliegħa*, would extend its foot and snatch away your cap. We used to tell them: It has a foot with many toes – not like ours – and it will steal your cap. When the water moved that would be the eel. At that time we used to place an eel in the well to eat up the small worms because in the past the well-water used to come from the streets; and the streets weren't clean like

ngħidulha dik il-belliegħa għax qiegħda tiekol id-dud il-kbir. (Konna nitfgħu sallura kbira jew tnejn biex tiekol dak id-dud li jkun hemm.)

the tarmacked roads of today. It used to be full of dust but then it settled and the water would become clear. We used to tell them that that was the *Belliegħa*, eating the worms in the well. [We used to throw in one or two big eels to get rid of the small worms in the well ...]

In the past, when my children were still young, everyone used to wear a cap because otherwise people would say: Poor boy! Why didn't you buy him a cap?

... Mort niġbor l-alka u l-baħar beda tiela', tiela'. Kelli digà ma nafx kemm-il xkora mimlija alka. U l-ilma wasalli sa rkubbtejja. Dejjem qed jogħla, qed jogħla, jogħla. U jien bdejt ngħid: Imma hawnhekk kien xott ... imma jien ma kontx smajt biha qatt din il-biċċa xogħol. U kien hemm mara qaltli: Itla' 'l fuq, għax ġejja l-belliegħa. – U l-baħar tela' sa triq il-Pwales, fejn kont. Tala' sat-triq u far għan-naħa l-oħra tar-raba. U jien li ma mortx dħalt għand mara kieku kien jeħodni. Dik il-belliegħa. Il-baħar ifur ... filli xott, filli jimla.

... I went to gather seaweed and the shore was dry. There was a big dry patch of sand and then, all of a sudden the water started coming in ... I already had I don't know how many sacks full of seaweed. The water had already reached up to my knees and it was all the time rising higher. And I said to myself: But this patch was completely dry ... I had never heard of this business! And then there was a woman who told me: Hurry up, and come in because the *belliegħa* is coming. And the sea reached the Pwales road where I was. It reached up to the level road and overflowed into the fields on the other side. If I hadn't gone into that woman's house, I would have been washed away! That's the *belliegħa*! The sea floods in ... at one moment it's dry and all of a sudden everywhere is full of water![12]

---

12. G. Borġ.

All this information, while showing the meaning of the *belliegħa*, also shows what a powerful deterrent it is.

Il-Kaw Kaw

The *Kaw Kaw*, or as pronounced in certain parts of our island *Gaw-Gaw*, was a slimy greyish sort of bogey man who strolled the streets at night. He could uncannily smell the breath of naughty boys and he would stretch his snail-like body until he reached the windows on the first floor, and he would then infiltrate himself through any crack or fissure, ventilator or other opening. Once inside the room he would grin with his toothless gaping mouth and frighten the naughty boy out of his wits or, worse still, make him have the most horrid dreams and wake up screaming with fear and sweating cold.[13]

Another variant of this bogey-man can be seen from this quotation:

... Some farmers imagine the *Kaw Kaw* slightly different, though none the less terrifying. At Wardija the *Kaw Kaw* is pictured as a huge giant who prowls the countryside by night and with his enormous strides steps from the heights of Gozo to the heights of Comino, thence to Mellieħa, and on to the hills of Wardija. Another step takes him to Rabat and then to Tal-Għolja. He could promenade from the furthermost tip of Gozo to the other end of Malta in just a few minutes. The naughty kids in the farmhouses can never hope to escape dreaming weirdly about the monster who could always get at them in any of his excursions around the Maltese countryside.[14]

These two variants of *Il-kaw-kaw*, which A. Cremona identifies with *babaw*, an imaginary monster for frightening

---

13. Gauci; for further information, see Bezzina.
14. Ibid.

children, is an onomatopoeic expression imitating the dog's bark, and show another type of 'extraterrestial beings', which are supposed to harass innocent children. Sometimes it was believed that this *Kaw-Kaw* or *Gaw-Gaw* went wild and took to harassing small children no matter how they behaved. However, there was a supposed cure if this *Kaw-Kaw* became a bully.

If at any time some *Kaw-Kaw* became a bully, one had to take a good pair of sharp scissors and a clean sheet of white cardboard, and await the coming of the bully to any ground-floor room making sure that the window on the first floor on top of his room was left ajar, he would grin ominously and stretch his body until his ugly head reached the first floor window. Then he would peep in and slide slowly inside the room. At that moment the fellow on the ground floor would throw open his window, with the sharp scissors cut the *Kaw-Kaw* in two, and while the lower half of his slimy body slid into the gutter, he would collect the upper half on the white sheet of cardboard so that the two halves would not be able to join up and throw it, preferably, into some empty well in the garden, but never in the kitchen sink. Thus the bully *Kaw-Kaw* would not be able to harass innocent children ever again.[15]

It was believed that the *Kaw-Kaw* favoured mostly the time between Christmas and the first week of February as the proverb shows: *Il-Gaw-Gaw joħroġ lejlet il-Milied f'nofs il-lejl; jekk isib mustaċċih miblula, jgħid: Ix-xita għaddiet; jekk isibhom nexfin, ighid: Ix-xitwa għadha ġejja*, 'The *Gaw-Gaw* comes out on Christmas Eve at midnight: if his whiskers are damp, he says: Winter has passed; if he finds them dry, he says: Winter is still to come.'

L-Imlejka (or *L-Imnejka*) which was supposed to be the female partner of this bogey man of Christmas Eve (because

15. Ibid.

it is also believed that the *kawkaw* is a phantom which appears on Christmas Eve, and that a person who is born at midnight on that day is also known by this name) was an old woman, believed to pass by during the night of New Year's Eve, and apparently symbolized the passing year, but the people wanted to make sure not to displease her in any way, lest the New Year be an unfortunate one, and therefore decorated their homes with flowers and also put flowers on the windows to placate the irritable lady.[16]

Other supernatural beings which are made use of in order to inculcate the behaviour according to the cultural norms prevalent in the Maltese society can be seen from these conventional expressions: *Toħroġx barra għax jaraw ħwejjeġ ta' barra minn hawn*, 'Do not leave the house because there they see evil beings not of this world'; *Fil-bir hemm l-imħalla. Ma tkun xejn. Tkun bħal sallura. Tiġi għalihom*, 'In the well we find the *imħalla* (a star).[17] It is nothing special. It resembles the eel. It comes to take them away.'[18] *Il-babaw jiġi għalik liebes l-għonnella u jieħdok*, 'The *babaw* will come for you wearing the faldetta, and he will take you with him';[19] *Jekk ma torqodx, jgħaddi waħx il-baqar*, 'If you do not sleep, the monster cow herd will pass by';[20] *Oqgħod kwiet u tisma' l-qanpiena*, 'Stay quiet

16. Lanfranco, 'Some Local New Year Customs' in *The Times of Malta*, 23.12.76.
17. These stars form part of a numerous group of the Pleiades. A.E. Caruana in his dictionary explains the Maltese word as 'la costellazione delle Pleiadi per la disposizione degli astri che la costituiscono in forma di aspo'. Information given by J. Aquilina, *Comparative Dictionary of Maltese Proverbs*, 512.
18. G. Borġ.
19. S. Borġ.
20. Ibid.

and you will hear the bell', whilst narrating the story of the driver who, while driving a Maltese cab, was assaulted, robbed, and killed; *Ara ġej Xaqq id-Dawl*, 'The Beam of Light is coming.'

All these supernatural beings or references to mysterious objects, together with an innumerable number of ghost stories, seem to have been widely used with certain effects in promoting the desired behaviour patterns.

The 'Why'

A question, which I often asked during my interviews with elderly people was *Il-għala*, 'Why', they believe in certain sanctions and act accordingly, although these are not prescribed by the Church's teaching. The most frequent answers were: *Għax hekk*, 'Because that's that'; *Għax hekk darrewna*, 'Because that's the way we were brought up'; *Hekk kienet tgħidli ommi*, 'That is what my mother used to tell me.'

Viewed in this light, folklore operates within a society to ensure conformity to the accepted cultural norms and continuity from generation to generation through its role in education and the extent to which it mirrors culture. It is an important mechanism for maintaining the stability of culture. Thus folklore is used to inculcate customs and ethical standards in the young, to reward an adult with praise when he conforms, to punish him with ridicule or fear when he deviates, and to provide him with rationalizations when conventions are challenged – the latter mainly based on the ritual dangers characteristic of taboo.

PUBERTY

The transitional period from childhood to puberty is considered a highly dangerous one in most societies. This marks numerous changes in both the personality and behaviour of yesterday's children who are now capable of reproduction. This is seen in the physiological maturity and the first functioning of the sexual organs.

In girls, puberty is definitely marked by the onset of menstruation, enlargement of the breasts, and other indications of maturity. Among boys, the period is not so clearly marked; there is only a gradual change, which is indicated by an increased growth of body and facial hair, the alteration of the voice, and changes in bodily weight and proportions.

Maltese society takes little or no cognizance of puberty in any ritual or ceremonial sense. The change in the cultural status of the adult is not marked in any way. Confirmation and similar Church rites marking transitions in the formal educational system have been suggested as attempts to find substitutes for puberty rituals which are still observed among many non-literate people.

Among non-literate societies young people in their puberty have to pass through various puberty rites, frequently involving circumcision for boys and artificially induced vaginal bleeding in girls. These rites serve as initiation into adulthood. In all these initiation rites there is the theme of rebirth which is parallelled by the equally-important recurring theme of death, which are closely linked structurally in the whole process of initiation.

These purificatory rites and the observation of precautions and avoidances also apply to boys who have to undergo periods of seclusion and retirement from the world, together with a severe restriction of the quality and quantity of their food, which correspond in character to those imposed upon pubescent girls.

In Maltese society the adolescent boy passes from childhood to puberty without any serious emotional disturbances although formal educational systems impress upon him a greater sense of responsibility about his changing attitudes towards girls and about the right use of the sexual organs. Girls, however, are more open to emotional stress and disturbance as a result of cultural causes rather than as an inevitable concomitant effect of physiological maturity. On reaching puberty the male adult is given more responsibility and is even given a key to the house. The adolescent girl, however, is not allowed to go about as freely as during her childhood. She runs too many risks which may clash with her 'honour' and 'prestige'.

Women

In order to understand the various beliefs about menstruation, one must first examine the social stereotypes and attributes surrounding women in the Maltese social structure.

A look at Maltese proverbs shows an anti-feminine bias. These proverbs may be described as characteristically aggressive, bearing the stamp of the male as the originator of most of them, a characteristic, however, which is by no means characteristic of Maltese paremiology. As one can see from the comparative sections, this anti-feminine bias occurs also in other languages.[1]

This aspect of Maltese paremiology is also reflected in the position and roles played by woman in the whole social structure, where segregation runs through many social activities. Sex differentiation is one of the main demarcation lines running through many social activities in Maltese society. Women are more than usually emarginated from important social roles and social functions. Up to a few years ago these prejudices were shared by the women themselves who held them as sacred from a very young age. Nowadays, the notion of emancipation is catching on among Maltese women who are shedding many taboos and fighting against social prejudices which have kept them marginal to the real issues of life. In this manner man's alleged superiority as the proverb, *Il-mara tilbes minn rasha u r-ragel minn saqajh*, 'A woman puts on her clothes from her head and a man [puts on his clothes] from his feet' seems to say, is beginning to be questioned.

In the outer social circle of Maltese society and even in the various institutions making it up, sex is a most important social difference. It demarcates structurally the bounds of

1. Aquilina, *Comparative Dictionary of Maltese Proverbs*, 149-50.

'A woman puts on her clothes from her head and a man [puts on his clothes] from his feet.'

social relationship. (In primitive cultures, almost by definition, the distinction of the sexes is the primary social distinction. This means that some important institutions always rest on the differences of sex.[2]) At school, in church, in public activities, and in all formal associations, with sporadic exceptions, there is the segregation of the sexes. It is only on rare occasions, such as the feast day of the patron saint of the village, that women are allowed to enter football clubs and band clubs. Those women who are seen going near, idling about, or buying from these clubs or 'bars' are held in low esteem and regarded as women of loose habits. It is quite

2. Douglas, *Purity and Danger*, 140.

normal to find women waiting outside these bars while someone attends to their needs. This, however, applies mostly to villages, for in towns the atmosphere is totally different.[3]

At the back of this segregation there is the division between right and wrong in terms of social mores regarding sexual activity, the morality of which depends on correct perception and due respect for the division of human beings into males and females. There is in this area a number of taboos whose ultimate purpose is to ensure that what should be kept apart shall not come together.

Some of these taboos emphatically state the differences between the sexes in such a way as to prevent dangerous situations in which confusion of identity or of roles could arise. This can also be seen from the taboos affecting dress and manners. The aversion of the older generation to the sight of girls who wear men's clothes and of young men who grow their hair like women is much more than anger in the face of a young generation which does not conform to the traditional patterns of fashion; this aversion springs from an instinctive fear of what could happen to society if human beings were to stop conforming to the basic patterns of their humanity.

Further examples of demarcation lines between the two sexes are to be found in language, where women experience linguistic discrimination in two ways: in the way they are taught to use language, and in the way general language use treats them. Both tend to relegate women to certain subservient functions. Girls are not supposed to use foul

---

3. For further information, see Boissevain.

language. When a girl uses certain harsh words, she is kept in line by her friends and parents by being scolded:

In some villages the old custom still prevails of having the women sitting on one side [in church] and men on the opposite side. This usage of splitting the worshippers into two separate groups according to sex harks back to the earliest periods of church history when men were kept separated from women by a screen of wooden lattice work.[4]

Boissevain speaks of what he calls 'a certain geographical separation of the sexes'. He writes:

The area of the village around the parish church and the small square and the streets leading into it are the territory of the men, when they are in the village. Here are located the clubs and wine shops which are their particular preserves. Moreover, men of various ages often congregate in small groups on the side-walk outside these clubs or on the street between them. The centre of the village, the *pjazza*, is, thus, a male area. In fact, women and girls, when they have to pass through this area in the late afternoon or evening, after the men are home, do so rapidly and often in twos. They don't linger there. Their area invocated away from the center, on their doorsteps or in their houses and in the numerous little grocery and notion shops, run, for the most part, by women; there, they meet with relatives and friends.[5]

The segregation between the two sexes can also be seen from the very structure of the rural traditional courtyard house, the typical Maltese village house, characteristic of the years before the nineteenth century, which saw the commencement of the Maltese people's transition from an agrarian into an industrially-oriented society:

The second house was, both a dwelling and a grinding store house. As a result, it was subject to an influx of males during the whole year and

---

4. Cassar, *The Meaning of the Maltese Countryside*, 44.
5. Boissevain, 42

Men of various age often congregate in small groups on the side-walk outside village clubs or on the street between them.

Village gathering

especially during the hot summer season after corn had been collected. The courtyard was not, therefore, a private part of the dwelling and, considering the social disparity between men and women in those days, it is no wonder that the owner built this house with all the rooms accessible from inside in order to get as much privacy as possible.[6]

More than anything this quotation shows a sharp division in territorial definitions of space in the settlement or living quarters in question, a sharp division which is also seen in the wide social matrix of society.

This sort of sex pollution arises from the desire to keep straight the internal lines of the social system. This separation of the sexes into their respective fields of action arises out of the instinctive feelings of attraction and repulsion which

---

6. A. Zammit.

emanate from physical needs. Its rules are phrased to control entrances and exits.[7]

This is only a glimpse into the web of the traditional female who is regarded as man's inferior. In the Jewish, Christian, and classical traditions, evil came into the world through woman. Up to our days the more important religious roles are still reserved for men and denied to women.

The prejudice against the female sex begins at the very outset, that is before birth itself.

Most parents, especially the mothers, prefer a boy to a girl. The reasons are several. Boys were more apt to contribute to the family purse, at a time when most of the Maltese extended families depended on agriculture for their livelihood. But the real reason at the back of this preference is one which is purely based on taboo, as the following proverbs show: *Ir-raġel dejjem bandiera bajda*, 'A man always carries a white flag', which means that a young man sows his wild oats but his folly is soon forgotten. Not so a young woman. If she behaves foolishly, her honour suffers seriously and irretrievably. The question of prestige, in a face-to-face community, depended on her behaviour. A foolish mistake on her part (viz. pre-marital pregnancy) would lose her her social status – *johorġuha fl-għarukaża*. Hence *Meta titwieled tifla sa l-ixkupa tieħu qatgħa*, 'When a girl is born even the broom gets a fright', while *Meta jitwieled tifel sa jġibu l-banda*, 'When a boy is born, they even call the band.' This apprehension about the child being a girl arises from the belief that girls, because of their alleged moral weakness, are more liable to fall into disgrace if they infringe any of the norms of conduct. *Meta xebba titlef unurha huwa diżunur kbir bħal min jaqa' fil-bir,*

---

7. Singer, *Taboo in Holy Scripture*.

Most parents, especially
the mothers, prefer a boy
to a girl.

'When a girl loses her honour, it is as great a disgrace as one who falls into the well', meaning that there is no hope of a remedy for a girl who has had pre-marital sexual intercourse. In the Malta context there is considerable bias towards a greater male participation in deviant behaviour than female one, although both sexes are responsible for a relatively large number of taboo violations.

Almost all elderly informants had the same idea about girls. In the way they expressed themselves, they showed the fear of disgrace and the prejudice against women in general.

The birth of a boy used to be followed by merry-making of all sorts, whilst that of a girl used to be kept as secret as possible. The birth of a baby girl seemed to be something shameful. A Birkirkara woman who only bore girls used to hide from her neighbours and avoid their visits by telling them that her baby was in imminent danger of death and was going to be baptized immediately:[8]

Meta titwieled xi tifla l-ġirien, skużi l-espressjoni, johor-ġulek l-ixkupa wiċċha 'l fuq. Iva ... jagħmlulek hekk. Darba kien hemm waħda u kellha ħafna bniet. Darba jkollha xi tgħid ma' waħda, jgħidu kellha seba' subjien u bdiet tinsulentaha u tgħidilha: Turtiera pastizzi ...	When a girl is born the neighbours put out the broom, pardon the ex-pression, face upwards by their door. Yes ... that's what they do to you. Once there was a woman who had many daughters. When she quarrelled with another woman who they say had

---

8. A. Zarb.

The birth of a boy used to be followed by merrymaking of all sorts ...

turtiera pastizzi. Qaltilha: Agħlaq ħalqek. Il-pastizzi li għandi kollha għad iridu jiġu għandek f'darek (għax is-subjien jiżżewgu l-bniet). seven boys, the latter began insulting her shouting: A dish of cheescakes ... a dish of cheescakes. She replied: Shut your mouth. All my cheescakes will one day be brought to your home (because girls marry boys).[9]

A woman who only bears girls is not held in high regard in the social consciousness of her milieu. This 'deficiency' is in fact made use of to insult one another, a common habit among lower-class women who are, however, also characterized by a deep sense of mutual solidarity.

9. A. Smith.

The following story is most fatalistic in character. Although it does not reflect the normal sort of repugnance felt towards girls in general, it still puts girls in a most unfavourable perspective:

Darba kien hemm raġel u qal lill-mara tiegħu li jekk ikollu tifla jaqtagħlha idejha t-tnejn. Mela titwieled it-tarbija u l-omm staqsiet lis-soru x'kellha. Is-soru qaltilha li kellha tifla. Hi bdiet tibki kemm tiflah. Is-soru qaltilha: Biex qiegħda tibki? Qaltilha: Għax ir-raġel qalli li jekk ikolli tifla jaqtgħalha idejha t-tnejn. Is-soru wegbitha: Tibki xejn ... għax it-tifla twieldet mingħajr idejha t-tnejn.

Once there was a man who told his wife that if she gave birth to a girl he would cut off both her hands. His wife gives birth to a child and asks the nun whether it was a boy or a girl. The sister told her that it was a girl. And she burst out crying. The sister asked her: Why are you crying? The woman replied: Because my husband told me that if I gave birth to a girl he would cut off both her hands. The sister said: You need not cry ... your daughter was born without hands.[10]

As has already been pointed out proverbs show an anti-feminine bias, a characteristic of all paremiology. In the light of the fact that proverbs serve as both charters for belief and models for action,[11] I am going to reproduce a selection of these proverbs so that, in the light of the ambivalent attitude of attraction and repulsion which surround women, the

10. M. Axiaq.

various taboos and other restrictions which surround women can be better understood.[12]

Mara daħket bix-xitan (or bid-demonju), 'A woman has even cheated the devil'; *Il-mara meta tidħak trid tqarraq bik; meta tibki tkun qarrqet bik,* 'The woman who smiles at you intends to deceive you; when she cries she has already deceived you'; *Il-mara dimonju (or xitan),* 'A woman is a devil'; *Żaqq ta' mara tesa' ħobża u kelma ma tesagħhiex,* 'A woman's belly can contain a loaf but it won't contain a word'; *Ilsien ta' mara jxoqq il-għadam,* 'A woman's tongue breaks bones'; *Ibża' minn geddum ta' ħanżir, sieq ta' tiġieġa u lsien ta' mara,* 'Beware of a pig's snout, a hen's leg, and a woman's tongue'; *Bosta drabi l-mara hi bħat-tuffieħa, minn ġewwa mħerrija (or mħassra) u minn barra sabiħa,* 'Very often a woman is like an apple, rotten inside and beautiful on the outside'; *Mara għandha sebat erwieħ,* 'A woman has got seven souls'. Seven lives are usually attributed to the cat, but a woman is believed to be as hard to beat. *Nisa fisa,* 'Women are tattlers'; *Seba' nisa f'sensihom miġnun jgħaddihom,* 'Seven women in their right sense are surpassed by a mad man'; *In-nisa laħam il-kelb,* 'Women are of the canine species'; *In-nisa xagħarhom twil u s-sens (or moħħ) qasir,* 'Women have got long hair and short sense.'[12]

Menstruation

The mystery, and therefore the assumed danger, of menstruation imposes many restrictions on women. These taboos with all their rigour are still widely diffused and survive in modern societies. This is a proof in itself of their antiquity. In many societies, including Malta, women's bodies

---

11. Dundes, *The Study of Folklore,* 275.
12. Aquilina, *A Comparative Dictionary,* Chp. XIV, passim.

are surrounded by a miasma of impurity and pollution which does not cling to those of man.

Most of these taboos have no practical value or specific utility and the trouble and hardship incurred in putting them into practice is often unnecessary. However, the popular mind does not fail to form various concepts on rational lines in its attempts to explain some of its behaviour.

Maltese society does not emphasize a girl's first menstruation but regards this event as a highly personal affair and even as something to be hidden or to be ashamed of. Education in this subject is passed in a rather distorted fashion from one age group to another, rather than by the other agencies of education such as the family, the school, or the mass media. At least such was the case up to a few years ago where the mass media were the prerogative of the few. The socio-cultural change taking place in Malta as a result of the rapid techonological change is bringing with it changes in different cultural values.

The transmission to the young of the knowledge necessary about the onset of menstruation is passed from mother to daughter, if the latter asks for it.

A blanket prohibition is placed on the transmission of knowledge necessary for survival as well as the dominant values, attitudes, and common behavioural patterns surrounding the onset of menstruation. *In-natura trid tgħallmek*, 'Nature itself must teach you.'[13]

Xejn. Proprju xejn. Xejn.	Nothing. Absolutely nothing.
Xejn. Għax kienu jibżgħu li	Nothing. Nothing. Because
jagħmlu dnub. Dak iż-żmien	they were afraid of com-

---

13. Il-Bukaċċina.

għalihom id-dnub kien dak il-kliem li jitkellmu quddiem it-tfal. Kienu jibżgħu li jiskandalizzawhom. It-tfal għalhekk ma kienu jgħidulhom xejn. Jien ngħid għalija meta żviluppajt min jaf kemm domt nibki. Ngħidilha 'l ommi: Mela jien se nibqa' hekk? Kienet tagħmilli: U kemm trid iddum hekk. Kont nagħmillha: Mela jien marida? Kienet tagħmilli: Kieku marida, kieku ma kontx issir xebba bħaxxebbiet tal-lum. – Illum littfal ngħidulhom aħna. Mhux bħal qabel. Id-dinja iċivilizzat ruħha.

mitting a sin. In those days talking about such matters in front of children was held to be a sin. They were afraid of scandalizing them. Hence they never told their children anything. God knows how much I cried when I came of age. I used to ask my mother: Am I going to remain like this for ever? She used to tell me: You cannot remain like that for long. I would ask: Am I ill? She would reply: If you were ill, you would not have become a woman like other women. Nowadays we talk to our children about these matters ourselves. Not like before. The world has become civilized.[14]

The categorical negation of any relevant knowledge about this life-crisis is clearly seen from the opening of the quotation just given. Although the girl continually pestered her mother with constant questions, she was given no information whatsoever, thus adding more mystery to this emotion-laden issue. A Sannat man referring to this subject said: *Meta tfajla tiżviluppa – l-istess natura trid li tiftaħlek moħħok. Kulħadd għami,* 'When a girl reaches maturity – nature itself must make you

---

14. S. Borġ.

conscious of certain things. Everybody is blind.' A Żebbuġ middle-aged lady said that when she was 18 years old she still did not know anything about menstruation.

Other girls used to get the relevant information and instructions from their mother in the form of whispered advice, full of intense preoccupation with danger:

It-tifla meta tiżviluppa, tiehu qatgħa. Tmur għand ommha u tgħidilha: Dan x'inhu? Imbagħad l-omm tibda tgħidilha: Issa din isservi għalhekk. Ara ma tersaqx ma' dax-xifer, għax jekk tersaq taqa' u tibqa' mejta. Fhimtni? Dik isservi għalhekk u għalhekk. Bħal certu żerriegħa li tnebbet biha. Niffiguraw dik bżar għar-raba. U dik bżar għalik innifsek. Jiġifieri oqgħod attenta għalhekk u għalhekk. Għall-minestra. Għall-minestra u għat-toqlija.

When a girl reaches maturity, she is shocked. She goes to her mother and arks her: What is this? And her mother starts by telling her: Now this serves for such a purpose. Beware of going too near the edge, because you might fall over and die. Understand? This is needed for such and such a thing. Like a certain kind of seed which is necessary for sprouting. Let us say there is manure for the fields. And that is manure for yourself. Hence beware of such and such a thing. For the *minestra* and for frying. For vegetable soup. For vegetable soup and for frying onions.[15]

15. Ż. Axisa, during an informal interview held in a bar at Għaxaq. Since, during the conversation, there gathered around us other persons, the informant had to use metaphors while he was talking. Still Zaren's words although metaphorical, were met with disapproval by those people around us.

The answer given by this informant is not completely evasive in character as the above quotation shows. Still the information given is indirect in character and shows certain feelings of embarrassment and secrecy. Resorting to a number of prolonged metaphors, the informant never mentioned the actual words. They are too taboo-ridden and straightforward. A crust of similes, metaphors, and circumlocutions overlays the information.

The following information contrasts the modern attitudes to this life-crisis with those prevalent in the past:

Ommha llum lit-tfajla saret tgħidilha bl-iżvilupp tagħha. Għax wasal iż-żmien tal-ħsad. Għax wasal iż-żmien tal-ħsad tal-patata. Allura ommha għandha tgħidilha hekk u hekk. Mhux hekk. Kemm-il darba inti tiġi li taħbat wiċċek ma' ħaddieħor, jista' jiġrilek hekk. Sewwa?

Mothers today do tell their daughters about their physical development. Harvest time is nigh. Potato harvest time has arrived. Mothers ought to explain the relevant do's and don'ts. If you have any relations with someone, such things might follow. Do you understand?[16]

The embarrased mumblings of their mothers and the confused tales of their friends usually had grave consequences:

Illum mhux bħal dari. Dari kienu jsiru disgrazzji aktar mil-lum għax kienu slavaġġ. Dari xebba ... qmis minn hawn s'isfel ... u mbagħad

Today it is not like the old days. In those days mishaps were much more frequent because people were savages. In my days a girl had a smock from

16. Ibid.

tilbes is-sufa ... issaħħan sidirha għax tibża' li tieħu xi bronkite polmonija u mbagħad ... blumer ... qalziet li jinqafel hawn (hawn fuq) ... u kien hawn mard tal-kliewi. Illum fid-dinja hawn movibment.

here downwards.. and then she would wear a woolen cloth ... in order ... to warm her: chest ... for fear of catching bronchitis in her lungs, and then ... bloomers ... pants fastened here (up here) ... and there was kidney disease. Nowadays there is a new movement in the world.[17]

Sometimes the information given was more apt to produce great emotional instability than the lack of knowledge itself. A woman from St Paul's Bay developed a crowd phobia because she was afraid of procreating children, after being told that if she touched a man she might have a child.

The ideas surrounding menstruation are part and parcel of the general ideas about how the relations between the sexes should be governed. In a place where having children out of wedlock was something really to be abhorred and a well-defined married state was the rule, the attitude to this critical moment had to be harsh and solemn. These taboos made menstruation an unmentionable subject which made the understanding of this natural physiological phenomenon very difficult.

The Touch Taboo

Beliefs in the harmful influence of a menstruating woman are widely held not only among non-literate societies but also

17. Ibid.

in Western 'civilized' countries. The attainment of reproductive power, which is marked by physical and physiological changes, is a dangerous state not just to the women themselves but also to others. Anthropology affords numerous examples of taboos which are mainly based on the psychological reactions produced in man by these physical and physiological changes. These have evoked feelings of repulsion, awe, and even hostility. The terms 'unclean' and 'defilement' show unmistakable traces of the thought idiom and world-view of the non-literate man. In their turn these views have excluded and restricted the role of woman, particularly at times when she is most womanlike. The periodic loss of blood is in fact regarded as one of the reasons which explain the physical inferiority of woman. However, while restricting her field of action, these taboos have also helped the woman and guarded her from danger and injury.

As explained in the chapter about birth, women, especially during pregnancy, during confinement, and after confinement are subject to many taboos. The same condition of inherent pollution is to be found during menstruation. Like most of the taboos inherent during birth, marriage, and death, these taboos are of a temporary nature.

Most of the specimen examples about sex pollution given hereunder are straightforward magical ideas on which the belief that certain normal bodily states are dangerously contagious is based. The very magical powers with which menstruation is invested underline the deep concerns of these beliefs. The contagious magic associated with this function shows the great concern with which the beliefs are held.

Menstruating women must not touch certain foodstuffs

such as vegetables, fruits, and meats, if not for immediate use. Otherwise these foodstuffs would become sour and unsuitable to eat. No harm would come to cooked food if touched by a menstruating woman. The popular mind support this belief by saying:

L-affarijiet li jkollok jekk tmisshom żgur jintnu, ngħidu aħna tadam, ħawħ, banana, u laħam. Kollha jintnu. Minnek innifsek. Int ikollok il-pori, il-vini ta' ġismek kollha miftuħin dak iż-żmien. Allura bil-fors irid ikun hemm iċ-ċirkulazzjoni. Din iċ-ċirkulazzjoni tibda toħroġ minn dawn il-pori. Għalhekk meta tmiss l-affarijiet ta' l-ikel, allavolja taħsel idejk, il-pori xorta jkunu miftuħin u li tmiss jinten. Għalhekk dak li tmiss trid issajru jew tużah, inkella jispiċċaw. Lanqas jekk tqegħidhom fil-friġġ, xorta waħda jmorru.

If you touch certain things such as tomatoes, peaches, bananas, and meat, these would become rotten. All of them would rot, because you yourself cause it. During this time all your pores and veins are open. Now since the circulation must keep going on, this circulation comes out from these pores. Hence whatever you touch, especially foodstuffs, even if you wash your hands, your pores would remain open and whatever you touch goes rotten. Therefore whatever you touch, you must cook or use in some way or another, otherwise, it would get rotten. It is of no use, even if you put the foodstuffs in a refrigerator.[18]

18. S. Borġ.

141

This belief is held by people of all ages who support it by examples, thus testifying the undying strength of this belief. A man was making wine in the traditional way and it turned into vinegar after it was touched by his daughter who was having her menses.[19] A young married man felt a certain repugnance about eating from a certain canteen because the bread was not good, owing to the same reason. Street vendors are most reluctant in allowing women to handle food in the market:

> Why? Because woman are thought to be unclean because of their monthly period. And because you never know when a woman is having her monthly period. The idea of her handling food then leaving it is a taboo....This is an area of straight taboo. And you have this in many Mediterranean countries.[20]

Per eżempju, din kulħadd jaf biha. Anke l-irġiel meta mmorru nixtru jgħidlek: Tmisslix b'idejk għax tnittinuli. – Huwa forsi jkollu kannestru mimli u tħassarulu. Tħassarlu waħda ... tħassarlu kollox, għax dak ikun velenu ivvelenat.

Thus, for example, everyone knows this even men themselves. When we go to buy, they tell us not to handle anything because 'you will contaminate it'. He might happen to have a basket full of fruit. If you contaminate one, all the other fruit would rot. Because that is poisonous and deadly venom.[21]

---

19. This information was given *en passant* during an interview held at Kirkop.
20. J.F. Boissevain, in an interview with the author.
21. S. Borġ.

'When you go to buy, they tell us not to handle anything because "you will contaminate it".'

Fearing lest the things they buy would be contaminated, buyers preferred buying salami, pig's trotters, and tunny from a man rather than a woman.

The following quotation refers to plants and the effect being touched by a menstruating woman has on them:

Taqbad xitla biex tħawwel oħra ma tgħixx. Tmut. U toqtol 'l oħra terġa'. Ma jgħixux. Min jaf kemm kelli affarijiet. Kollha jintnuli millum għall-għada, minn filgħodu sa fil-għaxija. Tibda

If you handle a plant to plant another one both of them will die. Who knows how many such things I have had which withered away within a short time, overnight. It will start to smell. And later on you can

143

trabbi r-riħa. U fejn tmiss tgħid: Minn hawn qbadtha. – Hawn għandek it-tebgħa ta' fejn qbadtha. Tittebba'. Tittakkalek. Tmurlek. Min jaf kemm kull tuffieħa u kull ħawħa jkolli jien ...

identify the place where you touched it because it carries a stain. It first changes colour, then it moulds, and then goes rotten. God knows how many beautiful peaches and apples I had ...[22]

Although the general tendency shows a great adherence to this belief, certain elements of scepticism are also found, as the following quotation shows:

Jiena kont immiss ma' kollox. Kont fil-forn u kont immiss ma' kull ma kien ikun hemm ... għaġina ... ħobż ... torti ... In-nies jgħidu li l-mara meta ma tkunx qiegħda sawwa f'saħħitha ma tistax tmiss l-oġġett għax l-oġġett jinten u jispiċċa.

When I used to work in the bakery, I used to handle everything, dough ... bread ... pies. People say that when a woman is not in good health she ought not to handle things for these things would start smelling and rot.[23]

This taboo greatly restricts the behaviour of woman when she is most womanlike, a restriction most common among non-literate cultures. It restricts women from continuing with their daily routine in certain areas and certain work. Old people, in their youth, used to avoid work altogether during the period, because if during the normal four days of this period the blood continues to flow abundantly, it was thought to be bad:

22. Ġ. Borġ.
23. M. Axiaq.

Anzi x-xjuħ kienu jgħidu li lanqas imorru jaħdmu għax jibżgħu li jmutu. Għax inkella tiġihom ħafna affarijiet. | The elderly used to say that they avoided going to work lest they should die due to the increased flow.[24]

Mgr. Pietro Duzina speaks of the practices of the Greek community in Malta and says that among the same community menstruating women were not allowed to enter the church, a custom which is still echoed in our society in the belief of the baneful influences ensuing from touching food with their hands.[25]

L.Bonelli recorded in 1895:

Quando i cocomeri siano stati coltivati da donne riescono amari. Lo stesso si afferma per citrioli quando una donna vi sia passata sopra colla gonna.[26]

This quotation further emphasizes what has already been said earlier because it speaks of cucumbers and marrows which turned out to be bitter when grown by women and the same thing happened to onions when a passing woman touched them with her skirt.

Mary Douglas writes:

The occult power residing in an object mystically dangerous is transmissible and therefore is capable of affecting whatever comes in contact with it. This notion must be regarded as a product of experience, however wrongly interpreted. The savage is aware that the bite of certain

---

24. S. Borġ.
25. Cassar Pullicino, 'Malta 1575, Social Aspects of an apostolic visit' in *Melita Historica*, Vol. 1, No. 3 (1956), p.39.
26. Bonelli, 30.

insects and snakes has painful and perhaps fatal results. He has learned, after long observation, that many plants and fruits, thought tasty, are not good for eating. He is familiar with various diseases which may be spread from man to man and from family to family, perhaps bringing death to an entire community. In all these instances the nature of the ill which happens to him is unknown; what he knows is that contact with the dangerous object has unpleasant consequences. How much more unpleasant must be the consequences of contact with anything mystically dangerous – with anything taboo! The contact which automatically liberates occult power is most often bodily contact. The object is something not to be touched – intangible in the strict sense of the word.[27]

This quotation shows that it is contact which automatically liberates occult power, most often bodily contact. The most intimate contact occurs in sexual intercourse; hence when women are unclean married couples must live apart. The absorption of certain food and drinks is also tabooed, hence the resulting alimentary prohibitions. Contact can also take place by sight as has already been seen in the section dealing with the looking taboo in the chapter about birth.

In spite of the prevalence of the above-mentioned beliefs, the popular mind did not fail to attempt to rationalize its attempts to explain mental illness. Suppression of menstruation, for instance, is believed to cause insanity. The idea is current that menstrual blood is 'bad' blood; if it is not shed when the period is due, it rises to the head and produces madness. Insanity is also held to occur if a woman washes her hair during her menses.[28]

These 'superstitions' with a taboo tinge shed more light

---

27. Douglas, 16-7
28. P. Cassar, 435.

on other ideas which are deeply embedded in the popular mind. If a woman washes her face or her head during her menses, she runs the risk of going crazy. Kissing leads to pimples on the face of the man. Swimming with girls during their periods is dangerous. Women themselves have pimples during their periods. Sexual intercourse leads to haemorrhage and the man *jimtela kollu imsiemer,* 'gets infested with boils'.[29]

Although these rules might be founded on rational lines, cessation of the usual activities and avoidance of the opposite sex during this period are normal features of taboo behaviour in this field. These taboos are especially rigorous when a woman is pregnant, gives birth to a child, or menstruates, since it is during such critical occasions that she is most a peril to herself and to her community. The conviction that women in their periods are unclean and consequently dangerous to themselves and to others is almost universal. This conviction lies at the back of the intensified restrictions. However, although certain impulses are vitally connected with the protection of the sexual functions, most of these restrictions are based on erroneous observations and false inferences.

---

29. Ż. Axisa.

MARRIAGE

Taboos gather around the marriage situation because it represents surviving *rites de passage* from one type of existence to another. The importance attached to the changeover and the various steps taken to ensure a successful marriage show the importance attached to it.

Marriage brings the parties into a new phase of existence. The supposed peril confronting them is increased because of the ideas so often entertained as to the defilement which is supposed to result from sexual intercourse.

Malta's past social structure was much more clearcut than today.[1] Hence it was bound to impinge heavily on the relations between men and women. Today, the social structure is not so clearly defined. Men and women are more free to choose and discard sexual partners, with no great consequences for society at large.

Social anthropologists speak of marriage as a contract,

---

1. For further information, see supra.

Donning her jewellery.

Handbags and women go hand in hand.

not solely between individuals but also between groups of persons. This is especially the case in Malta where the family of the bride and that of the bridegroom play most important roles in marriage. Both families exchange gifts and countergifts. This is seen in the dowry, which can take various forms. Still, one of the most important aspects of the marriage ceremony is surely the prestige attached to marriage, the resultant factor of many culturally-defined social and physical qualities.

It is not the case here to reproduce the rules of the game of marriage, taking into account all the ceremonies which surround the various phases of courtship, the dowry, the marital residence, and the religious ceremony itself. This chapter is mainly concerned with the taboos connected with this phase of human existence, adding the relevant information which enters into the game of marriage which will help to bring out the structural pattern or form which anthropologists try to describe.

It is most probable that many of the precautions and abstinences followed by newly-married couples, which now form part of nuptial etiquette, with a purely social sanction for their observance, were at one time genuine taboos.

Courting

Traditionally, in our society courting was restricted to a bare minimum. A girl and a boy running about by themselves were considered to be in danger of losing their chastity, especially the girl. This attitude, despite changes and the increasing numbers of people questioning old standards, still holds sway in many areas of local culture. Fear of defying this convention and especially of the dire consequences which may follow resulted in a marked segregation between the two sexes.

In the old days, especially in villages, marriage was contracted by means of a broker, a match-maker, *il-ħuttaba*, who agreed to bring about a matrimonial alliance for a small pittance. This way of contracting marriages sometimes made it somewhat hard for the couple to have frequent meetings between themselves before marriage. Usually such meetings were carried out clandestinely, but even such encounters were difficult to hold, since the solidarity of the community of which they formed part was strong against such meetings; everyone would have been ready to report to the parents of the couple concerned, especially the girl's. In order to avoid such happenings, marriages used to be hurried as much as possible, especially if an older girl should have already been married. It must be kept in mind that our forefathers were against marrying their second daughter before the older one was already settled and married.

In a closed community like Malta's, talking with your future husband in the streets by yourself with no one as a chaperone elicited unfavourable gossip. Such a habit was thought to be characteristic of girls of loose habits, although even such girls were supposed to do and in fact did their 'work' clandestinely.[2]

---

2. Traditionally the indication that there was a girl for marriage was a pot of basil. He (the lover) then employed an old woman as marriage-broker to bring about the match, for it was not becoming on his part to declare his passion in person to his lady love. When his suit had been accepted, the contract settled, and the dowry stipulated, the young man sent his beloved a present of a fish with gold ring or a costly jewel in its mouth. Then, on the day of the betrothal feast

The concept of 'sin' as denoted in the following information is applied to non-conformity to the norm prevalent among the face-to-face community we are speaking of:

Dari lanqas kienu jħarsu lejn xulxin. Meta kont għarusa jien, kienu jgħiduli li jekk indum inkellmu aktar minn nofs siegħa nagħmel dnub.	In my days we did not dare to look in each other's face. When I was engaged, they used to tell me that if I talked to my fiancee for more than half an hour, I would be commiting a sin.[3]

The concept of 'sin' here enforces the taboo character of the girl-boy relationship deeper in the psyche of the future wife. Keeping young engaged couples 'under the same roof' was also considered to be a 'sin'. The couple had to be kept apart from each other as much as possible.

Contact with a person leads to possession of the individual. This connotation perhaps explains better the

---

(M.*rabta*), he was introduced to her in the presence of her parents and friends and he offered her an engagement ring on which were engraven two hands joined in token of fidelity while she on her part reciprocated the gift with a handkerchief edged with lace. On the day of the wedding, musicians and singers celebrated in couplets the praises of the happy pair and handfuls of grain, rice, and wheat were showered upon them on their return from the church for the nuptial feast. The wife ate in a separate apartment but after the repast she went and sat near her husband and drank out of the same cup. Eight days after the marriage she joined her husband in her new home. J. Cassar Pullicino, *Studies in Maltese Folklore*, 38-40.

3. Il-Bukaċċina

taboo placed on touching, lest this would lead to undesirable results:

Jiena domt tliet snin imqaddsin inkellem 'il waħda mingħajr ma tħallini nagħmel idejja fuq tagħha. Minħabba f'hekk ma kienx hemm miġbda ta' grazzja.	For three whole years I used to keep the company of a girl who never allowed me to put my hands on hers. Consequently I never became attracted to her.[4]

This 'segregation' can further be seen from the following incident taken from written sources, in which the writer is speaking of long by-gone days, but from which it can be deduced that the restrictions and sense of shame which characterizes anything which has to do with physical contact were much stricter in the past:

Il matrimonio o sia sposalizio, ha qualche rarità. La messa si ascolta su due preparati cuscini; nella prima scala dell'altare del celebrante nella destra la sposa. Ivi risiede la sposa, non così lo sposo, con somma modestia, occhi bassi senza volger mai il capo per chicchesia. Il Signor Cav. de Guaft mi raccontò un fatto osservato da lui nella Parrochial Chiesa di Zurrico. Stando così la sposa, da una vertigne sorpreso lo sposo cade a terra, da parenti sollevato, dopo poco a forza d'acqua rimesso. La sposa – credesti mai! – restò qual colonna immobile, senza volgere il capo, o prestar mano a aiutarlo. Tanto è osservato questo ceremoniale tra le spose nuove.[5]

In this quotation the bride did not even move her head or extend a hand to help the groom when the latter felt dizzy

4. Ż. Axisa.
5. Cassar Pullicino, 'Antichi Costumi Nuziali Maltesi', *Malta Letteraria*, vol. XIV, 21-4

On the day of the wedding, musicians and singers celebrated in couplets the praises of the happy pair.

and fell to the ground during the marriage ceremony, an almost incredible anecdote.

The paternalistic attitude which directed the behaviour of girls in the choice of their future husbands is clearly manifested in the information given by iż-Żizu from Birkirkara:

Eħe ... darba niltaqa' magħha tal-Balal. Jien nieżel u hi tielgħa. Għidtilha: Fejn sejra Konz? Qaltli: Sa mmur l-barriera bl-ikel. Għidtilha: Sawwa. – Dakinhar iltqajt magħha. Qalet lil nannitha. Qaltilha: Iltqajt ma' Wenzu. Qalli: Fejn sejra? Għidtlu: Sejra bl-ikel. U qaltilha: Illum l-aħħar li tlajt. – Ara uuuuu dawk iż-żmenijiet x'kienu. Aħseb u ara kemm teħodha llum toknijiet waħdek, sqoq il-qasbi tiġri hemm waħdek iddimunjata.

Once I met her at Tal-Balal. I told her: Where are you going, Konz? She told me: I am going to the quarry with the food. I told her: Good. That was the day I met her. She told her grandmother: I met Wenzu. He told me: Where are you going? I told him: I am going up with the food. And she told her: Today is the last time you go to the quarry. You can see how things were in those days. You can imagine what they would have thought about today's girls and boys going about by themselves to the cinema and in dark lanes.[6]

---

6. W. Borġ, an 85-year-old informant from Birkirkara, in an interview by the author in August 1975

Karmnu Borġ from Birkirkara recalls the days when he fell in love with Gamilla and, in order to have a glimpse of her face, he had to take her faldetta off her face. During those days the faldetta worn by unmarried women had a round shape while that of married woman was pointed.

A girl who approaches a man and takes the initiative to propose marriage is looked upon as a girl of loose habits by the rest of the community, or at least as being *sfaċċata*, 'too frank and open', a characteristic which does not befit a serious woman. Such behaviour goes completely against the normal code of behaviour expected from a woman:

X'taqbad taqbad ... jekk ma jkunx irid x'taqbad. Hu jrid jieħdok. Taf x'nismagħhom jgħidu, li wiċċ ma jidher mad-deheb jinbidel u min iridek taħt is-sodda jsibek ... Dak iż-żmien jibgħat għall-ħuttab. Patti għal-lum, għax jagħmlu l-bejta quddiem.

Of course you wouldn't dare find a husband for yourself. He has to find you. I hear them say that the face which is kept hidden away is as valuable as gold, and the man who wants you will find you even under the bed ... In those days he used to send for the marriage-broker, totally contrary to what they do nowadays, because today they build their nest beforehand.[7]

W.R. Żahra writes that he was told that the cubicle (a sleeping alcove built at one end of a rather long room with

---

7. Il-Bukaċċina.

the bed installed in it behind curtains), apart from keeping the bed as private as possible, also served other purposes. He writes:

When the family had a marriageable girl and a suitor came to ask the father for her hand, he was entertained (in the master bedroom which was also the reception room), but was not allowed to meet the bride-to-be immediately. Although he would have seen her, coming out of church or on family errands, it was possible that she would not know him, so she was allowed to enter the cubicle before his arrival and have a peep at him through a very small aperture overlooking the room.[8]

Agius De Soldanis, writing about this topic in the eighteenth century, sheds further light on the strict segregation between unmarried men and women. He says that one can easily see how unmarried girls were guarded by their parents from the way in which women used to dress. It often happened that the nuptial feast was held by the parents of the couple and that a young man married a girl without having ever seen her even though Malta is such a small island.

Following this De Soldanis goes on to give a brief account of how all this happened. The father or, in his absence, the brother or, if there is no brother, the bride's mother is the person who deals with the question of marriage. But it devolves on the young man to ask for the girl's hand in marriage. It would be a shameful action if these members of the bride's family approach the young man themselves. They would want him, and they would do everything in their power to make him propose. The contract is made between the parents of the couple. The contract is made either

---

8. Zahra.

During those days the faldetta
worn by unmarried women had a
round shape, while that of
married women was pointed.

formally or, as they say, verbally. A ring is given by the bridegroom to the bride or else a handkerchief (the bridegroom never sends handkerchiefs to the bride; this gift would not be reciprocated).

De Soldanis continues to write that the people during the ceremony are given small baskets of *avellana* called *nucilli*. Then they send out small quantities of them to the neighbours. Some time afterwards the time comes for the first visit of the bridegroom to the bride. It begins with a kiss between the two. From that day onwards the bridegroom can go to the bride's house to see and talk with the bride. Eight days before the marriage, the bridegroom is obliged to send the bride a gift of fish! She then makes some fish pies and sends them to the bridegroom and to his relatives.[9]

All these case stories and anecdotes have provided a glimpse of the secrecy with which this would-be change in status generated in different times, a further reflection of the stringent way with which this phase was (and in certain areas still is) treated.

The chapter 'A Way out of a Question'[10] treated the secrecy with which the birth of a child is invested in order to ensure that no information whatsoever emerged, lest the young be scandalized. This dearth of information was also encountered during adolescence as shown in the chapter dealing with women and their physiological changes.[11] In this way women became ready for marriage and got married

---

9. Cassar Pullicino, 'Antichi Costumi', 21-22
10. See pages ff.
11. See pages ff.

without any formal information whatsoever about mating and its importance in marriage.

Here, the question, more than of taboos, is the safeguarding of the morality of the younger generation, but it generated various other taboos. The fact that pollution beliefs provide a kind of impersonal punishment for wrong-doing affords a means of supporting the accepted system of morality. Fear, which is systemized in taboo, in the lack of the necessary information leads to various emotional reactions which range from 'awful' to 'awesome'.

The classic example[12] of a woman who married at the age of 28 without knowing anything about sex amply demonstrates the great secrecy with which such matters were guarded.

The only code of ethics which our forefathers had to direct them in the kaxxa magħluqa, 'the closed box', as marriage was quite often referred to, are proverbs and sayings which reveal the general thought-idiom of the Maltese about marriage in general. Still, from these proverbs, it is very difficult to learn about the sexual side of marriage because this is tabooed, although it cannot be excluded that other by-ways by which this information is gathered are also to be found.

The following proverbs are relevant to marriage and, although not of tabooed character in themselves, are a part of the general picture of which the taboos tackled in this picture are found. They are in fact the wide context of the general thought-idiom of the people.

_____

12. See chapter on 'Transitions of Man's Life', supra.

Iż-żwieġ bħall-ħjar, 'Marriage is like cucumber'; *Iż-żwieġ dulliegħa,* 'Marriage is [like] a water melon'; *Iż-żwieġ kaxxa magħluqa,* 'Marriage is a closed box.'[13] As you never know the taste of a water melon before you taste it or what there is in a closed box before you open it, so you will know what your marriage will be like only after you are married. This was especially the case when marriage was contracted after a very short betrothal, before one gets accustomed to the character of his/her partner, owing to the fear of premarital pregnancy. *Iż-żwieġ lagħqa għasel (mgħarfa) bittija morr (mrar),* 'Marriage is a lick (or spoonful) of honey and a barrel of bitter.'[14] *Żwieġ li jiltaqa' Infern fl-art, u żwieġ li ma jiltaqax sewwa ħart,* 'Well-suited marriage is hell on earth; ill-suited marriage is cause of discontent.' According to this cynical proverb, marriage is always an evil.[15] *Żwieġ mhux imlaqqa' fil-qabar iwaqqa',* 'Ill-suited marriage leads to the grave';[16] *L-aħjar taż-żwieġ mill-kelma sat-tieġ,* 'The best part of marriage is from the day of engagement to the wedding';[17] *Iż-żwieġ qabel ma jinkiteb (jingħamel) fl-art, ikun miktub erbgħin ġurnata qabel fis-sema,* 'Marriage is decreed forty days in heaven before it is consummated on earth';[18] *Iż-żwieġ rabta tal-lsien li ma tinħallx bis-snien,* 'Marriage is (like a) knot made with the tongue which no teeth can untie';[19] *Iż-żwieġ xorti,* 'Marriage is a matter

13. Aquilina, *A Comparative Dictionary,* XVII, 167, p. 211
14. Ibid. XVII, 212, 173.
15. Ibid. 174.
16. Ibid. 176.
17. Ibid. 177.
18. Ibid. 179.
19. Ibid. 180.

of luck';[20] *Iz-zakak jaqbeż u jitfarfar, iżda l-ħamiem iżoqq u jgargar,* 'The wagtail hops and flaps its wings, but the male dove feeds and coos.'[21] Bachelors, compared to the 'wagtail' in this proverb, lead a carefree life, while married people, compared to the male pigeons, are full of worries and anxieties.

Second Marriages

There are various societal restraints on second and third marriages. In the people's consciousness, marriage should not take place more than once, for God ordained that marriage should take place only once. This is not the formal teaching of the Church but the product of bias which surrounds second and third marriages. The bias is the result of the association of second and third marriages with sexual activity, rather than with the primary aim of marriage, in the minds of our fathers, namely the procreation of children, although this is not the only variable. The concept of marriage in folk consciousness is one of emotional and sexual stability, where a man and a woman live together, indulging in sexual activity in a normative union.

Second and third marriages, on the other hand, are somewhat regarded as polluting because they are more associated with sex. Hence the expressions: *M'ghandux xebgħa*, 'He never has enough' (of sexual intercourse); *Lanqas Alla ma jxebbgħu*, 'Not even God can satiate him); *ħanzir*, 'A pig', an animal which is associated with *qżiżijiet*, 'repugnancy'.

---

20. Ibid. 213, 181.
21. Ibid. 184.

The following quotation explains more clearly the above information:

Bħal ta' l-ewwel la taqla' u lanqas thawwel; għax ta' l-ewwel, l-ewwel żwieġ. Jgħidu t-tieni min-nies u ta' l-aħħar mix-xitan. L-ewwel minn Alla – iż-żwieg ħalqu Alla – it-tieni min-nies – għax jgħidulek Ħudu – u t-tielet wieħed mid-demonju. Kristu hekk ħalaq. Darba ... darba taf x'qalet il-gawwija? Min jormol ma jiżżewwiġx. Hi romlot, reġġħet iżżewġet bħal ta' qabel ma qalitx. Telgħet fuq l-ogħla ġebel u tibki l-għarus ta' qabel.

You will never pluck or plant as your first one. Because the first one is the first marriage. They say that the second one is from the people because they tell you to take him and the third one is from the devil. God created it thus: Once ... once do you know what the seagull said? She who becomes a widow should not marry again. She became a widow and got married again and she did not succeed in marrying one as good as the first. She went up on the hills crying for her former fiancè.[22]

The association of the first marriage with God (the supreme good) shows that the first marriage is fully sanctioned. The second marriage as the outcome of pressure from society shows that it is a marriage of convenience. The association of the third marriage with the devil (the supreme evil) shows that such marriage is the result of evil, at least in the people's consciousness. Evil is here equated with sex.

---

22. Il-Bukaċċina

Pesce d'aprile

May and Marriage

Apart from the religious precept of avoiding weddings during the period *Minn Ras-ir-Randan sa l-Għid il-Kbir*, 'From Ash Wednesday to Easter', and a certain feeling of uneasiness regarding marriages on a Friday, there are no other specific days on which marriages could not be celebrated, with the exception of the month of May. This month is held to be a most unlucky month for a wedding. According to the proverb: *Xhur tajbin għaż-żwieġ, Jannar, April, Awissu, ix-xhur li fihom jiltaqa' d-demm*, 'The best months for marrying are January, April, and August because in these months the lovers' blood meets well.'[23]

The concept of the ill fate of May is encountered in many proverbs which, however, have an ambivalent character. *Mejju x-xahar (tqil) tad-diżgrazzji*, 'May is the (heavy) month of misfortunes'; *Mejju mirjieħ, b'kull deni stennieh*, 'Expect May, the month of winds, to bring all kinds of misfortune with it'.[24] Both proverbs show that this month is unlucky and apt to be full of misfortunes, although in no proverb is there a direct reference to marriage and the supposed ill luck associated with this month. On the other hand, in order to ward off the ill luck of this month and to celebrate its beauty, the Maltese placed this month under the protection of Our Lady as the saying *Mejju x-xahar tal-Madonna*, 'May is the month of Our Lady', directly shows. Such proverbs show

---

23. J. Aquilina, *A Comparative Dictionary*, XVII, 171, 211.
24. Ibid., XLV, 374, 569. Other variants of this proverb are: *Mejju l-mirjieħ, deni stenna bih*, 'From windy May expect all kinds of misfortune' and *Mejju bir-riħ u bid-deni stennieh*, 'Expect May to be windy and full of misfortune', Ibid., XLV, 383, 571.

that this month is invested with ill luck and this does not apply solely to marriages.[25] However, the taboo put on marriage is widely believed in. The taboo is supported by the belief that marriages entered upon during this month would lead to the birth of handicapped children or children of loose habits. The mutual love which is supposed to reign during marriage between a couple is itself at hazard .

The origin of this taboo goes far back in history. The Ancient Romans held May to be sacred because it was the month dedicated to the memory of dead friends. Hence it was held to be most unlucky for a bride to accept presents or hold a wedding feast during this month because most of her friends would be engaged in what we today call memorial services. Mary Queen of Scots married Bothwell in May 1567, a marriage which was to end tragically by the forced abdication of Mary two months later.

Among the Jewish people, those who got married during the month of *lyar,* which corresponds more or less to the month of May, were reckoned to be unlucky because it was unpropitious. In Palestine girls, used to be totally engaged in their work during this month, because this was harvest time and they had little time left for their private celebrations and no one felt free to indulge in merry-making until the harvest festival was over. In this case the restrictions are not the result of civil or religious laws but the outcome of necessity in the particular point in time – harvest time. The underlying motivation is therefore utilitarian not ethical.

---

25. A. Smith spoke of a certain kiosk that was blown away by unknown agency during this month. The people used to resort to the ill luck of this month as an explanation for this misfortune.

Of course, this historical information is not known by most of those who adhere to this custom. More than anything else, it is the fear of violating this time-honoured taboo which even keeps today's 'modern' people from marrying during this month.

Tempting the future

As the marriage ceremony approaches, 'taboos' tend to multiply, since the changeover from one state of existence to another becomes imminent.

Ritual abstention characteristic of taboo is seen in the custom according to which the bride must not be seen by the groom in her wedding dress prior to the ceremony nor must she look at herself in the mirror once she has completely dressed for it is dangerous to anticipate the future by projecting her image as a married woman into the mirror.

The same ritual danger is seen in the avoidance by brides or bridegrooms who happen to be seamstresses or tailors of making their own marriage attire. The spreading out of the blankets on the marriage bed is not supposed to be done by the bride herself but usually by her mother. Furniture for the new residence ought to be bought following the marriage ceremony. Losing the marriage ring leads to separation.

These popular 'superstitions', which in Malta are of recent origin, and which regard 'unlucky' objects, actions, words, and times, can be said to be transformed taboos. These are still adopted out of a vague fear of the evils which may follow from their violation, but without the importance, as regulators of conduct, which the original taboos assumed in non-literate cultures. However, there is a distinction between prohibitions whose infringement results automatically in a state of ritual disability (pollution or sanctity)which require a ritual purification, and prohibitions whose infringement does not taboo a person but only results in some misfortune for him if steps are not taken to avoid them.[26]

On the same line of thought there is the following taboo which centres around the threshold:

Nell'entrare a casa studia la sposa porvi la prima il piede in casa, credendo che quello sarà il dispotico del compagno. Che semplice credulità se non è superstizione.[27]

This belief, which led to the carrying of the bride over the doorstep into her new home, originated with the necessity of avoiding the threatening evil spirits that gathered outside the threshold. On the continent there was also a secondary consideration in that it was thought inappropriate for a girl who was so soon to lose her virginity to profane with her touch the threshold that in Roman times had been dedicated to Vesta, the goddess of virginity.

The First Night

The strictest continence may be required of newly-married couples on the first night after their marriage. A violation of this rule is sometimes believed to be fraught with possibilities of dangerous situations for the couple:

... è vietato allo sposo pernottavi colla sposa nella prima sera, alla considerazione d'essere illecita la coabitazione nello stesso giorno in cui ricevettero Nostro Signore Sacramento. Resta otti giorni senza sortirvi la sposa da casa, in sortirvi sarà accompagnata alla chiesa da poche donne

---

26. Webster, 369.
27. Cassar Pullicino, 'Antichi Costumi', 22.

parenti, poscia in casa dei genitori dello sposo, dove saranno i parenti della sposa a pranzo, e il restente è quasi uguale al di dello sposalizio.[28]

This is how Agius De Soldanis ended his writing under the heading 'Antichi Costumi Nuziali Maltesi' in which he gave much information about marriage customs in Malta. This quotation refers to the custom which prohibited newly-married couples from going to live together on the first day of their marriage because this cohabitation was considered to be illicit when they had just received the Sacrament of Holy Communion. The newly-weds could only cohabit after eight days. This custom recalls the Biblical episode which speaks of Tobias and his marriages, as the undergoing quotation shows:

Il carattere religioso o devozionale del trinoctium richiama alla memoria l'esempio di Tobia, il quale, secondo la tradizione, sposò Sara, astenendosi dall'avere contatto con lei per tre giorni: anzi in alcuni luoghi, e propriamente in alcuni paesi germanici, il trinoctium è conosciuto col nome di Notti di Tobia.[29]

The Biblical episode refers to Sarah and Tobias. Sarah had been married to seven husbands in succession but each had been killed by Ashmodai, the evil spirit which possessed Sarah, just when the marriage was about to be consummated. This evil spirit was, however, exorcised from Sarah by the burning of the liver of a fish and thereafter the marriage of Tobias and Sarah was consummated without mishap.

At the back of these rites and ceremonies there lies the concept of the power of evil spirits over the bride, or over both bride and groom.

---

28. Ibid.
29. Ibid.

J. Frazer is of the opinion that this *Trinoctium Castitatis*, as it is known in Italy, must have had a superstitious content in its origin. It must have been a form of taboo or temporary interdiction in the sexual relations between the newly-married because of the fear of occult and malevolent potencies which, in the minds of non-literate peoples, are always thought to be attacking the animal and vegetable life to bring about havoc in the life of the newly-weds.[30]

Like many pre-pagan or pagan rituals, the advance of 'primitive' religions put on new clothes, sometimes new forms, abandoning certain elements in order to incorporate others:

rispondenti alla mutat coscienza religiosa, al mutato ambiente ideale e morale; così quello del 'Trinoctium', eredità di tempi lontani e di superstizioni precristiane e, vorrei dire, prepagane, si cristianizzò, o meglio, continuando a vivere nel popolo, s'incardino' sul principio del timore riverenziale, ora sotto forma di penitenza impostata dai sacri canoni, ora sotta forma di voto in onore della Vergine Maria, del casto Giuseppe, del Signore, o della Santissima Trinità.[31]

As the above quotation clearly indicates, this taboo against the cohabitation of newly-weds on the days following their marriage ceremony is the remnant of pre-pagan modes of thinking which survived in the Christian world under the guise of devotion to saints. 'At times it took the form of penance imposed by the Sacred Canons of the Church; at other times it took the form of a vow in honour of the Virgin Mary, St Joseph, Our Lord, or the Blessed Trinity.'

This explanation is valid in so far as the taboo in question

---

30. Corso, 24.
31. Ibid., 68.

was current during the days of Aguis De Soldanis, but it is not applicable to the case of our elderly informants who were in their mid-eighties. As the information gathered *viva voce* from these informants shows, it is rather based on their own personal attitudes to sexual relations and marraige in the context of their ideological cultural patterns as expressed by the Church and other cultural factors which spoke of sex in a most clandestine manner. The taboo placed on sex and relations with the opposite sex made newly-weds (especially women, although not without exceptions) fear to infringe this once so tabooed issue after having kept this subject a secret for so long. The changeover from one phase of existence to another is difficult to cope with.

In the sixteenth century the newly-wedded couple were exhorted to abstain from sexual intercourse for at least three days. Duzina recommended a similar abstention – *triduo a copula carnali abstinenat.*[32]

Although marriage was held in high esteem in Maltese society because of important social functions, it also served for the sexual gratification of the couple. Lack of knowledge about this aspect of marriage seems to have generated a sense of guilt in the psyche of certain individuals. Another factor contributing to this gap of days between the marriage ceremony and its consummation is the fact that usually the couple were not allowed to speak to each other by themselves.

Eventually this could lead to a lack of intimacy between them, which kept them far apart from each other.

---

32. Cassar Pullicino, '1575 – Social Aspects of an Apostolic Visit', *Melita Historica*, vol. I, No. 3 (1956), 40.

Family reunion

The following information supports the above statements.

The periods of keeping the couple apart ranged from four to fourteen days, thus showing that the original reason which gave rise to this custom was not known. It appeared that informants had abstained during those days merely out of the habit of following traditional customs rather than because they understood the motivation or rationale behind them.

The following case histories do not give details of the customs surrounding the first night. From the information gathered it is not possible to sketch a normative model although the normal abstention can be said to have been not more than three days.

J. Fava from Qormi, on referring to this custom about 50 years ago, said that it was the custom for the couple to stay away from each other for three whole months in order to ensure that the girl had not become pregnant from another man. During this time they still visited each other's homes without, however, indulging in sexual relations. This explanation sheds light on the other socially respected customs regarding the preservation of a girl's virginity.

Waslet is-siegħa li niżżewweġ. Qalli: Meta trid tiżżewweġ? Għidtlu: Is-Sibt. Ħadna l-kunsens. Morna lejn id-dar – id-dar tagħhom – mhux bħal-lum tmur magħha. Mela, jien domt gimgħa ma mmur. (U mela xi ħsibt int?)

The time for my wedding was approaching. He asked me: (Her father) When are you going to get married? I told him: On Saturday. We got married, than we proceeded to their home, contrary to today's custom.

Ġimgħa domt. Jiġu għalija: Mela sa toqgħod hekk? Mela għalfejn iżżewwiġt? Kont bħal fatta nistħi, għax din ma tgħidx tifla kont inkellimha jien. Ma kontx inkellimha.

Of course, I spent a whole week away from our home. (Of course, what do you think?) I took a whole week. They used to approach me: How long are you going to stay by yourself? Why did you get married then? – But I was somewhat shy, because I had not even spoken to her properly. I had never talked to her.[33]

This case-story shows that the fear and shame of mutual relations between the opposite sexes was not solely the prerogative of the female sex. This sense of shame can also be seen from the undergoing information given by a female informant:

Jien domt erbat ijiem ma nitla' mar-raġel, għax kont nistħi minnu. Dari mhux bħal-lum. Illum jiġru daqs id-demonji, dejjem ma' xulxin. Dawk jixbgħu minn xulxin ta! Imbagħad x'ħin jixba' minn xi ħaġa jarma jgħajjarha … Jiena hekk kont ngħid: Jekk inkellmu jixba'

Four days went by before I went to live with my husband, because I was shy of him. People then were different from today. Today's couples run about like the devils – always together. These would surely get fed up of each other. Then it happens that when the man

---

33. W. Borġ.

minni … aktar ma niskartah aktar ikun ħsiebu fija. Hekk għidt jien.

gets fed up of something he starts to insult her. That is the way I used to reason things out: If I speak too much to him, he would get fed up of me … the more I stay aloof from him, the more he would think of me. That is the way I used to think.[34]

This informant, apart from stating that she was shy of going with her husband, justified herself by saying that the more one abstained from each other's companionship, which is risky in character, the more one's attraction increases, unconciously stating that love without inhibition would lose much of its strength.

The role of the priest in such matters is of the utmost importance, especially when one considers the fact that the word the priest said meant the shifting of responsibility from the individual in question to the spiritual father, who settles problems by giving the orders of God. This can be seen from this quotation:

Ta' dari ħamsin sena ilu, hi marret għand ommha u jiena għand in-nanna tagħha. Wara xi gimgħa għidt lill-qassis: Mela jien iżżewwiġt għalxejn. Mar

When I got married, about fifty years ago, she went to her mother's house and I went to her grand-mother's house. When a week had elapsed, I asked

34. Il-Bukaċċina.

għand ommha u qallha: Isma' Mattija – għax Mattija kien jisimha: Ilek tmint ijiem torqod għand ommok. Imbagħad ommha qaltilha: Issa mur ingabru go ħwejjigkom. – Iżżewwigt fit-18 u mort magħha fis-27.

the priest: Did I marry just to stay as I am? He went to her mother and told her: Look here, Mattija – because that was her name: You've been sleeping at your mother's house for a whole week. – Then her mother told her: Now it is high time you went to live together in your home ... I got married on the 18th and I went to live with her on the 27th.[35]

The following quotation seems to be simply based on the custom which prevailed at the time, and in which the couple give their mutual consensus:

Hi marret għand ommha u jien qgħadt waħdi d-dar. Kelli ħija żgħir u konna noqogħdu flimkien. Qaltli: Issa biex ma noqgħodx waħdi ... ikolli l-wens ibagħtu jorqod hawn għandi. Għidtilha: Iwa. Jien kont immur għax-xogħol, u hija kien imur joqgħod għandha. Imbagħad qaltlu: Mur ...

She went to her mother and I stayed at home by myself. I used to live with my younger brother. She told me: Now send your brother to live with me, so that I won't live by myself. At the same time he will serve as company. I told her: Yes. I used to go to work, and my brother used to go to sleep at her house. As time

35. Ż. Axisa.

mur ħija … mur ma' ħuk … Domna ħmistax-il ġurnata. Kienet l-użanza tagħna hekk. Imbagħad bdiet tersaq naqra naqra … ftit … ftit … insomma lejn id-dar. Ikkunsidra, kienet issajjarli għand ommha u ommha kienet iġġibli l-ikel jew kont immur niekol għandhom. Hemmhekk fit-telgħa ħdejn il-knisja ż-żgħira ta' San Pietru.

went by she told him: Go … go … go with your brother. We spent fifteen days away from each other. She used to prepare my dinner and her mother used to bring it to me or I used to go to eat at their home … over there on the slope … near the small chapel of Saint Peter.[36]

Ma kontx narah sewwa, 'I did not consider it to be right' – the concept of right doing is at the back of the following quotation, a concept which directed most of the behaviour of our forefathers together with the concept of 'sin' in general.

Jien biss biss domt għoxrin ġurnata ma morna jien u hu. U konna matul il-ġurnata mmorru fir-raba' niżirgħu l-qamħ u filgħaxija jien mmur norqod għand ommi u hu jmur jorqod għand ommu. U taparsi l-kamra lesta blgħamara u l-affarijiet. Domt

We spent more than twenty days away from each other before we went to live together. During the day we used to go to the fields to sow corn and at night I used to go to sleep at my mother's whilst he used to go to sleep at his mother's house. In the

---

36. Ġ. Caruana, 75-year-old, from Marsaxlokk, in an interview by the author in November 1975.

Just married

ma mort daqshekk għax ma kontx narah sewwa.

meantime we had our bedroom ready with all the furniture and things. I took such a long time before I went to live with my husband because I felt that it was not right to do such a thing.[37]

From all this it can be deduced that all these prohibitions and restrictions were either imposed by the arbitrary action of a superior authority – in our case customs and conventions – or were self-imposed by the newly-weds themselves who were still too shy of each other. There is also an inherent state of taboo in their new stage of existence. As already seen in the preceding chapters, women during childbirth, at menstruation, and so on, are inherently tabooed. This same condition of inherent pollution will be also seen in the chapters on death.

The prohibition of intercourse in the first days following marriage is of a temporary nature, although certain taboos connected with intercourse, as has already been seen in the chapter on menstruation, are permanent.

Il-Ħarġa, 'The Going away'

Il-ħarġa, 'The going away' brings to an end the long process of acquiring a bride, after having passed through the highlights of serenading, going to the match-broker, 'ir-rabta' – the ceremony by which the couple become engaged – and the marriage ceremony itself. Il-ħarġa was held eight days

---

37. M. Axiaq.

In the best of clothes

following the marriage ceremony. This consisted first of a banquet at the bride's home, where the bride was still living with her mother, then of another at the bridegroom's home. Following this they go to cohabit as husband and wife.

As far as my informants are concerned, the custom of '*Il-ħarġa*' goes farther back than their own time, and none of them could recall attending such a ceremonial banquet before going to their own independent home. As the information given in the preceding quotations and case-histories show, the way the newly-wed couple approached each other was devoid of any ceremonial activities. However, there usually was a go-between – the parish priest or the bride's mother – to act as an intermediary between the couple who were still shy of each other.

The following information seems to owe its origin to the pamphlets *Il-Mogħdija taż-Żmien*, published by Alfons Maria Galea, which were then still most popular. The informant told the author that she was an avid reader of these pamphlets.

Kienu jagħmlu tliet darbiet festa ... ir-rabta, it-tieġ, u l-ħarġa meta x-xebba tkun se toħroġ ma' l-għarus u tmur ġo darha. Kienu jagħmlulha pranzu ieħor imbagħad imorru. Ir-rabta, l-akkurdju, *engagement*, jiġi l-ħuttab u jgħid lill-missier: X'se tagħtiha 'l bintek, jgħidlu: Se nagħtiha tant flus ... intiha wejba qamħ ... intiha xkora tad-dħin ... intiha dvalja biex tagħġen il-ħobż u nagħġa.

They used to hold three feasts for the bride ... *ir-rabta* (engagement), the wedding ceremony, and *il-ħarġa*, (the going away) when the girl would go to her bridegroom and to her home. They used to hold a banquet and then leave. *Ir-rabta*, the agreement, the engagement, there comes the match-broker and asks the bride's father: What are you going to give your daughter? He tells him: I am giving her so much money ... a measure of corn ... , a sack for use in grinding, a table cloth on which to make bread, and a sheep.[38]

---

38. M. Muscat, 78-year-old informant from Mellieħa, in an interview by the author, April 1974.

Country folk – in typical farmhouse setting

The City 'belle'

Eighteenth century dandy

Maltese farmer

Maltese lady

Country fork in usual garb

Playing typical folk instruments

Ladies in walking dress

Lace-making

Country women and city ladies in typical faldettas

Paying visits to relatives or friends

Showing off their Sunday best

Valletta: cosmopolitan crowd in Merchants Street

Valletta: ladies going up Archbishop Street

Horse drawn hearse – last cab for the last journey

In procession – donning confraternity vestments

DEATH

The death-situation is a most complex one in which the human mind becomes irrational and is ruled by emotion. It involves a *rite de passage* in which the funeral formally separates the dead man from his previous status. It is, therefore, not surprising that this situation is separated and surrounded by various rituals, rites, and taboos of 'primitive' character which are still followed today. This situation is a phenomenon with world-wide distribution connected with certain human elements such as death itself, the various attitudes towards it, the fear of ghosts, the significance of burial, the specific attitude towards a corpse, and the problem of life after death. The negative regulations which characterize this situation are real taboos, and the entire period of their observance is a tabooed period.

The Maltese customs surrounding death share many ideas and observances with other parts of the world. This does not mean that all the taboos characteristic of the death-situation have been, so to say, imported from abroad. Similar ideas may arise from diverse sources and social environments and may bring about the development of psychologically similar traits from dissimilar or less similar sources in two or more cultural complexes.[1]

The rites of mourning among the Maltese contain many of the basic beliefs and customs observed among Semitic peoples, which in their turn resemble those observed in Israel in the Biblical and Rabbinic periods.[2] The customs of Southern Italy are also closely akin to Maltese mourning customs.

A. Cremona made comparative studies on local customs and beliefs surrounding the death situation. One of his articles,[3] first published in 1922, exhausts almost to the full the relevant material about the death-situation and the rites surrounding it. This chapter is partially based on the material gathered by this Maltese scholar.

It was Count G.A. Ciantar (1696–1778) who paved the way for the gathering of descriptive material concerning death in Malta and who included this material in his publication of the revised version of G.F. Abela's *Delle Descrittione di Malta*. In producing this material he took information and ideas from Agius De Soldanis (1720–70). Later research workers and novelists, who treated death in their novels, based their research on this original work.[4]

Taboos cannot be easily eradicated. It is a known fact that the human mind is mostly conservative with regard to matters connected to death. It is perhaps only to be expected

---

1. Bendann, *Death Customs*, 11-2.
2. Morgenstein, *Rites of Birth, Marriage, Death anomg the Semites*, 164.
3. A. Cremona, 'Maltese death, mourning and funeral customs'.
4. Cassar Pullicino, *Il-Folklore Malti*, 120.

that the superstitions associated with death should persist with much of their original vigour, for death remains an enigma, a state of complete lonliness, and the only completely uncommunicable experience undergone by man, as well as being the most fearful and at the same time most absolute of fulfilments.

Despite the decline of the stricter type of funeral ceremony, much of the old-fashioned taboo has survived into our age as stylized rituals. Flowers were laid on the grave originally as a sacrifice of a living object to procure happiness for the dead, but they are now placed there as a tribute of affection. The wreath was in ancient times a magic circle designed to enclose the soul of the dead and to prevent its return to haunt the living. The mourning dress was once the badge of spiritual contagion involving all those intimately connected with the deceased.

Although funeral rites still play an important role in our society, as they did in the past, the aims have to a certain extent changed. Our civilization sees to it that funeral rites are rightly carried out as an outward and external manifestation of inward desires, namely that the deceased will live for a long time in our memory and enjoy our respect. In the past, however, people organized these rites and ceremonies out of fear of the deceased himself. This does not mean that the 'death-fear' experience of the 'primitive' is to be totally excluded from the rites and rituals which surround the death-situation today.

Moreover, certain features which are associated with the death-situation also occur in other complexes. The horror associated with the corpse is also to be found with anything which is identified with the mystical, the uncanny, and the awe-inspiring. This is clearly demonstrated by 'taboo' which is not found solely in the death-situation but is also common in other human endeavours. Various precautions are adopted by the 'primitive' to get rid of the contagion which is thought to permeate the things which are considered polluted or sacred.

Violent Weeping and Lamentation –
In-Newwieħa

The custom of hiring of poor women and beggars to pray over and watch the corpse for the whole night prevails mostly in Gozo. In old days official female mourners called *newwieħa* (from *newwaħ*, 'to cry') were employed. The practice was abolished in Malta during the plague of 1676. Sicilians employed mourners called *praeficae* or *reputatrices*, a custom of Greek and Roman origin and practised by the Irish until 1849. It still prevails among the Corsicans and the Sahar tribes of Algeria. The old ceremonial of the Maltese is described by Abela as follows:

They wore trailing veils, *kurkar*, and when they entered the premises of the deceased they cut down the bower vines in the yard and threw the flower pots from the balconies and windows into the street. They searched the house for the finest pieces of china, dashed it on the floor, and mixed the fragments with ashes from the hearth. They boiled the whole together in a pot, and with the mixture washed the door posts and windows' shutters of the house. During these proceedings they sang couplets which ended in long-drawn sighs and lamentations. Then they gathered round the corpse and knelt down, extolling the virtues of the deceased, the relations joining in their mourning.[5]

---

5. A. Cremona.

If the dead man possessed horses, cows, goats, all their tails had pieces cut from them in token of mourning.[6]

All these customs which no longer prevail in our society are based on the motive, most common among non-literate peoples, which regards death as a 'mysterious atmospherical poison which extends its defiling influence far and wide'.[7] Consequently there arise the taboos of the corpse and those persons who had anything to do with the corpse, the relatives of the deceased, and the mourners in general.

The cutting down of vines and the throwing of the flower pots from the balconies together with the other expedients resorted to are based on 'primitive' thought which regards man's possessions as being saturated with his personality, and they form part of him, almost as much as his hair, his saliva, his footprints, and his name, which are so generally employed in magical arts.

To destroy a man's weapons, tools, ornaments, and clothing after his demise seems to the survivors an elementary precaution, and to make assurance doubly sure, not only on his personal property but on all objects even remotely associated with him are sometimes destroyed also. The custom, whatever its origin, will tend to be kept up as an expression of grief on the part of the survivors or as their tribute to the deceased, thus holding a place among the formal mourning ceremonies perhaps long after the ideas on which it was based have passed away.[8]

---

6. The reason advanced by E. Brockmann, *Maltese Memories,* for this behaviour is for the expiation of the dead man's sins. See also Cassar Pullicino, *Il-Folklore Malti,* 124.
7. Webster, *Purity and Danger*, 63.
8. Douglas, 177.

This custom is no longer followed today in all its details and has automatically passed into legend. However, there are still remnants of this once rather complicated ceremony of taboo character in the elimination of the dead man's clothes and most intimate personal possessions either by burning or by giving them to some orphanage or house for the elderly.

This practice is still attended to because of the dread of the corpse experienced by the living, although it also caters for the needs of the ghost as explained by Frazer.

The Mirror

The covering of looking-glasses in the rooms where the body is lying is also practised by several Maltese families. Some go so far as to remove the furniture, and turn round or take down the pictures in the death chamber and passages.[9]

These practices, perhaps, are reflections of the more complicated acts, followed by *in-newwieħa*, in past days, which in our time seem to carry the same psychological effect. Some hold that the mirrors in the house are covered to prevent the soul of the dead from being reflected in the mirror and carrying off with it any of the mourners.

However, the motives behind the covering up of the mirrors in the death-situation can be better understood if the many instances in our daily life where we find that looking in a mirror is regarded as almost 'immoral' are taken into consideration. Mirrors, to say the least, are objects which are surrounded by a feeling of uneasiness.

---

9. Cremona, 'Maltese death, mourning and funeral customs'.

An informant from Marsaxlokk[10] said that she was happy that she had gone blind because in this manner she wouldn't see the immoral behaviour of today's world. She believes that looking in a mirror is ample proof of vanity:

KIEN IKOLLKOM MERA D-DAR?
Leee. Anqas lampa u anqas xi nsajru. Huwa l-mera mhux kollha dimonji? Għax il-mera jħares lejha min mhux sewwa. Jien qatt ma ħarist ġo mera. Imma llum kull waħda tara minn saqajk sa rasek.

DID YOU HAVE A MIRROR IN YOUR HOMES?
Oh no. Neither a lamp nor any food. Isn't the mirror full of demons? Because those who look into the mirror do not usually lead a good life. I have never looked into a mirror. But today you have very big ones as big as the whole figure.[11]

Pawla Attard of Kirkop has more or less the same ideas:

Ħażin li tħares ġol-mera. Għax bħal speci timtela bik innifsek. M'għandekx tiftaħar bik innifsek lanqas. Jekk inti sbejħa ma għandekx toqgħod titpaxxa bik innifsek. Dnub ukoll dak. Għaliex inti ħadt pjacir bik innifsek.

It is wrong to look into the mirror. Because you would become very vain. You should not make much of yourself neither. If you are beautiful, you ought not take pleasure in your appearance. That is a sin too. Because you found pleasure in yourself.[12]

---

10. R. Bugeja, a 70-year-old informant from Marsaxlokk in an interview with the author in August 1975.
11. Ibid.
12. P. Attard.

Toni Mallia, an informant from Żebbuġ, speaks most solemnly about this subject, equating looking into a mirror with self-indulgence:

Kien hemm mara u qagħdet tħares lejn il-mera u rat ix-xitan. Dik iwa ... għax daħlet 'il ġewwa, għax kienet tant li tippretendiha bi sbuħitha, u 'tindrussa' u allura l-preġju tagħha kien fis-sbuħija. Allura flok rat il-figura tagħha, rat ix-xitan. Għax insiet 'l Alla. L-alla tagħha kienet figuritha. – Jien hu Alla sidek ma jkollokx Alla ieħor għajri. – Dik il-ħaġa kienet x'kienet tistmuha aktar minn Alla. Il-mera tfisser ħaġa wisq sabiħa. Jekk tara wiċċek sabiħ tgħid imma minn ġewwa iniex sabiħa: Ikollok kuxjenza pura. Dik il-mera.

There was a woman who stood looking into the mirror and she saw the devil. That is true, because she overdid it, because she was too proud of her beauty, and she used to dress up, therefore all her concern was for her beauty. Therefore, instead of seeing herself, she saw the devil. Because she forgot God. Her god was her figure. – I am the Lord thy God, thou shalt not have any other gods but me. – That thing, be it what it may, was something which she regarded as more important than God. The mirror can show a very beautiful thing. Like your face, for example. If you see it, you should say: Is my soul as beautiful as my face? You should have a pure conscience. That is the real mirror.[13]

---

13. T. Mallia.

A barber from Kirkop refers to this custom without giving any reason at all. Convention is what maintains this custom. *Użu kien hekk*, 'Such was the custom';

Ma kinux jaraw wiċċhom fil-mera kuljum bħal m'hawn illum. Dari le. Dari. Il-mera kienu jużawha ġol-kamra tal-għamara u l-barbiera biex iqaxxru l-leħja.

They did not look at their faces in the mirror every day as is the custom today. In my days they never used to do such a thing. They used the mirror in the main bedroom and barbers used it for shaving.[14]

Here the mirror was used solely for a utilitarian end and not for embellishment. The breaking of a mirror even nowadays is still regarded with apprehension by some individuls who believe that in some mysterious way they have condemned themselves to bad luck. These individuals make every effort to throwing away all the broken pieces because they fear that, if any piece is left in the vicinity, ill luck would persist. Following the breaking of a mirror, a family would have bad luck for a long time. The rationale behind this taboo is to be found in the assumption that one's reflection in water or glass, according to 'primitive' thinking is another 'self' or soul, and to damage the image automatically harms the original. This way of thinking generated a great number of taboos which are quite common, for example, in England, Ireland, and Italy.[15]

---

14. A barber from Kirkop, in an interview by the author in August 1974.
15. Maple, 22.

Meta kont xebba jien, mera d-dar ma kellniex għax ommi kienet tgħidilna: Jekk tħarsu ġol-mera tara d-demonju. U jiena kont xebba bħal ħaddiehor. Meta kont nagħmel xagħri, kont inkun irrid nara kif ġejt. Kont immur inħares fil-ħerza tal-bir biex nara naqra kif imxatt u ma mxattx … .

When I was a young girl at my mother's house we never thought of having a mirror, because my mother used to tell us: If you look into the mirror you will see the devil. And I was a maiden like other maidens. And when I used to comb my hair, I used to look into the well.[16]

The avoidance of the mirror during the daily activities and the taboos and 'superstitions' surrounding it, get increased doubly during the death-situation.

Għawi, 'Crying'

The extravagant grief expressed by the newwieħa in the olden days is no longer characteristic of our days. Still, the general rule holds, that mourners must show outwardly, by means of crying, għawi, and lamenting their great grief for the deceased. These lamentations are regarded as the duty of the mourners. Stories are told of mourners who were most adamant in not allowing the corpse of their beloved to be taken out of their homes. We do not find what in Sicily is called the piagnisteo and nenia, which is a lament by the living for the deceased. At least the author has not found any such

---

16. Ġ. Borġ.

lamentations in stylized forms, handed down from one generation to the other.[17]

Without any doubt this sorrow motive, which at first sight figures as a mark of sorrow, assumes an entirely different aspect when carefully investigated.

Taboo is entwined with social and political institutions; it is significant to note that everything sacred seems to be taboo, but not vice-versa, and that the belief may not be imposed, but spontaneous. Thus the death taboo seems primarily to be a result of the terror and bewilderment caused by the entrance of death into the circle.[18]

This is the first phase of the observance of the taboo period – characterstic of which are the violent weeping and lamentation.

Seclusion

Following death and burial, there is the second phase of mourning, during which traditional rites of mourning are observed.

Seclusion, the refraining from work, the discontinuance of public gatherings, and the closing of the house which are characteristic of every tabooed period, are mostly evident during the death-situation. These beliefs are often dictated by taboo, namely the temporary seclusion of individuals at times of social or physiological crises that have already been encountered during childbirth and menstruation.

---

17. For information about the *piagnisteo e nenie* in Sicily, see Pitrè, Vol. II, 212-9.
18. Douglas, 191.

Women keep indoors for a few weeks, only going out in the early morning to hear mass. In olden times such seclusion was much more strictly observed and the period was never less than forty days, now generally limited to three days. For men this sort of mourning did not exceed seven days, and is now generally limited to three days after the funeral. Business premises are closed and a mourning notice is affixed to the door while door knockers and knobs are removed; the front door of the house is kept closed for three days, whilst for 40 days it is kept half-open; neighbours half-shut their own. In some districts doors or knockers are draped with black crepe.[19]

The use of the numbers three, seven, and forty, during which seclusion and other mourning customs are generally followed is similar to the rites and other customs followed during birth.[20] This recurrent use of these days made Julian Morgenstern, president emeritus of the Hebrew Union College, come to the conclusion that, according to primitive Semitic belief, the power of evil spirits was thought to endure for three, seven, or forty days, usually reaching its greatest intensity upon the seventh day.[21]

A brief consideration of the time and duration of burial and mourning rites rounded up his conclusion that this same belief was basic to almost all primitive Semitic rites, including

---

19. Cremona, 'Maltese death, mourning and funeral customs'.
20. Another custom concerning the number forty is that in which a small glass of water is kept by the family of the deceased. It has to be kept until the water evaporates, because it is believed that the soul of the deceased remains restless up to forty days following death.
21. Morgenstern, 149.

those connected with birth, marriage, and death. The hypothesis often advanced that such long-persistent burial and mourning rites, which today seem to be primarily designed to maintain a bond of union with the deceased, all seem to have their origin in the superstitious fear of ghosts of the dead which were considered to be hostile to surviving relatives, friends, and associates with whom they had been in intimate contact during life.[22]

This consideration applies to most of the customs discussed in this book. It can therefore be said the adherence to these rules on these specific days is more the result of long-persisting customs, rather than anything else.

Sweeping

The seclusion and the stopping of the daily activities during the death-situation require that no sweeping, especially near one's door, should take place during the days following the death of one's relative. The broom, while it is associated with hygiene, it is also associated with dirt.[23]

The broom is, therefore, doubly tabooed during a death-situation which is regarded as something sacred.

Etiquette demands that no brooms should be left open to the gaze, especially of outsiders. Whilst sweeping in front

---

22. Ibid., 117.
23. The metaphorical use of the word *xkupa*, 'broom', is most derogatory. Metaphorically a woman of loose habits is referred to as *xkupa*, meaning that she does not make any difference between any of the male sex, in the same way as the broom does not make any difference among what it sweeps.

of the door, women stop whenever a person with a prestigious position in the village passes by. A male is often ashamed of carrying a broom in the street.

Keeping in mind this feeling of uneasiness which surrounds the broom, one can better understand the belief that sweeping after seven in the evening means that one would be sweeping on the souls of the dead. The reason for this belief is difficult to comprehend, although the popular beliefs which surround this period of the day are always associated with death and marauding spirits:

There is something unclean ... a vague feeling of contamination on touching a broom. There is something dangerous that emanates from this. It is a feeling of uneasiness.[24]

This sense of uneasiness can easily be seen in the ritual surrounding the broom in the Maltese lore. To begin with, people refrain from using the word *xkupa*, 'broom', and excuse themselves beforehand for using such a 'low' word. Hence: *Skużi xkupa*, 'Pardon me, broom' is often heard. The elderly still use the Semitic word *imselħa*, 'broom', but even in this case there is a certain feeling of contamination. The author remembers a middle-aged informant telling him to erase this word from the tape-recorder because she did not feel that it was appropriate to use, although her mother did not really mind about it at all.

The word *xkupa*, is often used by women, especially those of lower strata of society, to offend other women during a quarrel. This bears similarities with Sicilian usage, where the worst insult a woman can pay another woman is the placing

---

24. J. Boissevain, in an interview with the author.

of the broom near the door, while she shuts herself in. It is held that such a habit is injurious and at the same time a sort of blaspheming – an imprecation bearing strong power.[25]

In order to avoid the direct reference to this word there arose in Malta the custom of using the word *zija*, 'aunt', because as the aunt is always at home, the broom is also at hand.

The broom is always placed somewhere out of the gaze of outsiders. It is held to be a great offence to leave the broom outside, especially when a *viaticum* is passing by.[26]

The job of a health attendant, as he is being lately called in Malta, has a very low esteem. It is one of the worst jobs and it is something repugnant. Here the broom, which is the main tool of the health attendant, has contaminating influence. Obviously the supposed uncleanliness of the broom is the result of the nature of its work.

It is prohibited to sweep after the *Ave Maria* because that might lead to death of the head of the family, and one would be sweeping the faces of the spirits. The belief in witches might be the origin of this taboo because it was usual for them to leave their homes following this hour – the time for the malevolent spirits to roam about.

What is the reason behind all this repugnancy

---

25. At Modica, Sicily, when two women during a quarrel exhaust all their insults in words, they shut themselves at home and carry the broom outside seven times. In Malta, women insult each other by placing the broom face upwards and calling each other: *Ghandek wiċċ ta' xkupa*, 'Your face is like a broom.'

26. While the *viaticum* is passing no one is supposed to remain upstairs, watching it pass by, because no one is supposed to remain in a higher position than the Sacrament (Birkirkara).

surrounding the broom? It is a fact that the broom had a great part in the social, sexual, and psychic histories of humanity. There is the common popular belief that witches used to fly in the air on broomsticks, although few witches admitted this practice.

The broom is so often used by women during their daily chores that it has been deeply associated with them. In certain places in England, up to some time ago, when women were going to leave their homes they would place their broom near the door, or else they would leave it protruding in the chimney so as to make it known that they have left their homes. Orginally this represented the symbolic guarding of the house because the broom was a symbol of the woman.

Dietary Prohibitions

Old customs prohibited cooking for three days and the family of the deceased was provided with meals by friends or distant relatives. This rule was, and perhaps still is, followed in some districts of Sicily and amongst Arab tribes of North Africa. While meals were being served, the bereaved family sat with folded legs on the floor which was covered with a straw mat. The historian Ciantar relates in 1772 that these mourning dinners still took place in his early days. This custom has now been discontinued, and our village people merely abstain from having their pastry and other food prepared in the public oven for a period of some months after the death of a member of a family.[27]

---

27. Cremona, 'Maltese death, mourning and funeral customs'.

On the first day of the death of a member of the household, the food taken in the days of old used to be called the *għaza*, which used to be given to the relatives of the deceased by neighbours for three days following the death. This was eaten while seated cross-legged on a *ħasira*, 'straw mat'. One of the first things done by the *newwieħa* was to turn a *borma*, 'cooking pot', face-downwards, thus symbolizing that no cooking had to take place in that house for the coming days.[28]

The taboo placed on cooking, especially in public ovens, is followed out of respect for the deceased. The sackcloth-and-ashes psychology darkening the lives of those immediately involved in the death-situation does not condone cooking. The face-to-face communities in which they usually lived did not endorse having pastry prepared in the public ovens since, up to a few years ago, this meant that the family concerned was going to have a special meal. Public ovens were usually made use of on Sundays and feastdays.

However, what interests us most is the prominent part abstinence from food, especially cooked food, plays in the death-complex among many civilizations. This shows that, in days of old, dietary prohibitions were followed out of the sheer taboo fear instilled in the people's psyche. Today's more rationalized prohibitions are the remnants of yesterday's clear-cut taboos.

Effie Bendann states that food restrictions seem to be instituted for propitiation; as purifying agencies, to avoid any possible future defilement; to prevent danger because

---

28. Cassar Pullicino, *Il-Folklore Malti*, 124.

of the transformation of uncooked food to cooked food, because of the susceptibility of the hands to evil influences since they are regarded as carriers of ceremonial uncleanliness; and for the acquisition of supernatural powers.[29]

Some of these restrictions surely lie at the back of today's dietary prohibitions. These dietary prohibitions can be better understood in the light of the various taboos and restrictions which surround food in our daily lives.

Certain mild taboos which were followed in Malta in the past are connected with the table. Thirteen people sitting around the table will lead to the death of one of them, a belief associated with the Last Supper of Jesus Christ, in which there were thirteen people including Jesus Christ, who was crucified the following day, sitting round the table.[30]

Spilling oil is followed by bad luck, a belief of wide prevalence, deeply connected with a religious concept, since in the old days, oil was used together with balms, animal lard, and saliva in anointing important persons.

Spilling salt is also regarded as bad luck and to ward off the evil influences a little ritual is followed. While snatching a pinch of salt, one should stay with one's back against the spilled oil, throw the salt over one's right shoulder, saying: *Il-melħ idub, il-għali jmur*, 'The salt melts out, troubles depart.' Spilling wine, on the other hand, brings good luck.

Cooking in the baker's oven was strictly avoided during

---

29. Bendann, 108.
30. Customs of preventive character say that he who jams the fork on the table would be killing the angle ot the table, whilst ho who rotates the knife on the table might lead to his very choking, whilst eating. Crossed knives on the table lead to fighting.

the period of time when someone was abroad lest evil results follow. They also abstained from singing. A married woman waiting for her husband to return from abroad, so as to be sure of his arrival, used to keep an oil lamp or a candle alight near the door, on the inside, to ensure that her husband would arrive the following day. If, after the third day of this ritualistic act, the husband failed to arrive, this meant that the husband was dead.

Il pane è la Grazia di Dio per eccellenza: e non si posa nè presenta mai sottosopra, che è malaugurio, nè si taglia da quel lato (solu), che è disprezzo alla Provvidenza di Dio che ce lo manda, nè si segna o s'infilza col coltello, che è ferro e quindi maledetto; ma si taglia senz' altro, e quando vi si ha ad infilare dentro il coltello si bacia prima, si benedice poi e si protesta che è Grazia di Diu.

Quindi se il pane cade per terra, nel raccoglierlo, si bacia dicendo: Grazia di Diu. Se mangiando ne cascono per terra delle briciole e non si ha cura di raccattarle, si dovranno raccattare poi con le ciglia, morti che saremo.

E come grazia di Dio, si giura su di esso toccandolo: Pi Sta Santa Grazia di Diu e se ne vediamo cadere o buttare un bocconcino per terra, che non si voglia o non si possa altrimenti mangiare, ci affrettiamo a raccoglierlo e conservarlo in un bucolino pur di non farlo calpestare coi piedi. Il Signore potrebbe farci desiderare quel boccon di pane.[31]

In the above quotation Giuseppe Pitrè, while describing the paraphernalia of rituals surrounding bread in Sicily, runs parallel with the rituals surrounding bread in Malta. The adherence to these rituals stems from the common beliefs which, before the currents of secularization began to penetrate Maltese society, kept them alive, and held such customs to be one of their values. In dealing with these rituals

---

31. Pitrè, Vol.IV, 200.

surrounding bread, one must keep in mind that in Malta, especially among those coming from the lowest strata of society, bread is part of their staple diet. The idiomatic expressions *Naqla' l-ħobża ta' kuljum*, 'We earn our daily bread', incorporates man's vital need of bread.

A man from Sannat, Gozo told the author that the very first thing he learned when he was young was the sign of the Cross and the relevant ritual surrounding bread. He said that this was the right way to bring up children as good Christians and good citizens. *Il-Beżiża*, from Birkirkara, is of the opinion that if one thrusts a knife into a loaf it is a great 'sin'. The author personally witnessed the outrage of a young man who was shocked on seeing bread being thrown into the street.

The following quotations continue to shed light on the rituals surrounding bread, and expand on the information given in the above quotation by Pitrè:

Li ddaħħal is-sikkina fil-ħobża, dak dnub għalija. Jien ngħidlek il-verità meta t-tfal jaqtgħu biċċa ħobż, inkun irridhom sewwa ċatta. Meta jkollhom xi biċċa ħobż żejda jbusuha u jqegħduha gol-ħajt. Meta titqatta' santa jaħarquha.

To insert a knife into a loaf is a great sin for me. To tell you the truth, I am always telling the children to cut the bread in such a manner that the loaf falls on its flat side. When an extra piece of bread is left over, I ask them to kiss it and put it somewhere where no one can tread over it. When a holy picture gets torn, they burn it. [32]

_____

32. Il-Bukaċċina.

Naqilgħu l-ħożna ta' kuljum, 'We earn our daily bread', incorporates man's vital need of bread.

"I make the sign of the cross over the loaf so that God will give us more. If it falls on the ground I kiss it and put it in the wall."

This information shows how such beliefs and customs are transmitted from one generation to another, leaving a lasting influence on the bearers of such customs.

Ġ. Borġ, from Selmun, has this to say about this custom: *Il-ħobża nagħmlilha salib fuqha biex il-Bambin ikattar u anke jekk taqa' biċċa ħobż ma' l-art x'ħin terfagħha tbusha u tpoġġiha golħajt*, 'I make the sign of the cross over the loaf so that God will give us more. If it falls on the ground I kiss it and put it in the wall.' The reverence seen here in the handling of bread shows how clear is the association between the bread used in the Eucharistic Sacrifice and our daily bread.

Among English sailors the belief holds that if a loaf is placed face downwards, this may lead to the sinking of the ship; in Poland, the ghost of the house used to condemn any woman who, during her life, had treated bread carelessly to pick every piece of bread not well used. These customs, together with others to be found all over Europe, show the great importance given to bread.

Hair

A custom very popular in olden times required men not to shave for a fortnight or even a month after a death. Others say that this ought to be followed up to forty days, as a remembrance of the spirit, which remains on earth like Christ's did before going up to heaven. The male inhabitants of Malta go out on the seventh day with faces unshaven.

This mild taboo is similar to that followed in the districts of Southern Italy where custom dictates that men do not shave their beards for one month.[33]

---

33. Bendann, 72.

Among the Semites the custom prevails of avoiding cutting their hair until the end of the thirteenth day after death.[34]

This is the area of milder taboos, after the stronger taboos adhered to in the first three days following death.

The reason here might possibly be that the mourner is regarded as being in a state of extreme taboo, which however terminates automatically with the conclusion of the 30 days (month). Accordingly the cutting of the hair would mark the passing out of this state of extreme taboo into a state which, with the exception of a few minor restrictions, is the same as ordinary, profane, existence.[35]

Anthropologists hold, on the other hand, that the cutting of the mourner's hair was intended to furnish a ritual link with the dead. Primitive tribes express the same idea in cannibalism and in funeral mutilations.[36]

The hair of the deceased is coveted because it is supposed to affect 'a sacramental union with the dead and, for this reason, we only find the hair of the departed preserved as a precious relic.'[37] Perhaps one of the reasons for hair-cutting seems to be that this serves a substitution for the whole person who by this means need not offer himself as a sacrifice to the dead.[38]

The rite of cutting the corpse's hair immediately after death and in preparation for burial, according to Cremona, was probably done in order to have the openings of the

---

34. Morgenstern, 164.
35. Ibid., 261.
36. Brockmann.
37. Bendann, 94.
38. Ibid., 95.

corpse shut to avoid the return of the soul into the already-decomposing body.

Fire

Among certain peoples, all fires are put out after death. Among others, fire plays a most important part in death ceremonies, not only as regards cremation, but also in connection with the lighting of fires at the place of burial or on the spot where the deceased died. All these customs have various different motives:

In Malta an oil lamp is often lit and left for forty days before the Crucifix or the image of the Madonna in the death chamber. This is supposed to please the soul of the departed, whose ghost is in this way prevented from haunting the house. In some of the Gozo villages, the persons attending the corpse to the burial-ground return in procession after the funeral mass to the room of the deceased, where they kneel down and say the rosary before the Crucifix, placed on a chest covered with white cloth, and between two lighted candles which are afterwards replaced by the devotional oil lamps. The belief still exists that the lamp must remain lighted for forty days, during which the soul of the departed remains above the flame.[39]

Apart from the above motives given by Cremona, fire is lit for another purpose, although one cannot say whether this applies also to Malta. After death, fire is used to drive away ill-disposed beings and to light the spirit of the deceased to the other world.[40]

Another custom in which fire is used and which has led to another superstition regards the three candles which used

39. Cremona.
40. Bendann, 77.

to be lit and placed near the corpse.[41] This custom led to the superstition that no three candles ought to be kept in the same room because this is unlucky, a superstition also found in Sicily.[42]

No fire was lit in the house for three days after the funeral:[43]

U Allaħares tqabbad nar għax tkun għamilt l-ikbar ħmerija. Per eżempju ma nsajrux. Xejn. U la kafè. U la tagħmel xi ħaġa. U la tagħmel naqra minestra. Insomma ma tqabbadx nar.

And it would be a great sin if you lit a fire and you would be doing the silliest thing possible. Hence we do not cook. Nothing. Not even coffee ... You can't cook anything. You cannot even make vegetable soup. Anyhow you do not light fires.[44]

These quotations depict the way in which fire was regarded in connection with death by people in the past. Among many peoples, the extinguishing of all fires after death indicates the fear of attracting evil spirits or influences. The extinguishing of fire in Malta and Gozo is perhaps more due to the fear that other people might think that the family of the deceased are cooking food and are not mourning the dead properly.

41. S. Borġ.
42. See Pitrè, 211.
43. Brockmann.
44. Ġ. Borġ.

Morgenstern says that the original implication and purpose of the ceremony of kindling a light for a dead person is difficult to determine, since the rite seems to have a twofold meaning in Semitic religious practice. On the other hand, the burning light symbolizes the life or soul[45] and, when the light is extinguished, life is brought to an end – the soul has departed from the body. In this regard there are numerous Biblical references and ample evidence in the Orient in our modern times.[46] On the other hand, Morgenstern says that these lights, say in the rites of modern Egypt, do not symbolize the soul of the dead person, but are rather designed to illuminate the darkness and guard against the soul of the dead, conceived as a dangerous spirit, and particularly dangerous in the darkness of the night. Morgenstern comes to the conclusion that one of these beliefs certainly lay at the bottom of the current practice of placing lights in ancient Semitic tombs or of depicting lights upon the walls of tombs in the catacombs and elsewhere.[47]

Mourning Garments

Following the burial, both the mourners and the dead person's spirit enter a marginal phase which is marked by special modes of behaviour and lack of adornment as can be seen in the mourning garments.

Mourning garments are symbolic of the element of separation, transition, and reintegration, charaterisitic of the *rites de passage*. The surviving close relatives are separated

---

45. See A. Cremona, *supra*.
46. Morgenstern, 287.
47. Ibid., 289.

from everyone else by specific dress; they are 'in mourning' for a prescribed period, at the end of which they are reincorporated into society. During this period it is believed that the spirits of the deceased would be making its way to heaven.

Historically, this mourning custom was more rigid in character. Mourning began to lose much of its rigidity, after being partly mitigated by Grand Master Claude de la Sengle (1553–57) and commands expressed by nobles in their wills, in which they said that, if this mourning on a grand scale was to continue, *sisa*, 'excise duty', had to be paid, since this would mean that the mourners were not attending to the commands written in the knight's last will.

The Second World War, in which thousands died, brought with it, a sense that death is a common daily affair. This attitude, in its turn, once more diminished the rigidity of mourning costumes.[48]

The compact communities were always on the look-out for members who ought to be in mourning and were not conforming to the custom. Some families from lower-income groups used to borrow money to fulfil this requirement. They felt that it would be sinning against their 'beloved' if they did not conform to the custom. This is the last external sign of the union between the deceased and the living.

People of rank wear a mourning dress for a few days following a death in their family, but country people are satisfied with wearing a black felt hat and a dark sash round the waist. Women, if wives or brides, follow the continental style of full mourning dress in crape. Some women do not

---

48. P. Endrich, a 73-year-old informant, in an interview by the author at the Little Sisters of the Poor, Hamrun, in October 1973.

A horse drawn hearse was a common sight in Malta up to a few years ago.

wear a hat or bonnet during the first week of mourning, and go out in faldettas, a national head covering which is more commonly used when attending religious services.[49]

Some women in Gozo still wear a light black kerchief on leaving their homes up to a month or more following the death of some relative.[50]

As can be seen from the above quotations in regard to mourning garb as well as to the observance of taboos, these weigh much more heavily upon women than upon men. Perhaps the reason why the greater role in the mourning rites, for example in the attire, is imposed more upon women, is that the primitive mind sees the connection

49. A. Cremona, 'Maltese death, mourning and funeral customs'.
50. N. Vella Apap.

between life and women and at the same time feels that her connection with death is of equal significance.

An analogy

Without entering into the controversy about the influence of the Semitic culture on our own culture, but keeping in mind what has been said at the beginning of this chapter,[51] I am going to reproduce what Morgenstern has written about the periods of mourning in Ancient Israel. From this an important analogy can be deduced:

When we examine the rites of mourning in ancient Israel in the Biblical and Rabbinic periods, we find the same basic beliefs and the ame customs observed as among other Semitic peoples. In the Israelite practice the third, seventh, and thirtieth days after death and the first anniversary of death are of particular significance. In fact, traditional Judaism divides the time of mourning into four periods, marked off by these four significant days.

The first three days after death and interment are given to violent weeping and lamentation. During the next four days, i.e., during the second half of the first seven days after death, extreme rites of mourning are observed. The mourners may not leave the house and may sit only upon the ground or the floor or, at the very most, upon a low stool, but not upon an ordinary chair; nor may their beds be prepared in the ordinary manner for them to sleep in. They may not go about their regular tasks and duties, even within the house. These are neglected or lese are performed by friends. And even the food for the first meal after the burial is sent in from without. During this period the mourners wear torn and dishevelled garments, and in the Orient even strew ashes upon their heads, and keep the mouth and nostrils covered. The ostensible reason for this last custom is in order not to work harm to visitors who come to condole with them ... and finally, during this entire period, the

---

51. See pp. *supra*.

mourners give way to, or indulge in, expressions of loud and excessive grief. With the close of these seven days this extreme mourning, with its many restrictions and taboos, comes to an end and the next period, that of a milder mourning, begins and continues until the end of the thirtieth day after death. During this period the immediate relatives of the deceased are still subject to certain restrictions. They may not, for example, wash their garments, or cut their hair, or marry.

Finally, the fourth and last period follow after the thirtieth day and continues for eleven months, to round out the full year of mourning. During this period only the most immediate relatives, particularly children mourning for parents and parents mourning for children, are subject to certain mild restrictions. They may not indulge in excessive joy or visit places of amusement, or wear any but black outer garments. With the completion of a full year after death, or, among certain groups of eleven months as the substitute for the full year, the formal mourning automatically ceases entirely and all restrictions and taboos are ended.[52]

Apart from other analogies, in this quotation there is an analogy between specific periods during which the mourning takes different aspects. One should also notice the importance given to specific numbers – three, seven, and forty – all of which are to be found in the birth situation.[53]

Giving bread to the Poor

Some families give the poor bread. The love-feasts of the primitive Christians were in mediaeval times replaced in both Malta and Sicily by the distribution of meat and boiled wheat mixed with sesame. Distribution of meat and bread to the poor came also to be a custom at some feasts, but were

---

52. Morgenstern, 164.
53. For the recurrent use of these numbers during the birth situation, see pp. *supra*.

continued in Sicily mainly by the giving of beans and bread on All Souls' Day. In Malta on that day, however, the old custom has been replaced by the free kitchens or the *Borma tal-Fqar*, 'Pot of the Poor'.[54]

The very nature of the giving of this food marks it as a taboo-sacrifice and it bears similarities in its motivation with the *fedu'* of the modern native inhabitants of Palestine, where animals are killed and their flesh given to the poor.[55]

More information about this taboo-sacrifice can be seen in the following quotation:

Mons. Duzzina l'10 Febbraio 1575 nell'atto della sua Apostolica Visita ci fa sapere come i Maltesi nell'Uffizio di Requiem distribuivano la Coccia, che era una distribuzione di grano cotto con passoli, amandole, noci, e melagrani, parte poste in forma di croce in terra e parte nei bacili, sopra il monumento del morto, (et il Magri v. exequiai) come facevano sotto il cuscino del morto, facevano i fogli del cedro, ed ai poveri davano a il pane. Tutto a suffragio del morto. Perchè rito affatto gentile, ommesso.[56]

Mgr. Duzina, while describing the way the Maltese distributed the cooked wheat and bread to the poor, says that this was done for the repose of the dead man's soul. This shows that the sacrifice here has an expiatory force, to ransom the dead man from the consequences of his sins. In its turn this shows a progressively religious tendency almost divested of the taboo-character which was much more pronounced in its 'primitive' state.

---

54. Cremona.
55. Morgenstern, 118.
56. Cassar Pullicino, 'Degli Abiti, costumi, sponsali, matrimoni, e funerali dei Maltesi', taken from Manuscript no.142, vol 5, National Library of Malta, Conte G. A. Ciantar, in the appendix for vol. 1 for *Malta Illustrata* in 1770.

An informant from Birkirkara told the author that up to a few years ago they were accustomed to prepare a big cauldron in which vegetable soup with chick peas was cooked. This was distributed to the poor explicitly for the repose of the souls of the deceased.[57]

Another custom which falls under the same category of taboo-sacrifices comes from the abbattoir. It is believed that human beings have grown so callous because pigs had eaten up the plant of human conscience. At Qormi, in a rural chapel, people fattened a sow during the year and, on the day of the feast, killed it, melted its fat, and gave away the dumplings to the people present.

Il-Hanżira ta' l-Erwieħ, 'The All Souls' Pig', is another custom which has gone out of use since the Second World War. A pig was allowed to roam about the village, receiving food and delicate morsels from the villagers. On All Souls' Day (2 November) the pig was killed, flayed, and cooked; the poor of the village were called together and each received a good helping of pork.

According to supplementary information from Mġarr, usually about four months before All Souls' Day a piglet was given to the parish priest who then informed the villagers that the piglet had been given to him. It was now their duty to feed it, so that when it has been fattened it would be sold and the money used to celebrate as many masses as possible for the repose of the dead. *Il-Hanżira ta' l-Erwieħ* used to roam about the roam about the streets and regarded as a sacred object. To steal or kill it was held to be a sacrilegious act.

---

57. A. Zarb.

Taboo on Treading Over Tombs

Treading over tombs shows great lack of respect towards the deceased and even unwary treading must be avoided. If the burial took place in church a heavy black material (*faldrappa*) used to be put on the tomb, while a straw mat, '*ħasira*' used to be placed on the tomb if the burial took place in the cemetery.

Instead of a straw mat, sometimes the tomb was surrounded by candles.[58]

Lanqas it-trab ma rrid nirfes għax inħoss rogħda. Min jaf? Nittamaw jekk mhux kulħadd il-Ġenna, il-kotra l-kbira l-Ġenna. Għandek iġġiblu rispett. Il-qabar għandek minn fejn tgħaddi u bla bżonn anqas għandek tgħaddi. Lanqas tiġri. Il-bicca l-kbira tan-nies jekk ikollha tgħaddi minn fuq qabar tgħaddi, imma jien inħoss qalbi iebsa.

I don't even want to tread on the dust over the grave because it makes me shiver. Who knows? We hope that if not all dead people are in heaven, at least most of them are. You ought to show respect towards the dead. If you need to pass over the grave there is a passage where you can pass over but you should only use it if you really need to. You should not do so hurriedly either. Most people do not mind passing over the tomb, but I would feel really hard-hearted to do such a thing.[59]

---

58. Cassar Pullicino, *Il-Folklore Malti*, 125.
59. A sacristan from Sannat, Gozo.

The above information by an undertaker and a sacristan of a church in Gozo shows, apart from the respect towards the dead, a straight taboo on treading over tombs. It seems strange, however, that sacred places should be treated as polluted places. The explanation for this behaviour, however, lies in the ambivalence of the conception of taboo. 'Primitive' thought does not clearly distinguish sacred from unclean things but the all-important distinction is between anything taboo and therefore untouchable and anything which can be safely touched by all. The common characteristic of sacred places and polluted places lies in their mystic dangerousness.

The Death of Children

Taboos seem to be intensified when death is not the result of the natural process or order but has an unnatural cause. This is the case with persons who die on the gallows or who are murdered. Taboos are further intensified when people whom society regards as moral outcasts die.

However, although the death of children cannot be said to be the natural process, the Maltese, up to a few years ago, used to accept it the same way as the Victorians did.

The death of baptized children was regarded as a blessing from God. The idea of having children in heaven praying for you redeemed an otherwise mournful situation. The funeral and the heralding of the death of a baptized child were carried out in a spirit of triumph and rejoicing, reflected in the white colour of the coffin and the 'Glory' rang out from the belfries. *Mhux grazzja kbira*, 'Isn't it a great blessing?', exclaimed il-Beżiża, from Birkirkara, *ikollok 14-il tarbija jitolbu għalik il-Ġenna?*, 'having 14 children praying for you in

227

heaven?' The parish priest of the village used to congratulate the mother telling her: *Nifraħlek bil-Ġenna*, 'Congratulations for having a child in heaven.'

Il-mewt tat-trabi konna ngħidulha l-glorja u ta' l-oħrajn ngħidulha *Transitur*, jiġifieri l-mewt tal-kbar. Fil-glorja kienu jdoqqu b'qanpiena żgħira … tin … tin … tin … tin … bl-iżgħar qanpiena li kien ikun hawn. Ġieli mbagħad kienu jagħmlu *l-Lawdi*. Jeħduhom bil-qassisin flok qassis wieħed. Anke ġieli ħaduhom bil-kapitli wkoll, meta xi ħadd ikun jista'. Imbagħad kienu jagħmlu quddiesa hemmhekk, jgħidulha ta' l-anġli. U fil-quddiesa kien ikun hemm *il-Lawdi*.

We used to refer to the death of children as the glory. *Transitur* was the term used to refer to the death of adults. During the glory they used to ring a small bell … tin … tin … tin … tin … with the smallest bell at hand. Sometimes they used to sing the *Laudi*. The funeral procession consists not of one priest only, but of many. Sometimes, when the family was well-to-do, the Chapter used to accompany the funeral. And then Mass was celebrated – it was called the Mass of the Angels. Then the *Laudi* used to be intoned.[60]

All this rejoicing shows that, although faced by bereavement, there is no evidence of the usual taboos characteristic of the death situation.

The taboo character is intensified when an unbaptized baby dies. When this happens, according to information

60. A. Pace, a 75-year-old from Birkirkara, in an interview by the author in March 1974.

gathered from Birkirkara, a woman takes the baby in a box, concealed under her faldetta, straight to the cemetery. No ceremonies or religious observances accompany the clandestine burial of the child who, according to Canon Law, had to be buried in a *miżbla*, 'unconsecrated ground', separated from the rest of the Christians.

This custom bears similarities with others followed in Sicily during this period. G. Pitrè tells us that there are some differences and varieties in the customs accompanying the death of children. In the Roman Liturgy, under the heading *De exequis parvulorum*, death bells should be rung in a festive rather than a mournful tone. The common people call it the *Gloria*. In Palermo this custom lasted up to the times of Villabianca, that is up to the end of the last century when it was finally abolished. Outside Palermo, and in many localities in Sicily, the custom is still widespread. The news of a child's death is greeted with the consolatory exclamation, *Gloria e paradisu*, 'Glory and Heaven'.[61]

Texts

A faldetta placed on a bed leads to the death of the mother of the household and the father would surely marry again. The death of one person in a street leads to the death of another two raising the number to three. Too many people following the *Viaticum* procession means that the sick person is not going to die. Too few people means that he is definitely going to die. On hearing church bells tolling for the death of a certain person and you mistake it for the death of someone else, then you increase that other person's life. This is a kind of deception practised on death itself. When a

---

61. Pitrè, 240.

neighbour dies, you ought to place a slipper behind the door. This prevents the death of someone at home. Dreaming of candles means the death of one's relatives.

Following these miscellaneous examples, one should consider the following texts:

L-irġiel ma jqaxxrux il-leħja. Jibqgħu 15-il ġurnata biha. Tagħmel tmint ijiem ma titfaċċax 'il barra. Tkun għarukaża kbira toħroġ. Nilbsu l-iswed għall-ġenituri tliet snin. Imbagħad sena mezzu. U allaħares tqabbad in-nar għax tkun għamilt l-akbar ħmerija. Per eżempju, ma nsajrux. Xejn. U la kafè. U la tagħmel xi ħaġa. U la tagħmel naqra minestra. Insomma ma tqabbadx nar. Jiġifieri ma ssajjar xejn. Jekk il-ġirien ixommu xi riħa: Eh ... jinżlilhom ... allavolja għadha tmut ommha jew missierha.

The men do not shave their beard. They remain un-shaven for a fortnight. For eight days they do not leave their home. It would almost be a scandal if you went out. In memory of our parents we used to wear black clothes for three whole years, followed by a year of half-mourning. And God forbid that you should ever light a fire because that would be the greatest folly. For example, we did not cook. Nothing. Not even coffee. And you could not cook anything. You could not even cook some vegetable soup. Anyhow you could not light a fire. That meant you could not cook any-thing. If your neighbours smelt food cooking they would say: Eh ... they seem to be en-joying their food ... even though their father or mother has just died.

Ikel ... konna nieklu xi biċċa ħobż. Kellna l-ġbejniet tan-nagħaġ. Konna nduru għalihom. Kien ikollna l-ġbejniet maħżunin ġol-ġarra tal-bżar. Konna neħduhom u naqra żejt. U nixtru xi sold sardin ... Aħna għomorna kollu f'nofsinhar nieklu ikel xott għax konna nkunu fir-raba. Bilfors kien ikollna nieklu. Dak ix-xahar trid tagħmlu.

Meta jmut xi ħadd l-ewwel ma jagħmlu jaqilbu l-arloġġ. Għax dari kulħadd bl-arloġġ tal-kampnar; jaqilbuh wiċċu 'l isfel. Għax dik it-tektika ma jkunux iriduha. Insomma dak vistu. Kwiet. Dik it-tektika mhux sewwa. Vistu Ġieżu Marija. Għalhekk ikollok naqra gradenza mhux ħażin jgħattuha bil-liżar. Xogħol kienu jdumu ma jmorru ... biex ma jidhrux. Għax jekk imorru: Eh ... dak ma tantx ħassha bi kbira wisq! Ma tafx int, in-nies.

Food ... we used to eat bread. We had cheeses made of sheep's milk. We used to eat these cheeses preserved in pepper. We used to eat them with some oil and we used to buy a pennyworth of sardines ... Actually we ate such dry food all our life at noon because we used to be working in the fields and we could not do otherwise. You know, you had to eat such food for at least one whole month.

When someone dies the first thing that they did was to turn the clock face downwards. Because in olden days everyone had a wooden clock; they used to place it face downwards. Because they could not stand that ticking. That was a mourning custom. Silence. That ticking was not right. That was real mourning, of Jesus and Mary help us. If you had a hefty chest of drawers, you had to cover it with a sheet ... it was a long time before they went back to work, in order not to be seen. Because, if they went, people would talk: Eh that man ... he did not really feel badly about his loss. Don't you know, the people think.[62]

Following the description of certain customs which take place during the death-situation and the following days by an informant from the small locality of Selmun,[63] where the majority of the inhabitants are farmers, there follows an interview with a fisherman from Marsaxlokk, a fishing community, in which the homogeneous character of the occupation of its inhabitants brought about solidarity in most of the social occasions and times of need, which arise from time to time.

MISTOQSIJA: Kellkom xi drawwiet tagħkom meta kien imut xi ħadd, hawnhekk ġo Marsaxlokk?

QUESTION: Did you have any customs surrounding death here in Marsaxlokk?

TWEĠIBA: Iva ... leħja ma nqaxxruhiex. Konna nużaw il-ħmieġ għax dak ħmieġ, il-leħja, bħalma jgħidu, u hekk hu. Allura kien ikollna qalziet abjad, konna nibagħtuh għand wieħed raġel u kien

ANSWER: We did not shave. We used to remain dirty-looking, because the beard makes you look unkempt, dirty as they say. And it's true. Besides we used to send our white trousers to be dyed

62. Ġ. Borġ.
63. For further information see P.P. Borg, *Selmun u l-Inħawi*.

jiżbogħhulna iswed … ċertu wieħed minn Bormla. Ġo ħwienet ma konniex nidħlu aħna għax vistu. U ma nistgħux immorru ħdejn wieħed idoqq il-kitarra jew jgħanni. U vistu … għadu kif imut missieri, għadha kif tmut ommi, oħti, ħija, allura ma konniex immorru. Ara daż-żmien, per eżempju, t-tifla tgħidli: Missier baxxaqlu r-Rediffusion għax għadu jmut it-tali u t-tali. Għadha kif mietet it-talija. Aħna konna nagħmlu vistu anke għall-barranin, aħseb u ara għal ta' ġewwa. Ma konniex immorru għax-xogħol. M'hemmx daħk. M'hemmx ħruġ barra.

M. Jekk ikollok bżonn tmur għax-xogħol?
T. Imbagħad għall-bżonn … għax anke konna nżommu l-leħja. Ikollok bżonn tmur quddiem xi superjur jew il-qorti jew tagħmilha ta' xhud ikollok tqaxxarha l-leħja biex tmur sura ta' nies, u tilbes ġlekk u dan.

black by a certain man. A certain man who lived in Bormla. And we did not enter any shops because we were in mourning and we could not listen to a man playing the guitar or take part in folk-singing. And we used to have mourning when some relative had just died, be it father or mother or sister or brother. Even up to the present day my daughter tells me: Father, lower the volume of the Rediffusion set because that man has just died or that woman has just died. We used to be in mourning even for outsiders, let alone for relatives. No laughing. No going out.

Q. If you needed to go out?

A. Well, if the need arose … even as regards our beard. If you had to call on some superior or if you had to go to court or serve as a witness, you shaved to appear tidy. And you put on the jacket and the like.

M. Għalfejn ma kontux tqaxxru leħja?

T. Kienet sistema antika ... sistema antika.

M. L-iswed kien jidħol ħafna?

T. Uuuu anke fil-ħabbata wkoll. Kienu jaqilgħu anke l-ħabbata u jagħmlu ċarruta sewda. Anke l-buttuni kienu jinfurraw. Laħam anqas kien jidħol id-dar. Lanqas nhar ta' Ħadd. Lanqas kienu jsajru, per eżempju, fenek jew xi ħaġa stuffat biex ma jagħmilx ir-riħa u toħroġ mid-dar. Jgħidu: Ara ma jistħix ... għadha kif tmut ommu jew missieru u qed issajjar l-istuffat. – Lanqas il-forn biex ma jgħidux in-nies: Ara ġej bil-patata l-forn jew l-imqarrun il-forn għadu kif imut missieru jew ommu – Hekk kienu. Hekk konna dari ... Waqt li kien ikollna l-mewt id-dar il-ġirien min kien iġibilna buqar kafè biex nitrejqu għaliex meta jkollok dik it-traġedja d-dar ma jkollok aptit tieħu xejn.

Q. Why didn't you shave?

A. It was an old system ... an old system.

Q. Did black figure prominently?

A. Oh yes. Even on the knocker. They used to pull out the knocker and put a piece of black cloth instead. They even used to cover buttons in black. Meat did not enter our homes. Not even on Sundays. They did not use to cook rabbit or stew so that it would not be smelt from outside. Otherwise people would say: Look he is not ashamed of doing such things ... his mother has just died (or his father) and he is cooking stew. They did not bake in the public oven either so that the people would not say: Look, he is coming with his dish of potatoes or baked macaroni, whilst his father (or mother) has just died. – That is how we used to live in the past ... When we were visited by death in our homes

Allura kienu jġibulna l-ġirien imsieken.

our neighbours used to bring us a pot of coffee or tea to have something to drink because when you are visited by such a calamity you do not feel like having anything. So our kind neighbours used to bring us something to drink. They used to bring us some coffee, perhaps even some broth.

M. X'kien jiġri meta jmut xi sajjied?

T. Uuuu hawnhekk jaqa' vistu. Hawnhekk ġa Marsaxlokk jaqa' vistu kbir. Hawnhekk lanqas jekk bniedem jgħaddi minn ħdejk lanqas ikellmek u anqas tkellmu bis-swied ta' qalb li jibqa'. Anke jekk, per eżempju, ikun maltemp u dan lanqas inħarsu lejn xulxin għax kulħadd ikun qalbu sewda u qalbu ttaqtaq: Min jaf jiġix bis-sliem … min jaf jiġix bis-sliem?

Q. What used to happen when fisherman died?

A. Alas, such a calamity would bring deep mourning here in Marasxlokk. Even if your friend passed by you in the street, he would not stop to talk to you, and you would not talk to him – such was the sorrow that would prevail. Even if, for example, the sea happens to be very strong, we used to refrain from looking at each other because everyone would be sorrowful and terribly worried – Who knows whether he will return safely?[64]

---

64. The atmosphere following the death of a fisherman in Marsaxlokk, especially a tragic death at sea is clearly felt in *Il-Baħar Rasu Iebsa*, a series written for Xandir Malta by L. Psaila.

The Afterlife – Dread of the Spirit

The great importance given to the disposal of the corpse, which is a universal preoccupation, and the appropriate ceremonies with which this disposal is carried out, seem to stem from the belief that, unless these ceremonies are fulfilled, the deceased would return to the places which had been his haunt in life. Numerous stories are told in support of this belief. Hence a paraphernelia of rituals surround the shrouding of the corpse before it is taken for burial.

The corpse is first washed in order that the person in question appears 'in front of God' as clean as possible. The eyelids are shut, whilst the chin is raised by a band, usually a white kerchief, tied around the head. The hair of the corpse is cut immediately after death, in preparation for burial.

As Christians we Maltese believe in the survival of the human soul after death. As in some societies, including most Western ones, the condition of the soul after death is closely related to the behaviour of the individual during his lifetime. In this case the survivors have relatively little influence upon the situation, and rituals for the dead tend to be commemorative rather than manipulative but, as already explained in the preceding sections, the position of the departed souls is still influenced by the behaviour of the survivors, hence tending to make the situation manipulative.

In our culture the dead are believed to have left society and will not take part in the regular activities of the community. Their return is not desired (generally speaking) for the departed ones would only interfere with the social order and the business of the living. The dead are usually greatly feared, and at the same time respected. The Maltese try to help the deceased so that they would be as happy as possible in their other-worldly existence.

Regular sacrifices and offerings, which usually decrease with time, are a regular feature of the customs which follow death in the Maltese context. This is what anthropologists call the cult of the dead. This does not mean that no burial rites and elaborate precautions are taken to ensure that there is no return of the soul. As already described, *in-newwieħa* used to burn the possessions of the deceased and other precautions were also taken.

In spite of all precautions, the dead sometimes do return as ghosts and in dreams, taking various forms. Usually this is believed to be an indication that the souls have been neglected. Even when no direct manifestation of their presence is observed, they may signify their dissatisfaction by bringing disease or other misfortunes. Ritual actions will be renewed or intensified in order to appease them, and to send them back to their own realm.[65]

Although the following anecdotes were gathered from elderly informants, it does not mean that underlying today's sceptic attitudes, the age-old emotions of mourning and fear of the return of the dead to hunt the living do not persist.

Most of the funeral customs described in this chapter, although not all followed in our days, are the result of the conviction that the returned spirit will need most of the things it had in life in its future existence. This proves the antiquity of the elaborate burial of the dead which is one of man's earliest cultural achievements.

---

65. Case histories about the subject, apart from the ones presented can be read in Diacono.

In the light of this, such information about ghosts is of the utmost importance, since most of the taboos enjoined are the results of fear of the return of ghosts.

Kien hemm tieġ u stiednu sacerdot, u hu u tiela' ġo din id-dar, fejn kien qed isir *il-party* ra qassis ġo dil-kamra, jaqra l-uffizzju. U l-*party* bdiet. U dak il-qassis qed jaqra l-uffizzju. Qallhom: Intom stedintu xi qassis ieħor? Qalulu: Le ... aħna ma stidinniex qassisin iżjed. Qalilhom: Imxu ħalli taraw. U kellmu u qallu: Fl-Isem ta' Alla, inti xi trid minn hawn? Qallu: Jien ilni erbgħin sena fil-Purgatorju u llum wasalli ż-żmien li neħles, għalhekk il-Bambin ippermetta li jistidnuk biex tiġi hawn. Qallu: Hemmhekk, ara f'dak il-ħajt hemm armarju mkaħħal, iftħu, aqla' dik il-ġebla, għax hemm ktieb tal-qrar u dak qabel jinħaraq jien nibqa' nbati. Qallu: Issa daqshekk. Jiena sejjer il-Ġenna.

There was a wedding feast and people were invited and a priest was invited as well and as he was going up the stairs, in this house, where the party was going on, he saw another priest in this room, reading the breviary. And the party began. And that priest was still reading the breviary. He told them: Did you invite any other priest? They told him: No ... we did not invite any other priest. He told them: Let us go and see. And then he spoke to him and told him: In the Name of God, what do you want from here? He answered: I've been forty years in Purgatory and now it's time for me to be freed. That is the reason why God has permitted you to be invited here. He added: Over there, look, in that wall, there is a built-in cupboard, open it, pull out that stone

'He answered: I've been forty years in Purgatory and now it's
time for me to be freed.'

and there you will find a confession book and until that is burned I'll suffer in Purgatory. He told him: Enough now. I am going to heaven.[66]

Jien kont noqgħod ġo post. Kif mort ġo fih, sidu qalli: Tisma' x'tisma' u tara x'tara titkellimx. Qalli: Għax inkella jimmankak. Kif nidħol ġo fih, nara id tvenven u tajritli l-lampa minn idi, u l-lampa ma kissrithielix – Kienet lampa tas-sieq, tal-ħġieġ – U bqajt, bqajt, bqajt, kont noqgħod ġo fih u kelli l-bhejjem. U kont indaħħal bhima sewda, lanqas kwarta ma kienet toqgħod ġo fih, għax kienet tmut. Bajda xejn. Ħamra lanqas. U sewda joqtolhieli. Bqajt daqsxejn oħra ġo fih, imbagħad tlaqtu.

I lived in a certain house. As soon as I went in its owner told me: Whatever you hear and what-ever you see do not speak, otherwise he will maim you. As soon as I went in, I saw a hand shaking about and it waved the lamp from my hands, but the lamp did not break. – It was one of the glass lamps with a stand – I went on living in it, and I kept animals as well. And whenever I brought in a black animal, say a black goat, it wouldn't remain alive for more than a quarter of an hour, because it would die. Nothing used to happen to a white one. Nor a red one. But he would always kill a black one. I stayed on a bit longer there. Then I left the place.[67]

66. Ġ. Borġ.
67. Ż. Axisa, during an interview in March 1975.

In-nies ma tantx kienu jabbużaw jinfamaw post għax min jinfama post l-istess bħal min jinfama xebba. Tista' tfittxu bil-qorti u jkollu jħallas il-kera sakemm jinkera. Illum ma tantx għadna nisimgħu b'dan. Tgħidli qalbi l-blast tal-gwerra xorob kollox għax waqa' ħafna bini u minfloku sar bini ġdid. Fiż-żmien kien ikun hawn ħafna spirti għax kienu jgħidu li meta jsir xi delitt u joqtlu ruħ bl-idejn l-ispirtu tal-mejjet jibqa' ħaj.

People did not dare speak ill of any house, because he who speaks ill of a house is like the person who slanders a young woman. You can sue him in court. And he will have to pay the rent until the place is finally rented. We do no longer hear very much about this today. I dare say that the shell-blast of the war has swallowed everything up. Many buildings have been demolished and instead new buildings have gone up. In times past there used to be many spirits around, because they used to say that when a crime is committed and a person murdered, the spirit of the dead will remain on earth.[68]

Kien hawn waħda u kienet għaddejja minn triq, u kien hawn Madonna u dejjem kienet tgħidilha tliet Ave Marijiet. U kienet tisker u mara tagħmel kollox. Allura meta kienet tgħaddi minn hemm kienet tgħidilha: Int trid tkun is-salvazzjoni tiegħi.

There was a woman and she passed through a street where there was a Madonna. And she always recited three Hail Mary's. And she used to get drunk and lead a loose life. Therefore, when she used to pass that way, she used to tell Our Lady: You

68. A. Smith, during an interview in Febuary 1974.

Allura kienet toqgħod għarkubbtejha u tgħidilha kuljum Salve Regina u tliet Ave Marijiet. U meta mietet difnuha barra. Kien jgħaddi wieħed tal-karrozzin u hemm kien jara fanal jixgħel. Qallhom: Issa, meta tarawh, jixgħel ejjew għiduli. U meta marrù jgħidulu, mar fuq il-post u qallu: Part minn t'Alla, x'tinsab int? Qaltlu: Jiena ninsab mara, li kont nagħmel minn kollox, imma l-Madonna, billi kont ngħidilha tliet Ave Marijiet kuljum, ħelsitni. Mietet u marret il-Purgatorju. Qaltlu: Aqilgħuni minn hawnhekk għax jien m'arridx noqgħod hawnhekk. Allura qalgħuha u ħaduha l-knisja. Meta ħaduha l-knisja, qatt ma rawha aktar imbagħad.

are my only hope of salvation. She used to kneel down and everyday she would say a Hail Holy Queen and three Hail Mary's. And when she died, she was buried in unconsecrated ground. A cab man, who used to go by, was told that in that place people were seeing a lighted lantern. He told them: Now, when you see its light let me know. And when they went to tell him, he went on the spot and told the spirit: In the name of God, what are you? She told him: I am a woman who led a loose life, but Our Lady saved my soul, because I used to recite three Hail Mary's – she had died and gone to Purgatory – she told him: Take me up from this unconsecrated ground because I don't want to remain here. – So they dug her up and took her to church. After they took her to church, she was never seen any more.[69]

---

69. M. Borġ, a 73-year-old informant from Birkirkara, in an interview in August 1975.

Konna qegħdin Tunes u kien hemm il-ħares u kien joqgħod iħabbtilna u ommi ma ridetx toqgħod għax kienet tibża'. U mbagħad kien jgħawġilhom ħalqhom lit-tfal – il-ħares. U ommi qalet: Issa ma noqgħodx haw' ladarba lit-tfal qed jimmankahom. Imbagħad ġiebet wieħed Għarbi u qaltlu: It-tfal tiegħi qiegħed jimmankahom. Qallha: Ta' qablek kellhom għajnejhom juġgħuhom. Qalilha: Għax hawnhekk hawn wieħed ... kien Rumi, Mislem minn Rumi serqilhom il-post. Issa dawk marru ġewwa l-Asja, jiġifieri marru l-Infern, qalilha. Issa minn dak inhar 'l hawn dal-lok ma jistax joqgħod bit-taħbit u li ma jimmankax lit-tfal. Imbagħad ommi ħarġet minn hemm u t-tabib ħa kura tat-tfal u reġgħu ġew kif kienu.

We were living in Tunis. And there was a ghost. And he used to knock on our door. And my mother did not want to stay in that house because she was afraid. After this, the ghost began to twist the children's mouths. And my mother said: Now, I won't stay here, since the ghost is maiming them. And she consulted an Arab and told him: He is maiming my children. He told her: Your predecessor had trouble with their eyes. Because here there is a man. He was a Rumi, a Muslim from Rumi, who stole the place. Now these people have gone to Hades and since then, this place has always been full of noise and knocking and children always get maimed here. Then my mother left the place and the doctor cured the children and they became normal again.[70]

---

70. M. Axiaq.

Il-ħares ikun bniedem li jkun seraq oġġett fid-dinja ... ħaġa mhux tiegħu, imbagħad imur l-Infern u jibqa' dejjem iħabbat fuq dak l-oġġett li jkun ġo fih u biex ma jħabbatx iżjed min ikun ġo fih iroddu, jekk ma jroddux hu jmur l-Infern bħalu. Jekk ma jkunx seraq ikun wiret il-lok.

The ghost is a man who has stolen something during his earthly life – something that wasn't his. Then he would go to hell and goes on giving trouble, even knocking audibly on that thing or place, and in order that this trouble will stop, the new owner must return it to its rightful owner. Otherwise, if he does not do this, he will go to hell as well, even though he has committed no theft himself, he has inherited the theft.[71]

Darba kien hemm mara u raġel u kienu jdoqqu ta' l-imwiet u kif ħarġu mill-knisja jaraw żewġt iklieb kbar ġejjin minn fuq u dawn beżgħu u telqu jiġru lejn id-dar u x'ħin marru d-dar għaddew m'nejn tagħhom u baqgħu neżlin 'l isfel u mbagħad kien hemm mara u rathom u telqet tiġri lejn ommha u

Once there were a man and his wife and the church bells were ringing for the repose of the Dead. As soon as they came out of the church, they saw two big dogs coming towards them. And the man and his wife were very frightened and ran home. And when they arrived home, the two dogs passed

---

71. Ibid.

mbagħad qalet: Ha nittawwal mit-tieqa, ha nara dawk iż-żewgt iklieb nerġax narahom. U reġgħet rathom għaddejjin l-istess ħaġa mit-triq għal ġo l-għalqa u x'hemm ma jafux ... żewġt iklieb kbar daqs il-ħmir ta' l-Indi ngħidulhom aħna.

down a street and went on walking until they passed the house. Then a woman saw the dogs, and went running towards her mother, saying: Let me look out of the window so that I will see if the two dogs are really there. And he did see them again, walking through the streets and then into the fields. People don't know what they were ... two dogs as big as donkeys.[72]

Darba kien hemm ommi u kienet tmur toqgħod għand waħda mara għax kienet tibża' torqod waħedha, u mbagħad meta daħlu fis-sodda biex jorqdu kien ikun hemm dawl fis-saqaf ... jiġri daqqa f'kantuniera u daqqa f'oħra, il-lejl kollu. Ommi ma setgħetx torqod daqs kemm beżgħet. Imbagħad imma ma marretx torqod hemm iżjed. Iwa dak minnu għax ratu ommi stess. Ħwejjeġ li

Once my mother used to go to sleep with a friend of hers because she was afraid of sleeping all alone. Then, as soon as they got into bed, they always saw a light in the ceiling; all night long this light flickered from one corner to another. My mother was so afraid that she would not go to sleep. And so she never went to sleep there again. Yes that's true because my mother herself saw it. I

---

72. Ibid.

tghidhomli ommi kollha nemminhom jien.

Darba ohra kien hemm wiehed u kienet il-ġurnata ta' l-Għid u ried joqgħod jiekol xi ħaġa milli jagħmlu għall-Għid u qallha 'l ommu: Illum ma niġix il-knisja ħalli noqgħod id-dar. – Imbagħad insomma mar jiġri u ġewwa kellhom naqra ta' ġardina u sadattant tant beża' li ma marx jiekol u x'ħin ġiet ommu qallha: Kien hemm ħmar naħseb li ġol-ġardina ma ħalla l-ebda ħaġa tant kemm ilu jgħajjat u jiġri. – U mbagħad ommu marret u ratu u sabet kollox kien għadu kif kien għax dak insomma kien il-ħares.

always believe whatever my mother tells me.[73]

Another time there was a man who, in Eastertime, wanted to eat something that is usually cooked for Easter and so he told his mother, Today I'm not coming to church; I'm staying at home. – Then, to cut a long story short, he ran into the house. They had a small garden. In the meantime he was so afraid that he did not eat at all and when his mother arrived, he told her: There was a donkey, I think he has eaten up everything in the garden. He's been braying and running around for a long time. – And then his mother went into the garden and saw it but she found everything as she had left it, because in fact that had been an apparition.[74]

---

73. Ibid.
74. Ibid.

Jiena mhux l-ewwel darba li rajtu l-ħares għax meta konna noqogħdu fid-dar t'ommi konna narawh. Daqqa jiġi jmess il-qroqqa, daqqa narawh fid-dawl ta' qamar, daqqa jqabbad ħuġġieġa nar, filli jiġi ħafna dawl. Anzi darba minnhom kellna maqjel bit-tiben, u kien hemm iz-zija u qaltilna: Morru ġibuli qabda tiben. Qaltilna: Ara tieħdu sulfarina magħkom. Għidnielha: Le. – Konna, jiena, u oħti Karmena u t-tifel tagħha. Allura meta dħalna xegħilna ... xegħel partita dawl. – Ommi x'għamiltuli ... x'għamiltuli ... għandu jkun qed iqabbduli kull m'hemm – U ġiet iz-zija u kif ġiet id-dawl intefa u ma rajna xejn iżjed.

I've seen the ghost more than once because, when I lived in my mother's house, we used to see him. At one time he would touch the brooding hen, at another we would see him in the moonlight and at another he would light a fire – light would suddenly appear after darkness. Once we had a stable full of hay, and my aunt told us: Go and fetch me some hay. She added: See that you don't light any matches. We answered: Of course not. There were three of us, myself, my sister Carmen, and her son. As soon as we got in, a light suddenly appeared: My God, what have you done? Are you burning the place? And my aunt ran to the stable and, as soon as she arrived, the light disappeared and we could see nothing else.[75]

---

75. M. Borġ.

Darb'oħra ommi kienet rieqda. Kienet ix-xitwa u ġie jmissilha idejha. Qallha: Xi darba nħallilek il-flus. Qaltlu: Jiena m'arridx flus, għax jiena m'għandix bżonn tal-flus. Qaltlu: M'arridx. Qaltli ommi, għax jekk jagħtik il-flus u forsi titkellem, jista' joqtlok, qaltli forsi ngħidilhom. Qaltilna: Meta taraw hekk, xi spirtu jkun irid jagħtikom il-flus qatt taċċettawhom.

Another time my mother was asleep. It was winter and the ghost came and touched her hand. He told her: I will leave you some money. She answered: I don't want any money because I don't need it. She added: I really don't want any. She told me: If the ghost gives you money and perhaps you say something about it, then he will kill you. Probably I will blab. She warned us: If you see that a ghost is offering money, never accept.[76]

Ir-raġel tiegħi meta kien għarus lili kien isib daqqa soru tagħlaqlu t-triq, daqqa nagħġa … U meta kien ikun ġej bil-biegħa, filli jkollu l-mezzi bl-għeneb u filli ma jkollu xejn. U filli jerġa' jiġi kollox f'postu. Lejn l-Imtaħleb il-ħares jarawh veru. L-aħħar darba kont qed nitkellem ma' waħda u qaltli li rat servetta u ħasbitha

When my husband was bethroted to me, he used to find at one time a nun blocking his way … at another a sheep. Another day, whilst he was coming with his wares, his baskets up till then full of grapes would suddenly become empty. And then, as suddenly, everything would be as it was before. They really see ghosts

---

76. Ibid.

b'xi biċċa ħobż ... marret fetħitha u ħarġet ħuġġieġa nar. U dawn żewġt ixjuħ li qalu ... ma jigdbux ... għax issa minn dak inhar 'l hawn m'għadhomx joħorġu kmieni peress li fis-sajf imorru jaħsdu.

in the whereabouts of Mtaħleb. Earlier on this year I was speaking to a woman who told me that she once saw a napkin which she thought was full of bread. She went to open it and a flame burst out of it. And this was told to me by two old women ... they do not lie ... from that day onwards, they never left their house early in the morning, even though in summer they go in the fields to harvest the corn.[77]

L-aħħar żewġt itfal li kelli tewmin u ħsilthom insomma u fisqejthom u tfajthom ġol-benniena waħda 'l hawn u l-oħra 'l hinn biex neħles minnhom. Imbagħad qiegħda ngħid: Missieri ... jiġi missieri issa. – Għax jgħidu li fis-siegħa l-erwieħ joħorġu. U fl-istess hin nisma' l-lukkett jinfetaħ u dieħel missieri. U jien qed ngħid Missieri ... missieri ...

The last children I had were twins. I bathed them and swaddled them and placed them in the cot, one on either side, to get some rest of them. Then I was saying: My father, my father would come now ... Because they say that at one o'clock the spirits come out. I was saying this to myself. And at the same time I heard the latch of the door opening and my father coming in. And I

---

77. M. Muscat, a 50-year-old informant from Dingli, in an interview by the author in January 1974.

U għadda minn fejni hekk u għidt se jeħodli t-tfal ... se jeħodhomli ... u mar fejn il-benniena. Narah jikxef il-filoxx ta' fuq it-tfal u jħares lejhom. Imbagħad ħriġt barra. Niltaqa' ma' wieħed li qalli: Hawn fejn sejra ... għadek kif xtrajt dawk iż-żewġt itfal. Għidtlu: Hemm missieri d-dar. Qalli: Mela missierek ħa joqtlok. Għidtlu: Missieri mejjet. Qalli: Imxi ruħi, imxi tara kif m'hemm ħadd. Imbagħad mort u ma sibt xejn. U dan ir-raġel – Tas-Sanità – qalli: Talli semmejtu jidhirlek ... l-ombra tiegħu tidhirlek. – Allura bħal qisni seħħtlu. L-ispirtu mis-siegħa sas-sagħtejn ikollhom id-dritt.

said: My father ... my father. And he passed by me and I said: He is going to take away my children ... he is going to take them. And he went near the cot. I saw him removing the net which was covering the children and looking at them. Then I went out. He told me: (Because I met a man in the street) Where are you going? You have just given birth to those two children. I told him: There is my father at home. He answered: Is your father going to kill you? I told him: But my father is dead. He said: Come my dear and you'll see that there is no one. Following this I went and did not find anything. And this man told me. He was a sanitary inspector. Did you mention him? Because of this his shadow appears to you. Therefore it seems as if I had summoned him, since I mentioned him. Spirits are allowed to be about from one to two in the morning.[78]

78. P. Attard.

X'inhuma l-ispirti ... L-ispirti huma nies mejta li jkunu insewhom fit-talb. L-erwieħ jiġru jkunu. L-ispirtu tagħhom mhux se jiġi hu. L-ispirtu tagħhom jidher għax int m'għandekx tweġġa' l-erwieħ. M'għandekx ma tiftakarx fihom. Dawk għandhom id-dritt fuqek ... Jekk xi ħadd joqtol 'l xi ħadd l-ispirtu tiegħu jibqa' jidhirlu ... iħabbtu. Sakemm jgħaddu l-ħinijiet għax dak ikun bil-ħinijiet. Int weġġajtni allura għandi dritt sena nittantak dejjem.

Spirits are dead people not prayed for by their relatives ... these are spirits who roam the earth. Their spirit would not come for no reason at all. Their spirit would appear if you offend them, because you should not offend the dead. You should always remember them. They hold power over you. If someone kills someone else the victim's spirit would remain to haunt the murderer, troubling him, until his time has run out. You have hurt me, therefore I have the power of troubling you for a whole year.[79]

Jiena niftakar dar hawn il-Mellieħa, illi l-familja ma setgħetx toqgħod fiha. U bgħetha bi ftit flus 'il wieħed hawnhekk mill-Mellieħa. U dan kien ftit qabel il-gwerra. U peress li kienet vojta ħaduha f'idejn is-suldati għax is-suldati dak iż-żmien bdew jieħdu kullimkien.

I remember a house here in Mellieħa, in which the inhabitants could not go on living. And the house was sold for a small sum of money to a man from Mellieħa. This took place before the war. And since it was empty it was taken up by the soldiers, because the soldiers in those

---

79. Ibid.

Però xorta waħda s-suldati kienu joħorġu 'l barra, għax kienu jisimgħu ħafna ħsejjes. U minn fejn ġejjin il-ħsejjes ma kinux jafu. Allura sidha meta ra li anke s-suldati kienu qed jisimgħu l-ħsejjes meta spiċċat il-gwerra s-suldati telquha. Allura hu ried li jmur joqgħod fiha peress li xtraha. Iddeċieda li jagħmel somma flus il-Kurja, li jiena ma nafx kemm sewwa, imma hawn min jgħid li kienet bejn £300 u £500 u minn dak iż-żmien 'l hawn mar joqgħod fiha u ma ra xejn iżjed.

Il-waħx hu spirtu ħażin. Spirtu ħażin hu bniedem li jkun qiegħed l-Infern. Iħabbat fid-dinja lil min jaħti li hu qiegħed l-Infern. Il-waħx għandu l-almu jidher kif irid. Konna mmorru nirgħu n-nagħaġ u xid-

days were requisitioning everywhere. But still the soldiers used to leave the house because they used to hear various noises. And they did not know the whereabouts of these noises. When the war was over, the soldiers left the house. The owner wanted to go and live in it, since he had bought it. He decided to place a sum of money in the Curia, a sum which I don't know exactly but they say that it was between £300 and £500. After that he went to live in it and he was never troubled again.[80]

The ogre is an evil spirit, and an evil spirit is the soul of one of the damned. In our world he comes to trouble those who were the cause of his damnation. The ogre can appear in whatever form he likes. We used to go to tend

80. S. Muscat, a 65-year-old informant from Mellieħa in an interview by the author in April 1974.

disgħa ta' bil-lejl kien ikun id-dlam. U kien hemm blata u jien kont immur ma' oħra u f'din il-blata konna naraw żewġ qassisin wieħed tiela' u l-ieħor nieżel. Dawk kienu jkunu spirti ħżiena. Dan biex nuri li l-ispirti jidhru kif iridu. Hemm min jidher ta' baqra u hemm min jidher ta' ħaruf.

our sheep and at about nine o' clock in the evening it would be quite dark. There was a huge rock and here I used to go with another shepherdess and here we would see two priests, one walking up, the other down. These were evil spirits. I am saying all this to show that evil spirits may assume any form they choose. Some appear as cows, others as lambs.[81]

A host of stories support the popular belief that many houses have been haunted by those who lived or died in them, and sometimes by entities more difficult to account for. Sights and sounds outside normal experience have been heard in such places. Usually these were regarded as straightforward visitations from beyond the grave, or possibly instances of telepathy between the living and the dead. Others think that every such experience is purely subjective and due to hallucination on part of the 'observer'.

As seen from the above examples, ghostly manifestations take different forms. Some apparitions are no more than fleeting and elusive forms, suddenly perceived and quickly gone. Usually these appear several times. Others are distinct and recognizable figures and some are so normal in appearance that they are mistaken for living people, at first at least. Noises are heard, though nothing visible makes these

---

81. M. Axiaq.

noises. Sometimes these sounds are loud and terrifying, sometimes they are slight yet clearly audible, like the faint murmur of voices, or the sound of crying, or footsteps passing along a corridor or down the stairs. Certain houses contain rooms that produce restlessness in the inhabitant. This does not mean that they are haunted, but it is impossible to concentrate while one is in them.

The popular belief about these ghostly manifestations is that these ghosts remain strongly tied to their old homes. Usually these ties are the result of some past state of bitter unhappiness, or violent terror, or the guilt of an unexpiated sin.

This phenomenon is of wide prevalence and most of the informants always had some story to narrate, thus showing the tenacity of this belief.

Conclusion

In the popular imagination death is associated with the release from worries, return to God, uncertainty, finality, fear, futility, disease, mortality, ingratitude, hardship, survivors' interests, ineluctability, deterrence, reflection of life, equality, respect, heartlessness, suddenness, injustice, and hope. This is well illustrated from proverbs.[82]

These attitudes towards death, together with the taboo character of most of the rites and ceremonies surrounding it, some of which of Arabic origin, others local, and most of them traceable directly to Sicilian and Italian sources, show the importance given by the Maltese to this last taboo subject – death.

So far the various taboos through the full span of human

---

82. Aquilina, *Comparative Dictionary of Maltese Proverbs*, 28.

life from birth to death have been considered. Extensive space has been devoted to verbatim reproductions of information volunteered by the elderly, together with other usages observed by the author. Furthermore, various taboos and rites which manifestly were, and to some extent are still, an integral and indispensable part of our religious and social practice have been described. With the passage of time these taboos and rites began slowly to lose their intensity.

A look at the cultural evolution of these taboos will show that all these numerous and varied rites found during birth, puberty, marriage, death, burial, and mourning all had their origin and have their only possible logical and historical explanation in the cult of spirits of the past. In spite of over 1,900 years of Christianity in the islands, certain 'pagan' customs and beliefs are not yet extinct among the local people. Moreover, the Christian religion in its turn has generated other taboos. Since the days when Saint Paul was shipwrecked on the island in AD 60, religion has assumed an outstanding influence on the local population's daily habits and customs, with the result that many pagan customs and folk-ways that were too deeply rooted to be eradicated became adapted to the new religion after being given a different interpretation by the Church. At the same time, throughout the centuries Malta has come into contact with various other cultures, and this has resulted in a pattern of traditions which are in a continuous process of change.[83]

Having thus taken a look at the various taboos which surround the main life crises, the next step is to look at the taboos surrounding the year.

---

83. For further information, see Cassar Pullicino, *Studies in Maltese Folklore*, 40-54.

**Maltese landscape dotted
by chapels and farmhouses**

The water fountain: where needs and gossip meet

Posing for a picture: mule, cart and all

Street vendors: proudly displaying their wares

Valletta streetscape in the good old days

Country folk in typical Maltese costume

Valletta: inside old
del Monte gate

Gambling game:
playing at *'il-morra'*

Milk vendor with herd in a Valletta street

Village girl: goats, utensils and all

Milk on your doorstep before pasteurization

Gozitan country side with the Citadel in the background

Grand Harbour activity on the wharfs beneath Valletta

Xlendi, Gozo: so much has changed now!

Marketing the country produce in the city

Making the sacred and the profane meet: a procession going down Saint Paul's Street in Valletta

TABOO AND SOCIAL TIME

Among all cultures there are certain days in which various taboos are practised. Various negative regulations, such as refrainment from labour, fasting, and continence, characterize these days. These regulations, although burdensome and restrictive have a definite psychological value because, if duly observer, they help the community to face the future with renewed strength and confidence. They also help in social cohesion.

In general, any socially significant period which marks a transition from one state to another is invested with taboos designed to meet the threats facing the social life of the community. Such periods characterize the death-situation, unusual events, the transition from one season or year to another, and the celebration of various religious ceremonies.

Anthropological material[1] shows the taboos which characterize, for example, the Christian Sunday, the Jewish

---

1. See, for example, Webster.

Sabbath, and their historical and anthropological prototypes. This material investigates also tabooed days at critical epochs, tabooed days after death and on related occasions, holy days, market days, lunar superstitions and festivals, lunar calendars and the week, the Babylonian 'Evil Days' and the *Shabattum*, the Hebrew Sabbath, and the unlucky days.

In Malta, such elements of taboo are encountered on specific days, especially Sundays and Fridays, two days with which various taboos are associated, not only in Europe but even beyond it. These taboos were more prominent in pre-war Malta before socio-economic change brought about drastic shifts in the behaviour patterns.

Individuals seem to cling to tradition when they are living in a stable society because of the practical aid it provides in daily living. However, in present-day conditions, traditional methods often break down and hamper understanding of today's requirements. Adherence to traditions that are losing their relationship to the rhythm of life and are increasingly assuming the character of fixed obsessional ritual tends to be increasingly motivated by fear of a profoundly-changed environment.

The fear of breaking down traditions accounts in large measure for 'the conservatism among certain communities and their repugnance toward innovation of any sort, as will be seen in this chapter.[2]

---

2. Since this chapter was written, legislation has abolished the public celebration of mandatory feasts during the working week and transferred them to the weekend. Despite this, the Church has continued to practice the celebration of internal feasts, according to the liturgical calendar. During the last decade most of the mandatory feasts were once again transferred to their original days.

Days

Tabooed days are charaterisitic of every culture. Malta is not an exception to the rule. More or less, these tabooed days, as with the rest of Europe, are the result of pagan and Christian traditions.the supernatural element with which these days are invested is seen in the dedication of each specific day to a particular saint or devotion as shown hereunder.

It-Tnejn ta' l-Erwieħ	Monday is dedicated to the Holy Souls
It-Tlieta ta' Sant'Anna	Tuesday is dedicated to Saint Anne
L-Erbgħa tal-Madonna tal-Karmnu	Wednesday is dedicated to Our Lady of Mount Carmel
Il-Ħamis ta' l-Ispirtu s-Santu	Thursday is dedicated to the Holy Ghost
Il-Ġimgħa tal-Passjoni	Friday is dedicated to Christ's passion and death
Is-Sibt tal-Madonna	Saturday is dedicated to Our Lady
Il-Ħadd l-obbligu tal-festa, nisimgħu l-quddies.	Sunday is a feast of obligation.[3]

Among the peasants, the months are better known by the Saints' names which are associated with them. The following is the alternative list: January – *ix-xahar ta' l-Istrina*, 'The month of New Year gifts'; February – *ix-xahar ta' San Pawl*, 'St Paul's month'; March – *ix-xahar ta' San Ġużepp*, 'St

---

3. Ż. Axisa.

Sunday is a feast of obligation – villager in Sunday clothes.

Joseph's month'; May – *ix-xahar tal-Madonna*, 'Our Lady's month'; June – *ix-xahar ta' San Ġwann*, 'Saint John's month; July – *ix-xahar tal-Karmnu*, 'The month of our Lady of Mt. Carmel'; August – *ix-xahar ta' Santa Marija*, 'St Mary's month'; September – *ix-xahar tal-Vitorja*, 'The month of Our Lady of Victory'; or *ix-xahar tas-Salib*, 'Holy Rood Month'; October – *ix-xahar tar-Rużarju*, 'The month of Our Lady of the Rosary'; November – *ix-xahar tal-Qaddisin Kollha*, 'All Saints month'; or *ix-xahar tal-Erwieħ* or *tal-Mejtin*, 'All Souls' month'; and December – *ix-xahar tal-Milied*, 'Christmas month'.[4]

This information shows that each day of the week and each month of the year are put under the protection of some supernatural agency.

The following texts represent examples of ideal-normative patterns of culture which define what the Maltese would do or say on these particular days, i.e. if they were to conform completely to the standards set up by their culture. However, this does not mean that these ideal patterns of culture were, or are, always adhered to. In fact, with the passing of time, the natural process of change sets up new ideal patterns, either consciously or unconsciously. All this can be seen in the behavioural patterns of the Maltese, where divergent behaviour can be observed. This could be more readily seen in the past than in these days.

The following examples show us that those members of the Maltese society who are conscious of the ideal patterns of their culture tend to have a compulsion to conform to these patterns. The culture does not provide other acceptable means of meeting these customs.

---

4. Aquilina, *Comparative Dictionary of Maltese Proverbs*, 515.

Friday

Friday is a day fraught with taboos all over Western Europe. The ambivalent character of this day, however, is clearly seen when its positive significance for the Christian world is taken into consideration. The customs and beliefs characteristic of this day all centre on the death of Christ which is commemorated on this day. These taboos run analogously with the taboos found in the death-situation.

In the Middle Ages people were accustomed to date all the unfortunate events of religious tradition and history on a Friday. Synchronisms of this sort had a great attraction to the mediaeval mind.[5]

Friday is mostly tabooed when it falls on the thirteenth. The number thirteen is an unlucky number because of its association with one of the apostles who betrayed Christ and eventually was instrumental in his death. This taboo is of late British influence.

A Sicilian proverb collected by Giuseppe Pitrè explicitly says: *Nè di Vennari, nè di Martiri, nun ti moviri, ne ti partiri'*. No Maltese proverb is found to back this belief which says that it is unlucky to embark on a vayage on a Friday. A port director told the author that he follows this taboo because of a deeply-instilled fear which compels him to do so. The director also recounted instances in which bitter consequences followed the infringement of this belief.

A current belief holds that it does not augur well to begin a new piece of work on a Friday. The following information testifies this line of thought:

---

5. Webster, 273.

Trouble follows even if you enter into an unusual transaction.

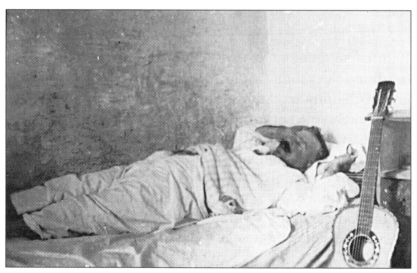

When you finish a set piece of work on a Friday, you are not supposed to enter upon other projects on Saturday.

TWEĠIBA: Meta tispiċċa biċċa xogħol il-Ġimgħa, is-Sibt m'għandekx għalfejn tibda oħra. Ibdiha t-Tnejn.

ANSWER: When you finish a set piece of work on a Friday, you are not supposed to enter upon other projects on Saturday. You should leave this for the following Monday.

MISTOQSIJA: Il-għala?

QUESTION: Why?

TWEĠIBA: Għax hekk darrewna. Jinqalagħlek l-inkwiet anke jekk tagħmel biċċa negozju mhux tas-soltu. Jinqalagħlek l-inkwiet. U konna nwaħħlu f'hekk dari.

ANSWER: That is the way we were brought up. Trouble follows even if you enter into an unusual transaction. We used to attribute such misfortune on the fact that it was carried out on a Friday in the past.[6]

L-aħħar tal-ġimgħa, is-Sibt, m'għandekx tibda xogħol ġdid. Nagħmlu mod tkun se tfassal bieb, jew tieqa jew xi apertura. Aħjar ma tfassalhiex. Din ġejja mill-antik. Kienu anke jekk jispiċċaw f'għalqa l-Ġimgħa, is-Sibt ma kinux imorru jibdew f'oħra. Iżda kienu jibdew it-Tnejn.

You are not supposed to initiate new work on a Friday. Thus it would be much better if, for example, you do not embark on such things as designing an aperture, a window, or a door. This is a custom dating from ancient times. If it happened in the past that our forefathers

---

6. Ż. Axisa.

Jekk jaħdmu jippretendu li ma tkunx ħaġa f'lokha. Ideat, dawn, l-istess bħal tal-baħrija.

finished working one field on a Friday, they would not begin work on another field on a Saturday. They used to begin work on a Monday. They felt that it was not appropriate to work on such a day. These ideas resemble those about the moth.[7]

This avoidance is of a precautionary and preventive nature. Since one of the precepts of the Church says that the members must observe all Sundays, the Maltese dreaded the idea of disobeying this injunction to such an extent that they even avoided beginning work on Fridays or Saturdays.

A common avoidance in this regard was (and still is) the designing of new patterns for clothes by tailors and seamstresses and the 'opening' of sewing machines.[8]

The beliefs mentioned so far are not purely native but the product of cross-cultural influences. Thus, in England it is supposed to be very inauspicious to start a new job, call in a doctor, move house, turn the mattress on a bed, begin a sea vayage or, if you are a criminal, come up for sentencing on a Friday.

Synchronisms of this sort had a great attraction to the mediaeval mind and numerous lists of them are preserved in manuscripts. A Jewish superstition reaching back to to the Talmud says that it is lucky to begin an undertaking on

7. T. Mallia.
8. H. Gauci.

Tuesday because, in describing the third day of creation, it is said, 'God saw that it was good'. Contrariwise, it is unlucky to commence anything of importance on Monday, as to which nothing at all is said.[9]

For thousands of years the inhabitants of the Maltese islands have depended for their livelihood on tilling the land. Consequently many of their taboos have been developed around the very land from which they drew sustenance. Their constant quest for food made them avoid tampering with the 'divine'. The taboo surrounding the uses of the plough and the cart belongs to the same thought-idiom.

The traditional Maltese plough, which is of the same genera as those which are generally found in the Mediterranean region, is of the *aratrum* and *ard* type. There are two kinds of ploughs, *il-Moħriet* and *il-moħriet taż-żewġ*. None of these must be used on this day because, as the following quotation says, both of them are emblematic of the cross.[10] This same taboo applies to the Maltese cart, which is an extremely simple affair, consisting basically of two poles that form the body of the cart and its shafts. It has no framed body: at one end a few slats are bolted across the poles and on these the load rests.

Nhar ta' Ġimgħa u fil-Festa   On Friday and on the Feast
tas-Salib ma konniex nużawh   of the Cross we did not use
il-moħriet. Għaliex il-   the plough. Because the

---

9. Webster, 273-4.
10. For further information regarding Maltese ploughs, see T. Zammit, 78-84.

The traditional Maltese plough is of the *aratrum* and *ard* type.

moħriet fih żewġ slaleb – tal-fekruna u tad-driegħ. L-istess il-karrettun – fih salib fuq quddiem. Għalhekk ma konniex nirkbu fuq is-salib iżda nirkbu fuq lura mis-salib, fuq id-dwali.

plough bears two crosses – *tal-fekruna* and *tad-driegħ*.[11] The cart also has the cross on the front part. Hence we used to stay back from the cross shaft and mount on the back shafts.[12]

Fasting is observed mostly during tabooed periods. While the observance of abstinence on Friday was specifically indicated by the Church, there was no obligation on Wednesday and Saturday, but many abstained as a devotion to the Blessed Virgin. Observances on Monday and Tuesday was less widespread and the origin of the custom is difficult to establish.

Dari, ħlief il-Ħamis u l-Ħadd, ma kien isajjar ħadd kwart laħam fl-antikitò. It-Tnejn, it-Tlieta, l-Erbgħa, il-Ġimgħa, u s-Sibt xejn. Kelli ommi ta' ħamsa u disgħin sena b'xejn ma kienet tniġġeż, lanqas meta kienet l-isptar.

In the past no one would cook meat except on Thursday and Sunday. No meat was served on Monday, Tuesday, Wednesday, Friday, and Saturday. My mother who was 95 years old would not break the abstinence under any circumstances, even when she was in hospital.[13]

---

11. *Id-driegħ* is the back part of the plough by which the peasant directs its movements.
12. Ż. Axisa.
13. Ibid.

This quotation shows the rigour with which our ancestors followed the penitential laws of the Church. More than this it shows their fervour for fasting, a spirit which made them add fasting days of their own. These in turn became observances of a taboo character, because as time passes people try to rationalize a custom, the origin of which they do not know.

Friday reminds us of the death of Christ. It is a day of general sadness on which all sorts of merry-making and unnecessary noise must be done away with, or else one has to undergo some evil consequence.

Fil-kampanja ma jiswiex għana. Għax jgħidu li jekk tidħak nhar ta' Gimgħa, is-Sibt tagħli ... jinqalagħlek l-inkwiet fil-familja. U veru ...

In the country-side folk-singing is prohibited on a Friday. It is said that laughing on a Friday leads to sorrow on the following Saturday. And this is very true.[14]

This belief was corroborated by a sailor's wife from Marsaxlokk who said that one of her neighbours who was singing on this day later received the tragic news that her son could not be seen in the rough seas, although he was supposed to have entered the harbour. This belief is parallelled with the one current among the Sicilians – *Cui ridi lu Vennari, chianci lu Subbatu*. Hence informants specifically refer to the Rediffusion, today Radio Malta, a most loved medium for the transmission of programmes and pop shows and say that it must be kept at a low volume:

---

14. Ibid.

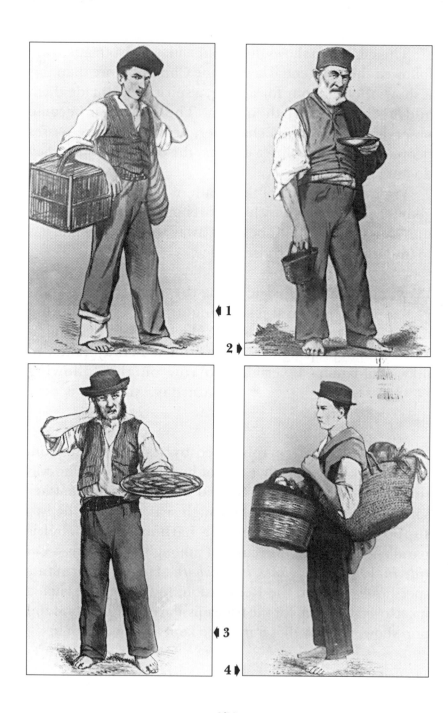

◀ 1

2 ▶

◀ 3

4 ▶

278

During these days work was kept to a minimum.

◀ *Opposite page:*
1. Poulterer   2. Shellfish vendor
3. Pie-man   4. Market boy

279

Nhar ta' Gimgħa sat-Tlieta ma jsajrux ... jieklu xott ... per eżempju ħobż u żebbuġ u hekk ... jew kien misjur il-bieraħ u jikluh illum.

On Friday up to 3.00 p.m. no cooking takes place ... unprepared food is eaten instead ... bread and olives and the like ... or perhaps food cooked on the preceding day and eaten on Friday.[15]

This quotation shows how the Maltese used to obey rigorously the Church's precept of abstinence and fasting. At 3.00 p.m. the church's bells toll to make the faithful remember the precise hour in which Christ died to save humanity. – *O ruħ x'għamiltlek jiena*, 'O Soul, what evil can you blame me for' or, as is commonly referred to, *Tat-Tlieta*, 'To be said at three o'clock' is a traditional prayer which the Maltese say at this hour.

Shaving and washing hair are actions mostly inappropriate on this day. A young informant from Żebbuġ, Gozo, told the author that she still follows this rule. She inherited it from her mother; when once she was about to wash her hair, she felt uneasy and changed her mind. She explains her behaviour by saying that she sticks to this taboo out of devotion to the death of Christ. The avoidance of shaving is analogous to the same avoidance still practised during the three days following the death of a relative.

These taboos ultimately rest on the notion that such actions as hair-cutting and shaving are ritually unclean, and hence performing them on a sacred day would defile the day.

---

15. Ibid.

Engagements and marriages are not entered upon on a Friday. The very joyous and gay atmosphere accompanying these two ceremonies are most inappropriate on the day commemorating the death of Christ. Again engagements and marriages are avoided in the immediate months following the death of a relative.

The proverb *It-tfajla li titwieled nhar ta' Ġimgħa fl-istess jum il-kelb jigdimha*, 'A girl that is born on a Friday shall be bitten by a dog on that same day' most probably means that Friday is a day of ill-omen, and therefore a most inauspicious day to be born on.

The contrast between the birth of the child and the death of Christ surely is at the root of this proverb. This bears no similarities with the belief current in Sicily where a child born on this day and even its mother are both supposed to be lucky. The child born on a Friday, *lu natu di Vennari*, would later in life be able to undertake with success the most difficult things and would be most successful in fighting. He would be able to face the *lupi mannari*, and make them recover from their *malu di luna*.[16]

It is believed that if one looks at one's image in a mirror after the *Ave Maria* on a Friday, the devil will appear. This behaviour, which is prohibited even on other days, becomes doubly tabooed because of the association of the devil with the day on which Christ died.[17]

---

16. Pitrè, 269.
17. Comments and analysis of these behaviour patterns will be given later on in this chapter, when dealing with similar taboos in conjuction with other days or feasts.

Sunday

The Christian Sunday, like the Jewish Sabbath and their common historical and anthropological prototypes, is a rest day for Christians. This is one of the Church precepts.

The Jewish Sabbath (from sunset on Friday to sunset on Saturday) was, and is, a positively blessed day, both holiday and holy day. It commemorates the last day of creation, on which God rested from his labours: 'and he rested on the seventh day from all his work which he had done. So God blessed the seventh day and hallowed it ... ' (*Genesis*, chapter 2). The fourth commandment instructs the faithful to keep the Sabbath day holy and to do no work on it (*Exodus*, chapter 20).

Jews and Christians have observed the prohibition of work on the Sabbath for centuries. However, the Christian transferred their Sabbath from the last day of the week to the first, the day on which Christ rose from the dead and the day on which they met for worship.

On this day Christians are not supposed to engage in manual work unless they have the permission of the parish priest of their village or town.[18] Through the ages the Maltese used to follow this precept scrupulously – abstinence from work, attending mass, and listening to sermons.

It is worth noting here that this custom of resting and refraining from labour on certain specific days is to be found

18. If needs arise – for example, fear of having the potato crop attacked by *ġlata*, 'blight' – the parish priest used to grant permission on condition that part of the harvest or earning had to be given to the parish priest for the maintenance of the parish church.

among peoples of totally different cultures. It might be thought that such observances originated from a utilitarian basis, namely relaxation and idleness after days of hard work. Yet, on considering the origin of these observances, it is found that they are purely based on an 'all-too-logical intellect or of a disordered fancy'.[19] They are the products of a deep-rooted fear of things unknown which find their clearest expressions in taboos and prohibitions. It can be said that the Christian Church somewhat rationalized this custom, but the faithful sometimes still became the slaves of taboo. Fear of some immediate ailment still grips many pious Christians if they do not comply with the precepts of the Church. If something sinister takes place on that day, they attribute it to their disobeying one precept or another.

On the other hand, the Sabbath of the Jews and the Sunday of the Christians still retain their characterisic of being positively hallowed days. This makes any breach of the precept all the more sacrilegious:

Il-Ħadd fl-antikament ħadd ma kien jaħdem. Isajru s-Sibt, u jikluh kiesaħ il-Ħadd. Għat-te lanqas kien hawn termosijiet. Kienu jagħmluh ġewwa l-fliexken tal-ġebel, tal-ħaġar, tal-ġinn, tal-ġnibru. Jimlewh bil-kafè u jagħmluh ġol-lożor, ġol-praken. U anqas jagħmlu

In the old days no one used to work on Sunday. They used to cook on Saturday and eat the cold food on Sunday. They had no thermos flasks to meet their needs. Instead they used to keep tea and coffee in gin bottles made of stone. They used to place these bottles

19. Webster, 1.

kafè dejjem ma kienu. Tarbija ġieli kienu jaħsluha u ġieli ma ħasluhiex ukoll. Ġieli qabdu biċċa ħarqa xotta, jitfgħulha t-terra, u ma jaħsluhiex ukoll fl-antikament ... fl-antik. Dan ma niftakrux jien.

between bed-sheets and blankets. They did not make coffee all the time. Sometimes they did wash their babies and sometimes they did not. Instead they often made use of a dry nappy with some talcum powder sprinkled on it. I do not remember these things anyhow.[20]

This information shows the puritanical behaviour characteristic of the Maltese of the past. Their deep urge to fulfil this precept made them resort to extreme methods which verge on the ridiculous. The above texts have been examples of taboo behaviour.[21]

Fishermen from the fishing communities of Malta also avoided work on a Sunday. An anecdote narrated by Ġużeppi Caruana, a fisherman from Marsaxlokk, confirms the taboo connotations of Sunday. Ġużeppi recalled that fishermen from Marsaxlokk never worked on a Sunday, not even during the high *lampuki* season which helped a great deal to

---

20. Ż. Axisa.
21. Since the author was rather sceptical about this somewhat exaggerated information given by this informant, he put the same question to the same informant a year later. The informant gave, more or less, the same answer. However, he added that they did not carry out any cooking in order not to kindle fire on a Sunday, *ma jkebbsux in-nar*, a custom which is to be found as far as Hawaii. Webster, 10.

"Fisherman from the fishing communities of Malta also avoided work on a sunday."

boost their income. But once, during this season, they went out to fetch *klamari*, 'squids' on a Sunday, so as to have enough bait for their fishing. When fishing, the following dayl, instead of catching *lampuki*, as they were supposed to do, they caught *xwabel*, 'needle fish', literally swords and swordfish. Since both fish in question have swords in common, a symbol of fighting, these were meant to be a portent of an imminent war or disaster. The informant said that this took place as a punishment for their having worked on a Sunday.

This anecdote shows the taboo mentality current among this Marsaxlokk community – although in it there is a mirror of a mentality common among humanity in general – where an inexplicable event, the catching of swordfish when they were fishing for *lampuki*, is attributed to their misdemeanour in the breach of the taboo. This event magnifies their fear of breaking the Church's law. There is also an erroneous association – the blade of a swordfish is associated with the swords of war, and so allegedly leads to disaster.

The farmer, like the fisherman, used to go to extremes to avoid working on this day, although no story could be collected to serve as an example of the scrupulousness with which this precept was enjoined. Farmers, however, all agree that 'modern' people, unlike their forefathers, work in their fields on a Sunday without in the least trying to conceal their actions.

This write-up illustrates the fact somewhat humorously:

Daż-żmien nhar ta' Ħadd sirt nistħi nersaq lejn ir-raba. Il-ġimgħa l-oħra ntasabt nindokra l-piżelli għax l-għasafar tal-bejt kienu sejrin biha daqs il-mniegħel u ħlief nies jaħdmu ma rajtx. Dari, xi kultant kont tara xi ħadd isaqqi naqra bis-serqa meta ma jkunx għadda riħ jew dawk li jkollhom l-ilma ġieri u la tkun il-ġurnata tiegħek, ikollok tagħmel li ma tridx. Fuq hekk, in-nannu kien bena għajn biex ikollu fejn jaħżen l-ilma ħalli nhar ta' Ħadd, ma jkollux għalfejn jersaq lejn ir-raba. Kilbet bl-ikrah il-lum in-nies. Saru jagħmlu kollox, jonqxu l-patata, jifflannaw u jbixxu. Rajthom saħansitra jgħaddu d-dwieli. Klibna hej. Tlifna rasna, donnu lanqas irridu nafu b'mistrieħ. Jew b'riħ jew b'riefnu, minn hawn ikollna nsiefru. In-nannu rabba familja kbira u għadda minn saram ma ngħidlekx, iżda nhar ta' Ħadd qatt ma niġġes. Kont nisimgħu jgħid li min jaħdem nhar ta' Ħadd, 'il quddiem ma marx u lura ma jafx kemm mar.[22]

In this write-up the author states that in the past it was extremely rare to see a peasant working in his fields on Sundays. Today it is completely different. The author says that his grandfather built a cistern in order to ensure that he would not work on Sunday. He quotes his grandfather saying that no progress was made by those who used to work on a Sunday. At the same time such miscreants never realize the loss which they have to suffer because of the breach of the taboo.

Deals entered into on a Sunday will not prove successful. A man who bought a horse on a Sunday found his horse dead the following week.[23] The informant attributed this to the transaction having been carried out on a Sunday and not to a change in environment which might have had a bad effect on the horse or some other consequence.

Changes in the modes of production together with the increasing tempo of life in general and the increase in education have contributed to a more rational conception of life and a decrease in the power of the taboo to regulate behaviour.

---

22. Peppi.
23. A. Zarb.

The decrease in the religious significance and connotations of Sunday have not been accompanied by a consequent decrease in holiday significance or connotations of this day.

Feasts

The religious year in Malta is marked by various feasts and rituals which reflect many of the organizational principles of the Maltese. The principal divisions of the year are emphasized by various feasts which are held either on a national or on a parochial scale.[24]

These feasts are of great help in understanding religion as a social product, since they are predominantly social in character and give expression to the feelings of the Maltese. Most of these feasts are celebrated as holidays, when secular occupations are given up and the Maltese devote themselves to religious exercises and relaxation. With the advance of culture, these feasts assume great importance from the economic and sociological standpoints, as is well shown by the feast of Saint Peter and Saint Paul (June 29); for our forebears, especially the peasants, it provided a period of relief from physical exertion.

For the community at large, these feasts provide an outlet for merry-making, as can be seen from the feasts dedicated to the titular saint of the parish. As referred to earlier on, the remission of labour during certain feasts has not always been dictated by practical considerations. In certain non-

---

24. For further details, see J.F. Boissevain, *Saints and Fireworks*, 74-96 and id., *Hal Farruġ*, 68-77.

literate communities abstinence from work during certain feasts is a part of the regular procedure for facing a crisis and the 'spiritual dangers' supposed to characterize such an occasion.

Perhaps the hypothesis can be advanced that what is holy can be contaminated by contact with the secular and the profane; hence the taboo on work. Furthermore, it can be said that the gods in a 'primitive' society are supposed to be pleased and flattered by the enforced idleness of their devotees. Abstinence from work, then, takes its place among other rites as a recognized way of expressing a proper reverence for the divinity; while, conversely, to work on this day implies a disrespectful attitude towards God.

Numerous examples of such tabooed days are to be found among non-literate societies.

In Bengal, Mother Earth is the object of much devotion. The goddess generally manifests herself as the benignant source of all things, the giver of the fruits of the earth. But sometimes she brings disease and hence requires propitiation. The chief festival in her honour occurs at the end of the hot season, when she is supposed to suffer from the impurity common to women. All ploughing, sowing, and other work cease at this time, and Bengali widows refrain from eating cooked rice. A very similar festival called *ucharal* is celebrated by the natives of the Malabar coast at the end of January, when Mother Earth has her annual menstruation. For three days at this time the people stop all work, except hunting: the house may not be cleaned; the daily smearing of the floor with cow-dung is discontinued; and even gardens may not be watered.[25]

After this sort of history of cultural evolution of certain feast days, there follow various examples from the Malta context, which still echo taboo modes of behaviour, especially

---

25. Webster, 89.

with regard to the stopping of attending to the body needs[26] and the cessation of labour.[27]

The Feast of The Cross

The Feast of the Cross is the most taboo-encrusted feast in Malta. Numerous anecdotes narrated by individuals all over Malta support this statement. Its taboo character is not only a thing of the past but still lingers on among certain individuals.

The Catholic Church used to commemorate the finding of the Holy Cross with two feasts, one on 3 May and the other on 14 September. Following the Second Vatican Council, the Church began to commemorate the September feast only. However, in certain churches of Malta, due to the extensive ties which traditionally connected it to 3 May, the feast is still celebrated on this day in Birkirkara and Valletta.

Santu Kruċ, 'Holy Rood' as this feast is colloquially referred to, commemorates the finding of the Cross by Saint Helen, the mother of the Roman Emperor Constantine.[28]

---

26. For further information and examples, see Ibid., 1, 9, 31, 39, 70, 71, 151, 155, 233, 289, 300.
27. For further examples, see Ibid., 88, 188, 303.
28. In 326, while Saint Helen was pursuing her excavations in Jerusalem, she succeeded in finding the three crosses connected with the death of Jesus Christ. Tradition says that Saint Helen succeeded in discovering which of the three crosses was the one on which Christ had been crucified, after it had been taken to a sick woman on her death-bed. The dying woman, on touching the cross on which Christ was crucified, recovered immediately. This information was given by Saint Cyril, at the time bishop of Jerusalem. The symbol of the cross was established as the emblem of Christianity, the official

This feast is the secondary feast of the parish church of Birkirkara, the titular feast being the feast of Saint Helen (18 August). Its characteristics are those of the local festa (i.e. religious ceremonies and secular celebrations) but on a smaller scale. The fireworks display and band marches together with the procession with the statue of Saint Helen constitute the outside festivities. The general feeling about this feast is one of celebration and joy. School children in government and private schools at Birkirkara on this day used to be given a holiday.

In Valletta, in the *Ta' Ġieżu* Franciscan church, the fraternity of the Holy Crucifix has been celebrating this feast on 3 May for a long time. Without going into details, it suffices to say that the Franciscan church used to celebrate this feast with great solemnity and since 1709, when the rules of the fraternity were officially recognized, the fraternity has 'obliged' itself to celebrate the feast on 3 May. In the past, religious ceremonies and secular festivities were celebrated on a grand scale. But with the passing of years other fraternities no longer took part and so the feast was reduced to a simple procession by the fraternity of the Crucifix and the Franciscan friars of *Ta' Ġieżu*.

Other parishes today celebrate the Feast of the Cross on 14 September, the day when the wood of the true Cross

---

Footnote 28 (continued)

religion of the Roman Empire, and crucifixion was abolished. Tradition says that Constantine was converted to Christianity when in 312 he saw a cross and heard a voice saying *In hoc signo vincis,* while he was going to attack one of his rivals. Following this event, which had a successful outcome, Constantine began to use the emblem of the cross on his armaments, coins, and statues.

was placed in the *Martyrium* of Constantine at Jerusalem in 336.

The general devotion towards the Holy Rood can be seen from the various niches and chapels dedicated to this religious symbol. It can also be seen from this quotation:

Kien hawn xi sajjieda, li kienu joħorġu għal wara Malta, u kienu jgħidu li meta kienu jkunu ankrata kienu jsibu ruħhom maħlulin. Huma kienu jaħsbu li kien hemm xi spirti. Imbagħad bdew jagħmlu għoqda forma ta' salib u ma bdewx jinħallu aktar.

There were some fishermen who used to go fishing off the southernmost part of Malta, and they used to say that while they were anchored they used to find the anchor ropes untied. They thought that this was the work of spirits. Thereafter they used knots in the form of a cross and they never found themselves loose.[29]

The general belief in the popular thought-idiom is that all sort of manual work must be suspended on this day. This day is also marked by the cessation of the usual daily activities and cares. Infringement of this custom leads to automatic punishments which vary in intensity according to the gravity of the act itself.

The man who forsakes the safe way of ancestral customs and who disregards the verdict of the gods or who infringes the sacred order is exposed to terrible spiritual and physical dangers. Such a man is regarded as the 'impious' man, the

29. A. Pace.

archetype of the sinner, and the criminal who is at once the object of divine vengeance and human abhorrence.

This is a universal phenomenon which is prominent in ancient mythology and ritual and which has entered so largely into modern psychological terminology of the unconscious. It is not difficult for us to understand it, since it still survives in the literary traditions of tragedy and in the basic religious concept of sin.

General opinion holds that all work is prohibited on this day. Nevertheless the prohibition is mostly connected with land cultivation and related work such as fruit growing, tilling, digging, planting, ploughing, reaping, picking, and gathering. Peasants are the most staunch carriers of this taboo-abstinence from work. For the Maltese agrarian communities it is an all inclusive prohibition.

The first spontaneous answer the interviewer is most likely to meet on asking questions about this feast is that this belief centres mainly around the peasant and his work. This is proved by the large number of stories related about this feast. Perhaps one may advance the hypothesis that the very first incident which gave root to the persistence of this taboo was closely connected with the fields. Hence the tradition moves on. It may also be because agriculture always played a major role in Malta and Gozo. Even today, although Malta is becoming an industrialized country, agriculture still plays an important subsidiary role.

All this does not exclude other trades and crafts from being put under a ban on this day. Stories are told about work which was followed by ill-luck such as stone-quarrying, fetching clay for pot-making, working in ovens, carrying of clover for animals, working in the Civil Service, hunting, and cutting grass.

Hunting and bird trapping were popular pastimes.

Although no marked geographical limitation is to be found regarding the taboo-character of this day, its strength is more clearly felt in certain localities. Hence the taboo persists strongly in Birkirkara, Mosta, and Mellieħa and their neighbourhoods. It is not felt so much in villages such as Mqabba, Kirkop, and Luqa.

This taboo is part and parcel of the mental make-up of human beings, although marked differences can be found among various individuals. Not even people of a high education are immune to this taboo. However, the ideal pattern of culture surrounding this day, although at first glance it could be categorized as compulsory, sometimes it could also be categorized as preferred, where several ways of behaviour are acceptable, but one is more highly valued than the rest; typical, where several ways of behaviour are more or less equally acceptable, but one is more often expressed than the rest; alternative, where several ways of behaving are acceptable, and there is no difference either in value or frequency of expression; or restricted, where certain ways of behaving are acceptable only for some members of society, not for society as a whole.[30]

The Feast of the Cross demands also the cessation of the usual daily activities. On this day it is prohibited to attend to such bodily needs as shaving, combing, washing oneself or infants, making bread, sweeping the floor, putting on new clothes, or milking the goats. These irrational sanctions are not attended to, to the same extent as the taboo concerning work. It seems as if they are more arbitrarily followed. However, the punishments are none the less harsh, although

---

30. Beals & Hoijer, *An Introduction to Anthropology*, 108-9.

"On this day it is prohibited to attend to such bodily needs as shaving ... sweeping ... milking the goats."

as far as the information gathered shows they are sporadic and not of the same significance as those that follow the infringement of the taboo of manual work.

These added prohibitions show the ways taboos tend to multiply on the same mistaken association of ideas that underlies sympathetic prohibitions: an object becomes tabooed because for some reason or other it reminds one of something else which is tabooed. In this way prohibition is piled upon prohibition to anticipate every single possibility of danger in the perilous maze of a world where all things are potentially dangerous.[31] Fearing that they might transgress the taboo in question and wanting to observe the rule to the letter, the Maltese added other taboos with regard to the daily activities of life. This shows the chaotic state of the mind which cannot decide which rules it has to follow and which to neglect. Consequently this leads to the piling of more taboos, for in such a situation the mind has to make decisions which are the least prone to dangerous consequences, like a direct punishment from the supernatural. They are ready to sacrifice even their property to follow the law to the letter. Sometimes this proves most detrimental to their well-being.

Ommi, nismagħha li ma nagħmlu xejn dak inhar. Li kien għaliha lanqas nagħmlu xagħarna. U lil missieri kienet tgħidlu: Tqaxxarhiex il-leħja. – U lanqas nikinsu għax niddewdu. U anqas

I used to hear my mother say that they used to avoid work completely. If it was up to her, we weren't even supposed to comb our hair. And she used to tell my father: Do not shave. – We did not even

31. Webster, *Taboo – A Sociological Study*, 5.

għaġina ma konniex nagħmlu fl-ifran. U darba minnhom kienet tirrakkontalna, ommi li darba meta kienu qegħdin jagħġnu daħal ħanżir u għaffiġilhom il-ħobż kollu. U minn dak inhar 'l hawn ma baqgħux jagħġnu ta' l-ifran. U veru ma baqgħux jagħġnu kienu. Jien niftakar il-bdiewa li ma kienu jagħmlu xejn.

Tarbija lanqas kienu jfisquha. Allura kif tkun ineħħulha l-ħarqa l-maħmuġa u barra. Il-mogħoż kienu jeħelbuhom l-għada.
MISTOQSIJA: Allura ma tagħmlulhomx ħażin?
TWEĠIBA: Allura, jissaportu. Sawwa? Jien anqas niftakar ta. Imma nisma' 'il missieri jgħid. Illum għad hawn min iħarisha.

sweep the floor. Fear of becoming lousy kept us from doing this. We did not work in our bakeries. And once upon a time my mother used to tell us, when they were preparing bread, there entered a pig which turned everything upside down. Henceforth work in the bakery was discontinued. I still remember the farmers avoiding work completely on this day.[32]
They did not even use to swaddle their babies. They used to remove the dirty nappy and leave it like that. They used to milk their goats the next day.
QUESTION: Wouldn't that harm them?
ANSWER: What can we do? They must bear it. You see? I do not remember this information I am giving you. But I remember my father saying this. Today we still find people who observe this custom.[33]

---

32. M. Muscat.
33. P. Spiteri.

Infringement of these rules is followed by immediate punishment which ranges from having one's crops infested with pests to the death of one's animals. Death of the transgressor himself is the highest supernatural punishment which can be inflicted.

Both men and animals must avoid work on this day, an injunction also found in the abominations of *Levictus*.

The consequences of taboo-breaking are, however, not always described in detail. They may be left to the excited imagination of the taboo-breaker who believes as firmly in the sequence of cause and effect (violation followed by punishment) as does the 'modern' man in the inevitable actions of natural laws.

The acts themselves many a time seem to recoil against the transgressor himself and push him directly for his misdemenaour. The acts are perceived by the people as ultimate causes of punishments involving the super-natural. It was the behaviour of the transgressors themselves which automatically brought on the punishments. This is an indication of personal guilt. The transgressor has offended the supernatural powers by breaking taboos. Many a time he may have neglected his religious duties, that is going to Church festivities or he may have exhibited anti-social behaviour. This is the explanation given to this taboo, an explanation which attributes death, illness, and other ailments to the transgressor of social or religious norms.

When a person commits an act culturally defined as wrong or evil, and he feels sufficiently guilty about it, his self-condemnation may well make him physically indisposed. This feeling may also lead to his death, so acute is the fear aroused by even an involuntary transgression. An old man from Mosta cried his heart out on telling the story of a friend of his, who died on this day while working in his fields.

In a much-quoted article, Cannon described in psychological terms how fear may cause illness and eventually can result in even death. Fear and rage, he states, have similar effects on the human organism, bringing the sympathetic nervous system into special action. Under normal circumstances, this system regulates the action of internal organs and blood vessels, but when the body is stimulated by great fear, the sympathetic nervous system accelerates the heart and other organs under its control. The blood vessels contract, the liver releases great quantity of blood sugar, and the adrenal glands send a large amount of adrenaline into the system. If this condition prevails over a period of time, the blood pressure may fall very low, and the patient dies. Persons thus knowing or fearing that they have been the victims of sorcery or supernatural punishment may well die from a true state of shock induced by prolonged and intense emotion.[34]

Among the punishments referred to by the informants there are seeds which do not take root; *baqta*, 'cream' used in making cheese which becomes worm-infested; whole stretches of fields which are attacked by pests; crops which are carried away by ants; cotton which is attacked by worms; a farmer who drowns in his cistern; a cow which is hit by lightning and killed; a balcony which falls down; a pig which attacks the baker while he is working; a cave which falls down on the workers; a hunter who is hit by his own gun; a cave which falls on the workers while they are trying to collect

---

34. Waal.

gravel; some boys who became lousy because their father had washed their heads on this very day ... however, there are other fearful and undescribed misfortunes which will dog the footsteps of the taboo-breaker.

As seen from these examples, the evils anticipated by the taboo-breaker are often identical with those which follow when a person is cursed.

In societies directly dependent on agricultural and stock-raising, it was a matter of the most immediate importance for seeds to take root in their time and plants to grow. The ever-present enemy was a failure of order, as can be seen from these accidents. Hence, when chaos came it was attributed to divinity. Their belief in the essential orderliness of the universe made them avoid work on such a day.

The persecuting tendency of such communities is that result of collective responsibility, the idea that all may suffer for the guilt of one. In this way hatred of the non-conformist becomes an expression of the sense of group welfare.

The observance of certain specific days is characteristic of all civilizations. Lucky and unlucky days are, however, a most common phenomenon in non-literate societies, although they are still to be found in modern societies. It is very difficult to assign reasons for the origin of the lucky or unlucky characteristics of these days. Usually the explanations provided, when they are provided, are based on hindsight and are not authentic reasons.

As is the case with most of these beliefs, the underlying source is to be sought in that erroneous association of ideas typical of many magical concepts. If an unfortunate event occurs on a certain day, the notion arises that all similar actions performed on that day will have the same result.

Instances of such erroneous association of ideas are

limitless. In the Middle Ages people were accustomed to attribute to Friday all the unfortunate events of religious tradition and history. It was on a Friday that Adam sinned and was driven from Paradise, Cain killed his brother Abel, John the Baptist was beheaded, and Herod slew the Holy Innocents. It was also the day of the Deluge, the Confusion of Tongues, and the infliction of the plagues upon Egypt.[35]

As regards the Feast of the Cross, owing to the financial hardship that resting from servile work implied in the past, on 8 March 1822, Pope Pius VII, at the request of Archbishop Mattei, reduced the holy days of obligation from 32 to only eight in Malta. Among these feasts which were suppressed and which were to be reckoned as feasts of half-obligation, *tal-Quddies*, on which the faithful were bound to hear Mass, but not to rest from work, there was the Feast of the Cross.

Up to this time the feasts of half-obligation were Easter Monday and Tuesday, the Finding of the Holy Cross, the Immaculate Conception, the Nativity and the Purification of the Blessed Virgin Mary, the Nativity of Saint John the Baptist, and the feasts of Saint John the Evangelist, Saint Anne, Saint Stephen, and Saint Laurence. The feasts of the titular saints of parishes ceased to be reckoned as days of obligation.[36]

Innovations find it difficult to take root. Tradition is difficult to do away with. The Maltese, accustomed for so long to innumerable days of obligation, still felt that they would be transgressing if they did not stick to the old custom of avoiding work at all costs. It might have happened that some sinister incident took place on this day which had once

---

35. For further examples on the subject, see Webster, 272-4.
36. A. Bonnici, *History of the Church in Malta,* Vol. III, 68.

been a day of obligation and this was attributed to the breach of the old custom. This established the taboo-avoidance which became deeply embedded in the minds of generations to come. These, in turn, forgot that this feast had once been one of obligation but they were still convinced that they must not work on that day. It can be said that once taboos are established and socially recognized, a condition of mind (the conscience or the sense of duty) impels to prompt unquestioning acceptance of them by everyone. Their character as 'categorical imperatives' applies equally to actions and states of being, devoid of ethical significance and to customs and institutions which the experience of mankind has proved to possess such significance.

Texts

These anecdotes which were narrated by various informants from different parts of the island shed light on the taboo-character of this feast day and its wide prevalence.

Aħna fil-Festa tas-Salib u fil-Vitorja ma konniex naħdmu fil-barrieri. Missieri darba fil-Festa tas-Salib ma ħadimx fil-barrieri iżda ħadem fl-għalqa. U ħawwel it-tuffieħ. U t-tuffieħ lanqas qabad. U mbagħad qal: La ma naħdmux fil-blat anqas naħdmu fir-raba ... Il-Festa tas-Salib kienet għażiża wisq għalina dak iż-żmien. Ħadd

We were not accustomed to work in the stone-quarries on the Feast of the Cross and on the Feast of Our Lady of Victory. One day, on the Feast of the Cross my father did not work in the stone-quarries but he worked in the fields. He planted some tomatoes. The tomatoes did not take root. And he said: Since we do not work in the

"We were not accustomed to work in the stone quarries on the Feast of the Cross."

ma kien jaħdem dak iż-żmien, ħlief iġorru xi qabda silla. Aħna qatt ma kellna l-ħila naħdmu f'xejn fil-Festa tas-Salib. Imma missieri dak inhar fettilu jiżra' t-tuffieħ. U meta ra li l-art m'għenithiex qal: Mela ma naħdmu f'xejn u la f'ħaġa u lanqas f'oħra. stone-quarries, we ought not to work in the fields either … In those days, the Feast of the Cross was most dear to us. No one worked on this day, except to transport some clover. We never had the courage to do any sort of work on the Feast of the Cross. But on that day my father thought of planting the tomatoes. And when he saw that it was of no avail he said: Then it is better not to work at all on this day.[37]

The expression *Aħna qatt ma kellna l-ħila naħdmu f'xejn*, 'We never had the courage to carry out any piece of work' suggests a deep sense of helplessness facing the taboo-day, as if some inward force was keeping them from indulging in any sort of work. At the same time this almost instinctive force was inexplicable.

Ra li l-art ma għejnithiex, 'He saw that the very earth had not been enriched' is an expression which implies a sense of solidarity between nature itself which is reluctant in conniving in any way in the infringement of the taboo and the taboo mentality itself which keeps in check man's instincts as implied in the above-mentioned expression. The coupled strength of these two forces enforces the observances of this

---

37. N. Schembri, a 70-year-old informant from Siġġiewi, in an interview with the author in September 1974.

taboo and its continuing importance in other fields of life as is suggested at the very end: *Mela ma naħdmu f'xejn. U la f'ħaġa u lanqas f'oħra*, 'Hence it is better not to work at all. Neither at one thing nor at any other'. All this shows that the ideal pattern of culture does not accept several ways of behaving, but one is more highly valued than the rest.

Another episode says:

Kien hemm wieħed u kien sejjer bil-bhima biex jaħrat l-għalqa. U n-nies qalulu: La tmurx għax illum il-Festa tas-Salib. U qallhom: La Kruċi, la Kruċetta u la Ħdud u anqas festa. – Imbagħad dik l-għalqa damet ma għamlet tliet snin. Ma nibet l-ebda ħaġa fiha. Kien wieħed mill-Għarb. In-nies kienet tgħid: Il-Bambin ikkastigah għax ma kellux imur jaħdem fil-Festa tas-Salib. Għax il-Festa tas-Salib kbira wisq. U la kellu ma jmurx jaħdem ma kellux imur jaħdem. U qal: La Ħadd u anqas festa ... – Ħadd, ħadd m'għandu jaħdem. Id-dinja llum tbiddlet. Xiħ ukoll. Marret għall-agħar. Taħseb li n-nies tal-lum sejrin il-Ġenna? In-nies jinħarqu jmorru. Ma

There was a man who, with the help of his beast, was going to till his field. And people told him: Don't go, because today is the Feast of the Cross. And he replied: Neither Kruċi nor Kruċetta, and neither Sundays nor Festas. From then onwards for three whole years that field did not yield any crops. Nothing grew in it. He was a man from Għarb. Thus people used to say: God has punished him because he should have not worked on the Feast of the Cross, because it is most holy. And as the rule is not to work on this day, he should have abided by the rule. To make it worse he said: Neither Sundays nor festas. – No one must work on this day. The

tarax kif jilbsu n-nies? Id-dbielet meta kont xebba jiena kienu jkaxkru sa l-art. U kont tagħmel dublett ieħor minnu bħal tal-lum.

world today has greatly changed for the worse. Would you ever think that today's people are going to heaven? It's to hell that they are doomed to go. Don't you see how people dress up? When I was a young woman, we used to put on skirts reaching to the ground. You can easily make two skirts, the kind they make today, from the ones we used to put on in our days.[38]

The style of the traditional narrative is perhaps even more effective in the repeated version of the *La Kruċi* story by the same informant:

Darba kien hemm wieħed mill-Għarb Għawdex. Qalulu: Toħroġx tiżra'. – U kienu jgħidulu l-Antikrist. U dan qalilhom: La Kruċi, la Kruċetta u la Ħdud u anqas festa. – U 'il bhima qallha: Ħaj, ħalli mmorru naħdmu. Minn dak inhar 'l hemm, dik il-għalqa m'għamlet l-ebda ħaġa.

Once there was a man from Għarb, Gozo. People told him: Do not go out into the fields to sow. And they used to call him the Antichrist. And he told them: Neither Kruċi nor Kruċetta and neither Sundays nor festas. And he said to the beast: Move on, off to work. From that day onwards, that field yielded nothing at all.[39]

This story is widely known especially among the

38. M. Axiaq.
39. Ibid. in an interview with the author in September 1974.

inhabitants of Għarb. Two brother priests who, for a long time, had lived in this community also quoted this story to the author. Another version of the same story given by another informant adds further information:

Kien hemm wieħed, in-naħa ta' Fuq ... it-Triq ta' Ċenċ. Kienu jaħartu l-maħluġ. Dal-qoton rama jġib ħafna flus. U sebħet il-Festa ta' Santu Kruċ. Qal: La Kruċi, la Kruċetta u la Ħadd u anqas Festa. U mar jaħrat bil-bhejjem – bil-baqar. Dik is-sena l-qoton intmess. U jekk inhu tgħaddi minn għala l-għalqa, tisimgħu d-dud jgħawwar ġol-ġewż tal-qoton. Rajtu kif il-kastigi t'Alla jaslu? Jaslu. Jaslu. Għax ikunu ġejjin minn Alla u ġejjin mix-xitan, mhux Alla jrid jippermetti?

There was a man who lived in the upper part, in Ta' Ċenċ Street ... The ploughing of the cotton fields was in full swing. This plant's produce was beginning to yield a lot of money. And there dawned the Feast of the Cross. He said: Neither Kruċi nor Kruċetta, and neither Sundays nor festas. And off he went to plough with his beasts – his cows. That year the cotton was worm infest-ed. And if by sheer chance you happen to be going alongside this field, you'll still hear the worms gnawing away at the cotton nuts. Do you see how God's punish-ments will eventually over-take you? They will overtake you sooner or later. They do. Because whether they come from God or from the devil; still it is God who allows such things to happen.[40]

40. W. Mallia.

The Maltese festa occupied an important place in the Maltese calendar.

These three variants of the same story are a clear example of a conscious almost vindictive transgression of taboo. The Anti-Christ, a nickname which in a closely-knit community such as Għarb's is a most sinister designation, stresses the irreligious behaviour of this man who consciously committed an act culturally defined as evil. This act in its turn brought about his very condemnation. Nature itself (his fields) ruined and brought to naught his activity. The informants attribute this to God the Supernatural Being:

Jiena naħseb li din il-Festa tas-Salib ftit ilhom jaħdmu fiha. Din l-iktar li ġiet mill-gwerra 'l haw'. Però anke jiena meta bdejt naħdem mal-gvern, 22 sena ilu, dik il-ġurnata kont neħodha *leave*. Jekk ma kontx neħodha *leave* kont nagħmilha *sick leave* biex tiġi. Imbagħad beda jaħdimha kulħadd anke t-Tarzna. U għalhekk ħadd ma beda ma jaħdimx. – Kienu jdaħħlulna f'rasna li jekk tagħmel xi ħaġa dak inhar, kollox jiġi bil-kontra. U għalhekk ħadd ma kien jaħdem. La fir-raba u anqas is-sajjieda. Għaliex jekk imorru s-sajjieda dak inhar tiġrilhom xi disgrazzja. U l-gabillott jekk imur jiżra' jew

I am of the opinion that it is only lately that the Maltese began to work on this day. This began to take place mostly after the war. When I was recruited by the Government, twenty years ago, I used to take a day's vacation leave on this day, or else claim it as sick leave. As time went by, people, including the workers of the Malta Drydocks began to work on this day. Henceforth the custom was no longer followed. Our fathers had instilled in our minds the idea that any work performed on this day would end badly. Hence farmers and workers did not work fearing some calamity would befall

ibejjet xi ħaġa ma kienx jitlagħlu. Jiena kelli żewġ ħut missieri, iz-zijiet tiegħi voldieri. Kienu gabillotti. U kont nieħu pjaċir immur magħhom fuq il-qiegħa, biex nidirsu b'xi ħmar. Però tiġi l-Festa tas-Salib u konna nitilgħu għassa biss fuq il-qiegħa. Anke jekk ikun riħ tajjeb biex idderri. Ma konniex naħdmu. U anke l-gabillott kien ikollu l-mitħna.

them. Neither farmers nor fishermen. Because if the fishermen were to put out to sea on that day, some tragedy would befall them. If the peasant were to cultivate the land on this day, the plants would not sprout. I used to enjoy myself very much, when in my young days I used to go with my father's two uncles, who were farmers, to watch them threshing the wheat with a donkey. But on the Feast of the Cross, we only went to the fields to keep an eye on the wheat. We did not do any threshing even if there was a good winnowing wind. The peasant did not work in his mill on this day either.[41]

Apart from the information that people ceased to observe this day as a feast of obligation after the end of the Second World War, a time which brought great upheavals in the behaviour patterns of the Maltese, this quotation sheds further light on the taboo character of this feast day. Although the informant is consciously aware that the fear of disobeying

---

41. S. Muscat.

this established norm was superimposed on them by their fathers, he still abides by the rule. Some inner feeling compels him to take a day's holiday on that day or, if this was not possible, sick leave. The informant also makes us aware that a taboo ceases to function, once infringement is not followed by the dreaded punishment. The taboo also affects the economic factor. This is exemplified by the cessation of labour even when wealth is favourable, which might increase the burden of the peasant's work. Since he depends wholly on the blowing of a favourable wind to continue his work, he may lose other work-days waiting for the right time to finish his job.

In the following anecdote we see that the authority of a taboo is unmatched by that of any other prohibition. There is no reflection on it, no reasoning about it, no discussion of it. A taboo amounts simply to an imperative thou-shalt-not in the presence of the danger apprehended. That any breach of the prohibition was unintentional or well-intentioned matters nothing; no allowance is made for either the ignorance or the praiseworthy purpose of the taboo breaker:

Jiena l-Festa tas-Salib nismagħhom jgħidu li hija għażiża wisq. Darba waħda meta kont żgħir kont il-Mosta ma' missieri. Kellu ġardina hemm. U jien kelli xi 12-il sena. U kienet il-Festa tas-Salib. Kien hemm wieħed mar għat-tafal minn Birkirkara. Kien jagħmel il-qsari. Mar għat-tafal – it-

I have heard people saying that the Feast of the Cross is very dear to our hearts. Once, when I was a young boy, I happened to be at Mosta where my father had a little garden. And I was 12 years of age. It was the Feast of the Cross. A certain man from Birkirkara – a potter – went to it-Taflija, as we call it.

Taflija, jgħidulha, aħna u sejrin Għajn Tuffieħa. U nisimgħu agħa kbira l-għassa – għax l-għassa kienet taħtna. – X'ġara? X'ġara? Qalulna: Miet tat-tafal. Mar għat-tafal u baqa' hemm. – U kulħadd jgħid: Iwa illum. Illum għażiża tant.

It is situated on the way to Għajn Tuffieħa – to collect clay. And beneath us, where the police station was situated, we heard a loud clamour: What has happened? What has happened? They told us: The potter has died. He went to fetch clay and died on the spot. – And all the people were saying: Why did he go on this day? A day which is so holy![42]

This anecdote was confirmed by another informant – Stella Debono from Birkirkara – who added that this man called *il-Banni*, did work inadvertently on this day. As seen from the above quotation, no direct reference is overtly made to connect the man's death with his work on this feast day. But in their heart of hearts the people surely attribute his death to his actions, as seen from the exclamation: *Iwa llum! Illum għażiża tant!*, 'But why! Why on such a holy day?' What seems to be sheer coincidence to the outsider of the community in question, is seen as a punishment from God for the man's misdemeanour.

The following anecdote speaks of automatic punishment as a result of the infringement of this taboo:

Fost l-oħrajn konna naħdmu jien u missieri l-Gudja

Once upon a time my father and I were working in a

---

42. K. Sammut, a 70-year-old informant from Dingli, in an interview with the author in March 1975.

313

f'maqjel (il-maqjel kien mithna qabel) – mithna tal-miexi ngħidulha aħna. Kienet ir-rota kbira, idawwarha ż-żiemel, jew inkella bagħal, proprju bagħal dak iż-żmien kienet u kif qed idur dal-bagħal kienet il-ġurnata tas-Salib, u għadda sid il-bagħal u qagħad fil-bieb. Għadda raġel u qallu: Jaqaw qed taħdem illum … ma tafx li llum Santu Kruċ? Qallu: Ħallini minn Santu Kruċ. Qallu: Il-bagħal idur qiegħed. Daħal biex jagħtih daqqtejn ta' nerv, ta' frosta, u l-bagħal sabu wieqaf bix-xokk. Ma ndunax mill-ewwel il-bagħal għaliex wieqaf. Kif tah id-daqqa ta' frosta l-bagħal waqa' għax kien mejjet. Il-bagħal kien miet dak il-ħin li qallu dak ir-raġel u s-sid wieġbu: Ħallini minn Santu Kruċ.

stockyard in Gudja. Before it had been a mill … it was worked by an animal. It had a huge wheel turned by a horse, or a mule – to be more precise, a mule at that time. It was the Day of the Cross. The mule was at its work when its owner passed by and stood in the doorway. A passer-by told him: What! Are you working today? Don't you know that today is the Feast of the Cross? And the miller replied: What care I about the Feast of the Cross? The mule is still working – nothing has happened to it. – He went in to strike the beast with the whip, and he found it standing still. At first he did not realize why the mule had stopped. As soon as he struck the mule, it fell down – it was dead. The beast had died at the very moment when the other man had talked to the owner and he had replied: What care I about the Feast of the Cross.[43]

43. P. Spiteri.

Tempering with the divine many-a-time means one's own condemnation and punishment. However, such punishments usually make the transgressor repent and once more behave himself according to the prevalent code of ethics. This can be seen from the following anecdote:

Fost l-oħrajn waħda Għawdxija (in-nanna) kellha l-forn u ma kinetx taħmi nhar il-Festa tas-Salib. U marru xi persuni u ġegħluha minn hawn u minn hemm ... ġegħluha tiftaħ il-forn u taħmi. X'ħin tefgħet in-nar, in-nar ma bediex jaħdem kif is-soltu jaħdem. Deher nar barra minn loku. Il-fjammi barra minn lokhom. U għamlet wegħda. Qaltlu: Jekk terġa' toħroġli kollox sewwa, jiġifieri l-ħobż, jien fil-ġurnata tiegħek ma naħdimx iżjed.

Once upon a time, a certain Gozitan (my grandmother) had a bakery and she never used to bake anything on the Feast of the Cross. Now some people went to her and, somehow or other, they managed to persuade her to work the oven and bake something for them. As soon as she lit the fire, it did not burn as usual. There was something strange about the fire. The flames were not in their usual place. So she made a vow. She said to the Holy Cross: If you permit everything to come out right, that is my loaves, then I promise you never to work any more on your feast day.[44]

Animals, as has already been noted, are not immune from

---

44. Ibid.

the baneful influences of this day, once infringement of the normal rules take place.

Darba waħda kien hawn wieħed minn Ħad-Dingli u kien qed jaħrat bil-baqra nhar il-Festa tas-Salib u nħallitlu l-maħanqa. Mela kif ikun qed jorbothielha ma tagħmilx sajjetta. Is-sajjetta toqtollu l-baqra u lilu ma tmissux.

Once a man from Dingli was ploughing his fields on the day of the Cross, and the cow's yoke got loose. While he was trying to fasten it – would you believe it – there flashed a bolt of lightning. The bolt of lightning killed his cow but he was un-touched.[45]

The following quotation does not have the pristine strength of the behaviour patterns of taboo character of the other anecdotes. Here, the avoidance of work in part is more as a means towards an end – that is to attend the religious functions of the Church. No severe restrictions are prescribed:

Le ... fil-Festa tas-Salib kienu jaħdmu fir-raba. Fil-barriera ma kinux jaħdmu. Ikun hemm xi ħaġa tal-bżonn ngħidu aħna tagħmel sad-disgħa u l-għaxra u taqta'. Wara nofsinhar taqta'. U xogħol imkien. Naqra ġorraba biss. Għax dak iż-żmien

They used to work in the fields on this day. But they did not work in the stone quarries. They used to attend to those chores which were really necessary up to nine and ten in the morning and that's that. No work was carried out in the afternoon.

45. Ż. Mifsud.

tal-Festa tas-Salib kien ikun hawn is-silla għar-rbit. Xogħol ta' filgħodu. Allura l-għodwa ma titlifhiex. Imbagħad wara nofsinhar kien ikun hawn il-knisja; għasar, priedka, purċissjoni, u dana kollu.

On this day no work at all could be done except in the fields, because on this day clover would be ready for stacking, a type of work which had to be carried out in the morning. Hence they did not waste the morning. In the afternoon they used to go to church to attend the religious functions.[46]

These anecdotes shed further light on the taboo character of this feast and its social significance in the past.

The Feast of Saint Catherine

Saint Catherine is the patron saint of Żejtun and Żurrieq.[47] The titular feast, normally celebrated on 23 November, is characterized by the cessation of all labour involving the use of wheels. Ill luck follows the transgressor of this rule.

Erroneous associations are at the back of this taboo.

Saint Catherine of Alexandria is the patron saint of lacemakers, spinners, rope-makers, wheelwrights, carpenters, spinsters, young women, and girl students. Her emblems are a sword and a wheel with strong spikes on its circumference. Usually she is represented as a princess, crowned and magnificently robed. Such emblems can be

---

46. M. Callus, a 75-year-old informant from Kirkop, in an interview with the author in September 1975.
47. The feast is also celebrated at Tad-Daħla, Rabat, Malta.

seen on public transport buses belonging to Żejtun and Żurrieq owners.

The proverbs which mention Saint Catherine do not hint at any taboo. They are predominantly concerned with weather-lore and landcraft, collected from personal observation, which serve as a guidance, especially for the tillers of the ground.

A story popular among the inhabitants of Żejtun and Żurrieq tells of a stubborn woman who wanted to grind her corn at all costs on the feast of Saint Catherine.

F'Santa Katerina m'għandekx taħdem, għax billi Santa Katerina kienet mitħuna, imdawra ġor-raddiena, ir-raddiena xorta waħda m'għamlitilha xejn. Fi żmien il-Gwerra l-Kbira tal-Kaiżer, kien hemm mitħna tan-nar, ta' l-*isteam*, u din il-mitħna kbira tar-riħ ... Marret mara biex titħan il-qamħ li kellha u t-taħħân ma riedx jitħan. Qallha: Illum Santa Katerina. – U sfurzat u sfurzat u sfurzat u qabbad il-magna. X'ħin qabbad il-magna, hi, il-magna qabditilha l-għonnella u taħnet lilha wkoll – iż-Żejtun, quddiem il-mitħna tar-riħ.

One must not work on Saint Catherine's Day, because although Saint Catherine's body was broken on the wheel, the wheel still did not harm her. There was, shortly after the First World War, a large steam mill at Bir id-Deheb, Żejtun. Once this woman went to have her corn ground at the mill but the owner refused saying: Today is Saint Catherine's Day – Being pestered by her, however, he turned on the engine. As soon as the engine started the woman's faldetta got caught in it and the woman was pulled and ground herself.[48]

_____

48. P. Spiteri.

A look at Maltese proverbs shows an anti-feminine bias.

Once again, while working in his fields on the Feast of Saint Anna
a farmer had his animals killed by lightning.

In a similar story the owner of another mill, sceptical about this belief, even tried to make fun of it. But while he was working, the mule which was providing the power became paralysed.

It seems as if this prohibition has to be followed only by those who come under the patronage of Saint Catherine. It is not followed on a national level, or by the rival faction, in the case of Żurrieq, who honour Our Lady of Mount Carmel as their patron saint. To spite the supporters of the titular of the parish, the supporters of the secondary feast often do just the opposite.

Informants state that those who work on their sewing-machines, grind corn in their mills, or ride bicycles on this day would be intensifying the pain felt by Saint Catherine who died on the wheel.[49]

The Feast of Saint Anna

Il-barba tiegħi f'Sant'Anna kien sejjer għad-dulliegħ. Kien hemm wieħed u talbu dulliegħa. Il-barba niżel biex iġiblu waħda. Il-baqra tatu daqqa ġo rasu u qatlitu. Jgħidu għax kienet Sant'Anna ... Darb'oħra kien hemm wieħed qed jaħdem

On the feast day of Saint Anne, my uncle went to pick water-melons from his fields. A passer-by asked him for a water-melon. While trying to fetch him one, the cow kicked him on the head and killed him. They say this happened because it was the feast of

49. For further information about the folkloristic aspect of the feast of Saint Helen, see Żahra, 'S. Katerina fil-Folklore Malti', 11, also Żurrieqi, 'Santa Katerina matul is-Sekli', 8.

| għal Sant' Anna, għamlet sajjetta u qatlitlu l-bhejjem. | Saint Anna ... Once again, while working in his fields on the Feast of Saint Anna a farmer had his animals killed by lightning.[50] |

These two passing references to incidents which took place on the feast of Saint Anne place this feast among the tabooed days of Malta. No reason could be found for the origin of this taboo, although erroneous associations must lie at the back of it. It must be kept in mind that the feast of Saint Anne had ceased to be a day of obligation on 8 March 1822, when Pope Pius VII, at the request of Archbishop Mattei, reduced the holy days of obligation from 32 to eight.

Although the incidents which were collected about this day are limited to just two, these were confirmed by various informants, among whom K. Camilleri and K. Galea, both from Mġarr. Apart from this in past days, as T. Muscat himself put it, people were afraid of speaking about such issues but today *qed jifthulu*, 'They are becoming more outspoken.'[51]

The Feast of Saint Laurence

Cooking in the oven, according to a custom prevalent among the inhabitants of Birgu, is tabooed on the feast of Saint

---

50. T. Muscat, an 82-year-old informant from Mġarr in an interview with the author in October 1975.
51. Ibid.

Laurence, which is celebrated on 10 August. This is another belief based on erroneous association because Saint Laurence was martyred on a grill.[52]

The Feasts of Saint George and Saint Sebastian

Qormi is a typical case of a village divided into two rival factions supporting different titular saints: Saint George (St George's Band Club) and Saint Sebastian (Pinto Band Club), both clubs being also known as *Tal-Werqa* and *Tal-Qalba* respectively. The taboos characteristic of these two feasts concern the colours associated with the saints in question.

Once more, these two customs are based on a loose association of ideas. In the case of Saint George, since red, the colour of blood, is associated with the saint, his protegés do not attend the celebrations performed on the feast day if they cut some part of their body: indeed, they do not even leave their residences. Similarly, vegetables are not cooked, on the feast of Saint Sebastian, whose colours are green. Infringement of both sanctions is followed by ill luck. Stories are recounted of men who, having infringed the rule, got drunk and were beaten up. A young boy was hit and gravely hurt because he did not observe the custom.[53]

The obligations attending one feast day are only binding on the faction celebrating that particular feast. The

---

52. Information given by Ġ. Cassar Pullicino to the author. Other informants from Birgu, among them 83-year-old G. Pullicino (August 1974) could not confirm this belief.
53. M. Schiavone, a 12-year-old informant from Qormi – September 1975. This information was confirmed by other informants who said that they have relatives who still observe the custom

supporters of the feast of Saint George and those of the feast of Saint Sebastian do not consider themselves affected by the other faction's custom. A story is told of a group of supporters of Saint Sebastian who in order to insult those of Saint George killed a lamb, ate it in a restaurant, and wandered around the village with the blood of the lamb in a dish. This insulting behaviour outraged the rival faction and a row ensued.[54]

Lent

The forty days of Lent, between Ash Wednesday and Easter Sunday, apart from their religious significance are a period rich in customs and taboos which come from the distant past. Most of them originate from Sicily and most of the celebrations which take place during Lent go back to the Middle Ages, towards 1300. More customs were introduced during the rule of the Order of Saint John (1530–1798).

Special ceremonies have been performed during the week preceding Easter, Holy Week, since the fourth century. The dramatic Gospel accounts of Christ's last week in Jerusalem provided a series of events that could be ritually commemorated. Most of these ceremonies originated in

---

54. As regards the popular etimology of the nicknames of the two respective band clubs – *Tal-Werqa*, 'of the leaf' and *Tal-Qalba*, 'of the sprout' we can say that up to 1893 there was only the Pinto Band Club at Qormi, founded, it is claimed, in 1862. Some of its membres left the club in 1893 and formed rival organization. To emphasize seniority the supporters of the Pinto Club said: Well, the leaf shoots forth from the sprout, and this gave rise to the two nicknames. G. Cassar Pullicino, *Studies in Maltese Folklore*, 1976, 131.

Jerusalem and were soon adopted in varying forms throughout the Church.

Good Friday, which is the end of the religious year in Malta, has the same taboo characteristics as the other Fridays of the year.

However, these prohibitions and negative sanctions are more deeply accentuated on this day.[55] On this day the Maltese follow the precepts of the Church, some of which are of a taboo character in themselves. They also add rules and customs of their own. The connection between the negative prohibitions surrounding this feast and the death-situation is evident.[56]

As has already been noted, the Church in Malta orders the rhythm of the life of the Maltese and governs it in social space and social time. This is clearly manifested in this feast where several restrictions of a taboo character are to be found not solely in the 'sacred' Church, but also in the 'profane' world. Both worlds seem to become one whole world with the procession of the Way of the Cross joining them.

The blessing of palms and olive branches on Palm Sunday gives a start to the Holy Week. After the blessing, a procession is held in remembrance of Christ's entry into Jerusalem. These olives are used during the year for fumigation to drive away the evil eye.

Back in church, the Passion of Jesus Christ is read during the Mass, as is later on done in the Masses during the Holy Week.

On Holy Thursday the functions proper to this day take place in the church. The end of the function is the rite of the

---

55. See *infra*, 142 ff.
56. Ibid.

Seven Visits. This consists of visiting seven different altars of repose or seven visits to the same altar of repose, if there is only one church in the vicinity.

On Good Friday the faithful attend the 'sermon of the three hours' and the taking down of Jesus from the cross, which is then taken in procession and placed on a side altar, followed by the 'Adoration of the Cross'. Afterwards the narrative of the Passion is read and the Blessed Sacrament is brought in and distributed to the faithful. In the afternoon, processions take place commemorating the Way of the Cross. Scenes from the Bible are enacted and the members of the Fraternity wear all-black, grey, or violet habits. The faithful follow the procession, barefooted, carrying wooden crosses on their shoulders, or with heavy iron chains shackled to their ankles. These are usually hooded in penitential robes. Funeral marches are played by bands accompanying the procession.

On Easter Eve, the churches take on a new aspect. The climax of the church's function is the *Gloria*. As soon as the *Gloria* is intoned, the whole church bursts forth into a joyous pealing of bells and the chanting of the *Gloria* by the celebrant. In the morning the statue of the Risen Christ is taken around the streets, accompanied by processions.

These secular and religious celebrations are one aspect of Holy Week. This week and Lent in general are characterized by other customs and behaviour patterns which mingle with these official and semi-official regulations of the Church to provide one whole atmosphere of gloom, with the characteristics of tabooed periods, seclusion, cessation of labour, fasting, abstinence, and other prohibitions, most of which have been dealt with in preceding sections.

The silence injunction demanded of such periods is obeyed not solely by the people but also by the Church itself.

In the morning the statue of the Risen Christ is taken around the
streets, accompanied by processions.

Bells are banned from calling the faithful to service and are tied up. A huge wooden clapper is instead set up in the belfry. The church's windows are kept shut and covered with black damask. No liturgical functions take place in the church. No entertainment is admissible. The general atmosphere is one of mourning. Clubs, cinemas, shops, and other commercial establishments are shut. Police stations, government offices, clubs, and other public centres fly their flags at half-mast. No daily papers are published.

Many individuals refrain from smoking and drinking. Women wear dark clothes and men black ties. Children are not allowed to play in the streets. Fasting and abstinence is a precept of the Church on this day. The most popular food on this day is *qaqoċċ* and *bebbux bl-arjoli*. *Karamelli tal-ħarrub*, 'carob sweets'[57] are bought in the evening from vendors on the pavements, while the procession is going by.[58]

Dire results follow if work is done in the afternoon. This is not a Church precept, but work done in the afternoon clashes with the Church's functions. This information speaks for itself:

| Omm ir-raġel kienet tgħidli | My mother-in-law used to tell |
| li fil-Ġimgħa l-Kbira jaħdmu | me that on Good Friday |

---

57. A saying about these carob sweets goes like this: *Karamelli tal-ħarrub, jekk tikolhom tagħmel dnub,* 'You'll commit sin if you eat carob sweets'. These carob sweets, which are made out of boiled carob syrup and sugar and wrapped in paper, are not to be eaten, since this day is a fasting day. Children, although not obliged to follow the fast, must try to make a sacrifice on this day.

58. More information about Maltese traditions during Lent and Good Friday is found in Cordina.

sa nofsinhar. U dak il-bidwi li jġorr is-silla wara nofsinhar mill-għalqa tiegħu sakemm jasal id-dar fl-art isirlu kollu dud.

work was only done until midday. If a farmer carries clover from his field on the afternoon of this day, it will be infested with worms by the time he gets home.[59]

Another story sheds more light on this taboo:

Darba kien hemm wieħed fettillu li kellu farka xogħol ried jagħmilha. U l-mara tagħmillu: Le tagħmilhiex illum għax illum il-Ġimgħa l-Kbira. U dak ma tax każ. U wara ftit ġiet maltempata u waqqgħetlu kollox. – Għax meta ma jkunx waqt tagħmel dak l-oġġett m'għandekx tagħmlu għax dak skandlu.

Once there was a man who had some work to do which he wanted to finish. And his wife implores him: Do not do it on this day because today is Good Friday. But he did not heed her. A little later a storm broke out and destroyed all his work – When you are not supposed to do certain work you must not do it because that is a scandal.[60]

The general gloom referred to earlier, together with the partial ban put on work, is clearly seen from this quotation:

Ara mbagħad fil-Ġimgħa l-Kbira, ġieli konna mmorru sa nofsinhar inlaqqtu żewġ

On Good Friday sometimes we used to work up to noon doing such work as picking

59. M. Callus, a 75-year-old informant from Kirkop, during an interview with the author in September 1975.
60. M. Axiaq.

piżelliet jew inlaqqtu magħlef ħaxix. Imbagħad fil-għaxija ma mmorrux għax immorru l-knisja. Il-Ġimgħa l-Kbira konna ngħożżuha bil-mewt ta' Kristu. U la daqq … lanqas qanpiena f'għonq ta' żiemel … xejn … vistu kbir. – Għax hawnhekk (f'għonqhom) dari l-bgħula kienu jorbtulhom qanpiena … kienu jkunu telgħin minn hawnhekk … tkun tafli ġejjin … ċikk … ċikk … ċikk.

peas or gathering a handful of fodder. Then, in the afternoon, we would not go back because we would go to church. This feast was very dear to us because of the death of Christ. Hence no ringing … not even a bell attached to the horse's neck … nothing. A great mourning. – Because here (around their neck) in my days mules used to have a bell fastened … they came up from hereabout … you would know that they are coming … ċikk … ċikk … ċikk.[61]

Fasting is a characteristic of any tabooed period and not solely of Good Friday. Like the Muslims and the Jews, the Maltese had the concept of some food being unclean or polluting. The act of eating meat during Lent was regarded as unclean, hence the expression *niġġeż*, 'to pollute'. No meat was eaten during these forty days. Certain informants said that they did not eat meat neither on Sundays during these forty days. It was regarded as a time in the year dedicated to prayer and *ċaħda*, 'continence'. It was normal practice for individuals to weigh their bread in order not to run the risk of breaking the fast. Thus vendors of *ftajjar tar-Randan*,

---

61. M. Muscat.

'Lenten pancakes' which consisted of fried sausages, black-pudding, liver, and kidney, at Rabat, Gozo, used to put them up for sale only during the evening.[62]

During this period, pious Maltese abstained not solely from meat but also from milk and cheese. During Lent street vendors going around with their flock of sheep used to tone down their usual cry *Ħalib*, 'Milk here' to *Hawn ta' l-abjad*, 'Here is the vendor of the white stuff' – as if to hide the fact that anybody is buying milk on a day of fasting. Unmarried girls used to perform a special form of fast called *Tas-Seba'*

The feast was very dear to us because of the death of Christ. Hence no ringing … not even a bell attached to the horse's neck … nothing.

62. Scicluna,110
63. Ġ. Cassar Pullicino, *Lenten Customs and Traditions in Malta.*

Bukkuni, Sette Bocconi, 'The Seven Mouthfuls' a rigorous fast in which not even coffee or tea was allowed and they used to go out in the morning to beg a mouthful of food.[63] The seven mouthfuls recall the seven sorrows of Our Lady. The evil consequences that followed a breach of the Lenten fast are to be found in the proverb, *Min ma jsumx f'Ras ir-Randan, imut f'denbu,* 'He who does not fast on Ash Wednesday, will die before Lent is out'.

The numerous restrictions to be found during Lent, especially on Good Friday where, together with the usual restrictions followed on this day, there are other prohibitions which show clearly that Friday is a day fraught with taboos, many of which have become part of religion.

Bells used to regulate the social time of our forefathers.

---

63. Ġ. Cassar Pullicino, *Lenten Customs and Traditions in Malta.*

The New Year

With the start of the New Year the Church bells, which up to a few years ago still directed the social time in Malta, acclaimed the presence of a renewed first moment in time in which all enter a state of ritual rebirth. The actions performed on this day are a portent of the future because this day combines sorrow for the passing year and joy for the coming year.

The completion of one phase of existence and its re-emergence into another has always been an occasion of ceremonial importance in human affairs. However, this time of the year, although representing a transition has nothing of the taboo atmosphere characteristic of tabooed periods or days of the year in general. The atmosphere is gay and full of joy. Still the sense of wonder tinged with alarm at the transition provides the motive force for various magical ceremonies which are characteristic of primary situations. Such rites in the celebration of the New Year take place all over the world.

The first of January introduces the New Year to a world of sanguine expectations. According to a folk belief, on that day the *sultan*, 'king' whitewashes the threshold of the house for us to welcome the New Year. The *sultan*, impersonated for the purpose by some needy person, asks for a favour in return – money or alms of some sort – to feed his children.[64]

The folk-rhyme uttered by the above-mentioned *sultan*, while daubing the threshold with lime, runs thus:

---

64. Aquilina, *A Comparative Dictionary of Maltese Proverbs*, 515-6.

L-għatba mbajda;	The threshold is whitewashed.
Bajjadhielek is-Sultan;	The *Sultan* whitewashed it for you;
Tih xi ħaġa karità,	Give him something of your charity,
Ħalli jitma' 'l dawk it-tfal.	so that he may feed his children.
Flok tiġieġa, tih dundjan.	Instead of a hen, give him a turkey.

This custom is now discontinued, but the Maltese author Ninu Cremona told Prof. J. Aquilina that he remembers how, when he was still a boy, a man in Rabat, Gozo, called *is-Sultan*, used to carry a sack of lime with which he smeared the thresholds of the houses and asked for some food, while offering the good wishes on the occasion of the New Year. The *Sultan* used to start his round early in the morning. The custom survives in some parts of Malta.

Why the whitewashing? The white colour of the lime is pleasant to the eyes; it suggests happiness and joy to come. It is significant that in San'a, to wish a man a happy journey, one tells him *tarig bayda*, 'Triq bajda', as in Maltese.[65]

An eighteenth-century diarist records that early in the morning on New Year's Day the doorsteps were all daubed with lime thrown by friends as a sign of good wishes for the coming year.[66] Agius De Soldanis, the Gozitan scholar who was the first librarian of the Malta Library, throws further light on this custom. Year after year, he says, this custom is

---

65. Ibid, 516.
66. Cassar Pullicino, *Studies in Maltese Folklore*, 26.

carried out by an unknown person who forms part of the *Qarinża*, which consists of a group of idle but good-humoured fellows who, on the last night of the year, go about the village playing on rustic musical instruments. One of them feigns death and lies prostrate on the ground. After much playing and singing, the leader of the company lifts up the arm of the 'corpse' and makes as if to give it to Titus; he takes the leg and gives it to Sempronius, and other parts of the body to others. This scene takes place inside the home of friends for their amusement, while food and drink are freely given to the joyful company. This goes right on throughout the night, but only in the country and not in the towns of Malta. In 1904 A. Preca recorded that a group of singers and players carried 'two enormous puppets, dressed up as a male and a female, but presenting a grotesque aspect'.[67]

These ceremonies combine the elements of birth and death. They correspond to the rites of passage of an individual's life. This is symbolic of the year that went by. On the other hand there is the symbol of life (the birth of the New Year) in the feast which takes place, which the ceremony is taking place.

In a practice that extends from East to West, the household prepares to usher in the New Year in a symbolic form. Except in the inevitable instances where sons or breadwinners had to work away on ships, all the family forming part of the household should stay at home to eat together. Non-conformity may result in the absentee expecting to die within a year. The symbol of prosperity is seen in the abundant food which is eaten on this day. Poor

---

67. Ibid.

food means a poor day. Sometimes fish was eaten as a sign of hopeful future. This is based on the belief that actions taken on the first day of the year determine the character of the ones that follow. The *strina*, which is a very ancient custom and involved the giving and receiving of New Year Presents, was meant to insure that the New Year began on an auspicious footing. In the main the *strina* in Malta consisted, and to a smaller extent still consists, in donating a coin or two to children, from relatives, shopkeepers, and neighbours.[68]

Change

On Wednesday 17 March 1977, Prime Minister Mr Dom Mintoff announced in the House of Representatives that eight feasts were no longer to remain public holidays. A Press Statement, issued simultaneously by the Church authorities on the island also revealed that following common consideration between the Government and the bishops of Malta and Gozo, the Vatican – at the request of the Church authorities in Malta approved that seven of these feasts, excluding the feast of Saint Paul (10 February) were not to remain holy days of obligation. The feasts were: St Joseph (19 March); Ascension Day, Corpus Christi, St Peter and St Paul (29 June), All Saints Day (1 November), and the Immaculate Conception (8 December).

Economic considerations were at the back of the suppression of these feasts. The news of the suppression of these feasts disturbed and saddened many individuals who

---

68. For further information about *Il-Qarinża and il-Gawgaw*, see Bezzina, 5-7.

are conscious of our national heritage, besides those who objected for religious reasons.

In the light of the information given in this chapter, and the way taboos concerned with certain days evolved, the question may be put as to whether new taboos will evolve out of this change.

Human cultures and their institutions are subject to continual change. The transformations may be so gradual that they are barely noticeable from generation to generation, or they may proceed so rapidly that they become conspicious from year to another. These rates of change are not random but are a function of numerous internal and external factors.

The cancellation of these feasts took place at a time when change in Maltese culture and its institutions was perhaps greatly being affected by internal and external conditions. These included the relative degree of cultural receptivity to new ideas, the amount of freedom of inquiry, the population size and density, and the presence of innovators and inventors.

Among increasing discrepancies between the attitudes and beliefs of an industrial age and the traditional culture the external conditions affecting this change, it is important to take into consideration the degree of contact the Maltese are having with other groups of different social and religious values and the mode of production. There has been a change in the nature of cultural contacts between the Maltese and foreign cultures. Previous cultural contacts were always associated with cultural impositions owing to the colonial status of Malta. Thus cultural change tended to be resisted.

Taking into consideration all these causes and functions of change, the effect of the cancellation of these feasts from days of ecclesiastical and legal obligation to normal working days will not have the same connotations as the above-mentioned feasts.

As regards religion and economic life, it can be said that there would have been a much more overt cultural resistence, had these or similar changes, taken place a decade or two ago. Economic activities which are basic to the survival of a group were often reinforced by religious definitions and sanctions, while today they lead almost an independent life.

Apart from all this, the essentially irrational power of the taboo has decreased. This does not mean that such empirical demonstrations will destroy the taboos at once, but many of the taboos will change.

Taboos which may have an adverse effect on the economy are common among certain communities who observe many taboo days in such a way that the pace of work is slowed down; production diminishes and, in extreme cases, this may result in the impoverishment of the community.

Too many compulsory holidays, especially when not periodic in character, result in fitful, intermittent labour rather than in a steady and continuous occupation. On the other hand, the negative regulations have often a definitive psychological value. They represent a kind of folk technique for the avoidance of possible pollution or the unwelcome attentions of the spirits. The consciousness that all precautions have been taken is itself invigorating; the social group goes forward, henceforth, with renewed strength and confidence to the tasks which lie before it.[69]

---

69. Douglas, *Purity and Danger*, 252.

Unusual Natural Phenomena

The belief in unusual phenomena as the heralds of evil events and the punishments of 'sin' and illicit behaviour is a belief of wide prevalence. It is clearly manifested in the beliefs surrounding the sky and the planets, with special reference to the moon, the sun, meteors and meteorites, comets, and the other planets, especially when these do not keep constant to their normal rhythm. Such periods have great social significance and hence generate taboos.

This taboo mentality pertains to the mode of thinking which sees unusual phenomena in the cosmos as being the automatic result of non-conformity with the norms of the community in question. This is clearly explained in the following quotation:

This taboo mentality pertains to the mythical thought-process, the logic of which rests upon the experience organic unity between man and the cosmos and leads to a magical vision of the universe in which bringing disorder in the community is thought to disturb the harmony of the cosmos; in that perspective it is to be expected that the divinity (the quasi-personal forces of the cosmos) or the ancestors (who stand for tradition) will react strongly against the human offender – all the more so since primitive societies see their universe not as an entity that can be improved upon but as a given order which it is imperative to keep intact and urgent to restore when interfered with.[70]

The Maltese, like many other peoples adhering to this 'mythical thought-process', based many of their decisions and most of their behaviour in certain periods of crises or transitions on the planets, seeing in them the regulators of many important decisions in their lives. It is this great

---

70. Bowin, *A Positive Approach to Taboo*, 100-7.

importance which in itself generates that feeling of uneasiness, characteristic of taboo, which follows the breaking of the normal rhythm of the planets, such as an eclipse, the appearance of a comet which is not a common phenomenon, or a meteor moving out of its orbit.

Taboos, according to their scope, can be either individual or social. Individual taboos affect the persons in question or at the most his family or nearest of kin and immediate connections. Social taboos, on the other hand, are binding on a group, such as a village community or a whole country.

What applies to the taboo itself applies also to the consequences of a broken taboo. The breaking of a taboo does not have effect solely on the breaker himself, but also on his fellows. The welfare of a whole village or country might be at stake for the misdeed of one of its members.

In the following examples epidemics and other catastrophes are attributed to the misdeed of particular individuals who bring the wrath of the supernatural on the whole community or country, in our case Malta. Maltese history is replete with such stories. Terrifying natural phenomena, such as thunder and lightning, violent storms, and earthquakes, are ascribed to the infraction of a taboo in the popular mind. In such instances the community should purge itself of the dangerous contagion and seek to appease by a particular sacrifice the angered divinity held responsible for the visitation.

However, these communal taboos have a positive aspect in that they help in securing the social cohesion of the community, for each individual tries to restrain himself so that no misfortune will overtake the entire social group of which he forms part.

Kewkba tax-Xuxa, 'Comet'

The sky, the thoroughfare the stars systematically go through, has been a fruitful source of omens. The process of nature is sometimes disturbed by unusual phenomena which cause anxiety and are interpreted as good or evil omens. The meteor, the eclipse, and the comet have perhaps created the greatest dread of all.[71]

Numerous stories are narrated about the comet and the catastrophes following its appearance. Most of the informants who witnessed the appearance of a *kewkba tax-xuxa,* 'comet', a long-haired star,[72] refer to the comet seen before the First World War. All of them, however, have their idiosyncratic way of narration, seeing in it a punishment for non-conformity with the norms of the community.

The belief in comets as portents of cataclysmic disasters such as war, famine, plague, the downfall of kings, or even the end of the world is worldwide. It can be presumed that this belief is based on the comet's swift and unexpected passage throughout the sky which was seen as a disruption of the orderly regularity of the heavens, heralding a parallel disruption on earth. Giuseppe Pitrè, writing on the comet, said:

Stimano alcuni che le comete presagiscono gravi calamità, morti di re, infortuni, guerre, strage, ed altri gravissimi danni: onde i più timidi sono

---

71. For further information, see Aquilina, *A Comparative Dictionary of Maltese Proverbs,* 512.
72. The designation *bix-xuxa,* long-haried or long-maned, goes back to the ancient Greeks who called stars that 'suddenly come to birth in the heaven itself ... comets ... long-haried stars because they have a blood-red shock of what looks like shaggy hair at the top'. Quoted in Ibid.

sorpresi da spaventi temendo i mali che minacciano, secondo il panico lor timore.[73]

The belief that coming events cast their shadow before them is a deeply-entrenched belief. An omen (as is the case with the comet) has been defined as some phenomenon or unusual event taken as a prognastication either of good or evil.

Omens show that men usually do not accept the rigorous fatalistic belief that the future is predetermined, but rather that they are warnings of dangers to be avoided or signals of opportunities to be seized. The information gathered so far in this regard shows that seeing a comet was taken to be not only a sign of a forthcoming disaster but also as the cause of the disaster itself.

In their turn such events, which in contrast to a secular, profane, or 'common sense' realm, belong to a sacred or supernatural realm, make the people 'repent from their sins' and change their behaviour, lest dire results should follow. As a result of events such as these, disturbing to the even tenor of daily activity, every society develops certain patterns of behaviour designed to guard against the unexpected, by one means or another, and more important still to control man's relationship with the universe in which he lives.

In the following anecdotes, mainly referring to the comet seen preceding the First World War, one can notice the great impact such an unusual event had on people and how the taboo dread instilled in them made them modify their own lives:[74]

---

73. Pitrè, *Usi e costumi, credenze e pregiudizi del popolo Siciliano*, 200.
74. For further information, see Micallef.

Din il-kewkba tax-xuxa jien niftakar kont għadni xbejba u kulħadd kien raha. In-nies kollha: Dehret kewkba kbira, b'xuxa twila. – In-nies jiġru għax kien is-sajf, għall-ħabta ta' Awissu. Kulħadd jiġri fuq is-swar ħa jaraw din il-kewkba tax-xuxa. U min jgħid ħaġa u min jgħid oħra. U kulħadd jgħid li se tiġi disgrazzja kbira fuq id-dinja. U mbagħad qamet il-gwerra. Naf ingħid li qabel il-gwerra kienu mietu salt nies kbar ... l-Isqof Pace u l-Isqof t'Għawdex. Jiena kelli n-nanna tiegħi, li kellha mitt sena nieqes ftit xhur, mietet ukoll. Xita minn dik il-qawwija. U għamel dilluvju bil-lejl. Niftakar nies kulħadd imqajjem. Imbagħad qamet il-gwerra. Dan wara li dehret il-kewkba. Jiena kelli in-nanna kienet temmen b'dawn l-affarijiet. Kienet tgħid: Dak sinjal ħażin. Gwaj kbir ġej fuq id-dinja.

I still remember this long-haired star which everyone, including myself, saw when I was a young girl. All the people said that they saw a bright long-haired star. It appeared in summer during August and one could see people running about on the bastions trying to get a glimpse of it. Everybody gave his personal opinion about this star. Many great people died at the time, Bishop Pace and the Bishop of Gozo. My grandmother, who was a hundred years old less a few months, died that year too. At night rain poured down heavily. It was a deluge! Everybody stayed awake. Then the war broke out. This happened immediately after the appearance of the comet. My grandmother used to believe strongly in these things. She used to say: That is a bad sign. A grave warning of great danger for the world.[75]

---

75. A. Smith.

Darba rajt oħra. Ħadd ma jaf x'inhi. Ħadd ma jista' jitla' fuq il-bejt, lanqas biex tonxor. Imbaj, imbaj, int. Għax dak iż-żmien meta jaraw biċċa kewkba taqa' missema, kulħadd jiġġennen, jistaħba bħallikieku Alla ma jilħqekx. Dan bluha talmohħ, ngħidlu jien, għax Alla fejn iridek isibek. Dan jiġri meta l-qalb t'Alla tkun muġugħa u ma jkunx jiflaħ iżomm bil-proxxmu. Tkun tbeżbiża ... għal dan l-ilbies li qed jilbsu u min jibqa' ħaj min jaf x'għad jaraw, għax dawn l-iskandli barra ma jistax ikun ... daqs dawn skandli. Anke fil-karozzi tistħi tirkeb għax ikun hawn nies iregħxuk. Ngħid għalija nistħi.

Once I saw another star. No one knew what it was. No one could go up to the roof, not even to hang out the clothes. All huddled up! Because in those days when they saw a shooting star falling from the heavens everyone ran to find somewhere to hide as if God would not be able to reach them there. This is a sheer craziness. That is what I call it, because God will find you whenever He wants to. This takes place when God's heart is full of pain and He cannot bear it any longer. Such events are a rebuke. A rebuke for the sort of clothes people are putting on. Who knows what scandalous things people will witness in the future. There is so much wrong-doing in the world. Today you feel ashamed when you get onto a bus because certain people's behaviour makes you shiver. I myself feel most ashamed when I see such things.[76]

76. P. Attard.

Darba fl-1914 fuq Għawdex rajna ħafna nar – sħaba tan-nar, kbir, għaddej. U rajna l-kewkba hawnhekk fil-Majjistral, bix-xuxa fuq Ġnien Ingrew. Kienet tidher kewkba b'ħafna stilel mdawrin magħha. U n-nies kienet tgħid: Imma dawn x'inhuma? Imma dawn x'inhuma? – Imbagħad ġiet il-Gwerra l-Kbira. L-ewwel waħda. U f'Santa Marija konna sejrin ix-xalata ta' Santa Marija. U qalulna: Fejn sejrin? Ma tistħux? Haw' kastig bħal dan. – Iltqajna man-nies minn Għawdex u qalulna: Illum Santa Marija … tmorrux għax waslet il-Gwerra. – U veru. Għax imbagħad bdiet il-Gwerra l-Kbira. – Is-sema kienet ħamra. U Dun Belinn qalilna: Oħorġu biex taraw xi sħaba għaddejja tan-nar. – Kien filgħaxija.

Once in 1914 we witnessed a big cloud of fire over Gozo and we saw the star in the north-west, with its hair over Ġnien Ingrew. It used to appear with many other smaller stars around it. And people used to ask: But what are these? What are these supposed to mean? Then the First World War broke out. We were going to celebrate the Feast of Saint Mary by means of an outing. And we met people coming from Gozo who told us: Today is the Feast of Saint Mary … do not go because war is imminent. – And this turned out to be true. Because not long afterwards war broke out. The sky was red in colour. And Dun Belinn told us: Come out and see for yourselves what a big cloud of fire one can behold in the sky. It was in the evening.[77]

The informant added:

---

77. M. Muscat.

Fl-antik kienu jibżgħu. Illum ma jibża' ħadd. Jiena l-Mellieħa nafha. U min jiġi minbarra 'Art Qaddisa'. In-nies kienet tiġi biex tagħmel wegħda. Mhux bħal-lum. Il-Mellieħa ma kinetx kbira daqskemm hi kbira llum. Dak li jgħidulu Ta' Snajjin, naf kamra waħda u dar waħda. Tliet toroq kien hawn. Allura min kien jiġi xi ħadd minn barra n-nies kienet tidħol tiġri ġewwa. Kienet tibża' min-nies li jiġu.

In days of old people were afraid of such happenings. Today no one fears such things. I remember Mellieħa as being a 'Sacred Place'. Even those coming from abroad used to refer to it in such a manner. People used to come on pilgrimage. Not like today. Mellieħa at that time was a very tiny village. The whereabouts of Ta' Snajjin consisted of just one room and one house. There were only three streets. The villagers were afraid of all strangers. They used to hurry indoors when they saw a stranger.[78]

This particular anecdote, apart from its vivid narration, is given in its specific context of time and place. It shows the contrast with the modern world, and the diminishing impact of such beliefs. That which once was an isolated close-grouped community, with no contacts with the outside world, has now become absorbed in the life of the nation. It also shows us that, for 'backward' people, strangers are regarded as enemies and their intentions are suspected and dreaded. This distrust and even hatred felt towards them seems to be

---

78. R. Bugeja.

based on the very fact that they are strangers. Perhaps this echoes the primitive mode of thinking, namely that strangers, since they are unknown, are invested with mysterious and dangerous qualities, which makes them carriers of evil, and hence taboos are regularly attached to them.

Another anecdote says:

Qabel il-gwerra rajt waħda ġot-Tramuntana. Kellha xuxa 'l isfel. Kienet akbar mill-bieb. Allura ommi staqsiet 'il sacerdot li kien jiġi iqaddes miż-Żejtun. Qaltlu: Dun Mabb qed titla' kewkba, rajtha? Qallha: Le, Grezz ... Kif inhu s-sejf li għandha? 'Il fuq jew 'l isfel? Qaltlu: 'L isfel. Qallha: Mela gwerra ġejja. U ġiet fl-1914 – bdiet il-Gwerra l-Kbira, avolja din kienet ikbar. U wara ħafna snin dehret oħra hawn fuq Delimara, ngħidulu għal-Lvant aħna. U qalet ommi: Qed tidher kewkba oħra. Ġej xi ħaġa. Staqsiet lill-istess sacerdot. Qallha: Mard (għax kienet immejla mhux 'l isfel u ġie mard). Kien hawn il-kolera. Veru ġie mard. Dan ilu ...

Before the First World War I saw one in the north. Its hair was long. It was bigger than the door. My mother asked a priest who used to come from Żejtun to celebrate Mass here in Marsaxlokk about it. She told him: Dun Mabb, I have seen a star rising. Have you seen it? – No, Grezz. In which position is it pointing – upwards or downwards? She told him: Downwards. He told her: Then war is close at hand. And in 1914 war was declared – the great war, although the last war we had was bigger. And after long years elapsed there appeared another one to the east of Delimara. And my mother said: Another star is making its appearance. Something is going to happen soon. She asked the same priest. He told her: Sickness (because it was tilted and not facing downwards and there really came sickness over the land). Cholera broke out. This took place a long time ago.[79]

Eclipses

According to modern anthropologists, the scientific knowledge of the causes of eclipses has not succeeded in dispelling some of the fears accompanying them. The basic reaction to a major natural disturbance like an eclipse still contains a certain amount of fear. In an age when solar eclipses were not understood these phenomena were the cause of great alarm and were generally ascribed to some supernatural agency. The Romans considered blasphemous the saying that an eclipse was the result of natural causes. During an eclipse dawn seems to happen in a few seconds and there occurs a gradual weakening of the sunlight as the moon moves across the sun, even though the sky remains clear and blue. For thousands of years astrologers have predicted eclipses and usually interpreted them as omens of disaster.

The following quotation speaks in terms of the fear which captivates the mob mentality of masses in Malta.

Meta titgħatta x-xemx isir qisu qed jidlam u kulħadd:

When the sun gets covered it seems as if it is getting dark.

---

79. Ibid.

Hi ... x'dalma ... x'dalma din! L-eklissi ... ha naraw kemm se jdum. – U kulħadd bħal speċi jibża': Tgħid donna se taqa' d-dinja? – Għax konna ngħidu: Jekk tirbaħ ix-xemx, taħraq id-dinja imma jekk jirbaħ il-qamar, dak jirbaħ dejjem għax dak magħmul raġel għax donnu l-espressjoni tal-qamar donnu espressjoni ta' raġel.

And everyone says: Oh what darkness ... what darkness! It is an eclipse ... let us see for how long it is going to last. – And everyone is terror-stricken. We used to say: Is the world going to fall? If the sun wins, it will burn the earth, but if the moon wins, it will always win, because it is quite manly, as can be seen from the expression on its face, an expression of a man.[80]

The fear that most people felt on seeing this unusual phenomenon, and which usually made them hide away to avoid being the target of this ominous spectacle, did not affect everyone. Hence when an eclipse occurred:

Konna nagħmlu fliskatur bl-ilma, nagħmlu biċċa sewda fuqu, nitilgħu fuq il-bejt, u naraw ix-xemx u l-qamar ġo fiha jiġġieldu.

We used to prepare a basin, full of water; we place a piece of black cloth over it, go up on the roof, and there watch the sun and the moon fighting.[81]

Today the moon moving across the sun is followed by means of a piece of tinted glass.

---

80. A. Smith.
81. Ibid.

Meteors

Meteors, like comets, have always been interpreted as portents of unlucky events. In an age lacking scientific knowledge about such events, people associated such unusual phenomena with the gods and their wrath for the bad conduct of Man. Scientific knowledge has made us aware of the fact that these meteors which can be seen by themselves or in showers at regular times of the year are interplanetary matter, varying in size from a mass of many tons to less than a grain of sand, which blaze by atmospheric friction.

Many tribes and peoples have their own myths surrounding these meteors, each of which directly influenced their way of living and patterns of behaviour. In Malta, like the rest of the world, shooting stars have been associated with the souls of the dead who are lost, *rwieħ mitlufa*. On seeing such a shooting star, the Maltese say *Nostrok biex tostorni sa ma tiġi l-mewt tiġborni*, 'I hide you so that you will hide me, until Death takes me with her', because if they fall on earth they will burn it.[82] In classic times a popular notion held that every human being had his star in the sky, which used to shine according to his fortune and fell down to earth under the form of a meteor when the man died.[83]

On seeing showers of meteors the populace used to fast, make vows to God and the saints, as well as perform penance, so that none of these meteors would fall on earth and burn it.

---

82. Ibid.
83. Frazer, *The Golden Bough*, Vol.II, 19.

Lacrime di San Lorenzo – għax dawk it-tlett ijiem hekk kienu jgħidulhom. Illum minħabba d-dawl elettriku ma tantx għadhom jidhru. *Bu lidi*, jgħidulhom bil-Malti. Iħobbu jidhru dawk it-tlett ijiem ta' San Lawrenz, f'Awissu – kwiekeb jiġru li kienu jibżgħu minnhom ħafna. Kienu jaħsbuhom waqgħet kewba. Kienu jmorru jistaħbew. Jibżgħu minnhom bħala xi ħaġa ħażina.

They used to call these three days *Lacrime di San Lorenzo*, 'Tears of Saint Lawrence'. Today electricity has made it almost impossible to see them. In Maltese we call them *Bu lidi*, and usually they appear in August – a shower of stars moving around which bring dread to many because they think of them as falling stars. In fact they used to hide, fearing them because they considered them as bad omens.[84]

Fire Balls

Since fire-balls are unusual phenomena, they are regarded as portents of some punishment or as a means of punishment themselves for non-compliance with the will of a supernatural agency. The following story amply supports this notion:

Meta kelli xi tnax-il sena kont sejra norqod man-nanna, minn hawn ... minn Selmun għall-Mellieħa. U x'ħin tlajt it-telgħa tal-Mellieħa, x'ħin tlajt fuq ngħidulu l-

When I was twelve years old, I was going to sleep with my grandmother. On my way to Mellieħa, on reaching the hill known as *Il-Migduma*, I saw a fire-ball coming from over

---

84. Two priests from Għarb, Gozo.

Migduma, kienet ġejja minn fuq Għawdex, balla nar xi daqs xkora mimlija ... balla nar xi daqs xkora mimlija ... balla nar xi daqs xkora. U jien ġrejt u bżajt. Imbagħad kienu qaluli li baqgħet sejra, marret daħlet minn tieqa, u ħarqet it-teatru tal-belt. Daqshekk ilu maħruq it-teatru tal-belt. Ma kienx inħaraq it-teatru tal-belt? Dik il-balla nar jien rajtha ġejja minn fuq Għawdex.

Gozo. It was as big as a full sack. And I ran because I was afraid. Later on they told me that this fire ball kept moving on and entered through a window and burned down the theatre at Valletta. The theatre at Valletta has been burned down for so long. Wasn't the theatre at Valletta burned down? I saw the fire-ball coming from Gozo myself.[85]

The informant added that this fire-ball served as a punishment for the 'great immorality' taking place in the theatre:

Dawn kollha kastigi t'Alla għax il-bniedem ma jkunx jimxi sewwa miegħu. It-Teatru Irjal qabad minn fuq l-artal għax jgħidu kienet toħroġ tqaddes minn fuq l-artal. U ġo fih kien hemm minn dawn in-nies li jieħdu l-pjaċiri, biex ngħiduha sewwa.

All these are punishments coming from God because men were not obeying Him. The fire at the Royal Theatre began on the altar where a woman used to celebrate Mass. And in the theatre there were people who used to take illicit pleasure, to tell you the truth.[86]

---

85. Ġ. Borġ.
86. Ibid.

The mystic danger of these unusual natural phenomena, which are attached to occasions when the normal current of the community life is interrupted and when what may be called a crisis presents itself, are invested with taboos to meet the emergency and to ward off the threatened danger of disaster. As seen from the given examples, on these occasions periods of abstinence and quiescence are rigidly enforced. Although the informants only gave passing information about negative regulations which are followed during such periods, it is a characteristic of such periods to follow customs which resemble some of the observances which mark the great crises in human life at birth with the deepening sense of social solidarity. During such periods the observances are not solely confined to the individual but extended to the community at large. Among such restrictions there is the suspension of the ordinary occupations, the discontinuity of public assemblage, and the prohibition of usual daily activities.

This chapter in no way pretends to be exhaustive. Various other taboos are imposed during such periods as the undertaking of a military expedition (history provides a great number of taboo characteristics of such periods); the commencement of the fishing season, a time which today is accompanied by a religious ceremony, as can be seen from the religious ceremony celebrated every year at Marsaxlokk before the opening of the *lampuki* season; the first planting; harvesting; and house-building. All these rituals and ceremonies characterize the social time in Malta.

BIBLIOGRAPHY

AQUILINA, J., *A Comparative Dictionary of Maltese Proverbs*, Malta, 1972.
–, *Papers in Maltese Linguistics*, Malta, 1970.
–, *Teach yourself Maltese*, London, 1965.
– & J. CASSAR PULICINO, 'Lexical Material in Maltese Folklore', *Journal of the Faculty of Arts*, 1 (1975), 10.
BADGER, G.P., *Description of Malta and Gozo*, 1838.
BASCOM, M.R., 'Folklore and Anthropology' in A. Dundes, *The Study of Folklore*, Prentice Hall, 1965.
BEALS, R.L., H. HOIJER, *An Introduction to Anthropology*, New York, 1971.
BENDANN, E., *Death Customs*, 1st ed. reprinted, London, 1969.
BENEDICT, R., *Modelli di cultura, un classico dell'antropologia*, Milan, 1974.
BEZZINA J., 'Il-Qarinża u l-Gawgaw' in *Il-Qawmien*, Nov./Dec. 1972, no.555.
BOISSEVAIN, J.F., *Hal Farruġ a Village in Malta*, New York, 1969.
–, *Saints and Fireworks: Religion and Politics in Rural Malta*, London, 1965.
–, *The Italians of Montreal: Social adjustment in a Plural Society*, Ottowa, 1970.
BONELLI, L., *Saggi del Folklore dell'isola di Malta*, Palermo, 1895.
BONNICI, A., *History of the Church in Malta*, Vol. III, Floriana, 1969.
–, *Malta u l-Inkisizzjoni f'Nofs is-Seklu Sbatax*, Malta, 1977.

–, 'Superstitions in Malta towards the middle of the Seventeenth Century in the light of the Inquistition Trials', *Melita Historica*, Vol. 4., No. 3 (1966).

BORG, P. P., *Selmun u l-Inħawi*, Malta, 1989.

–, *Selmun: a Story of Love*, Malta, 1996.

BOWIN, M.W.F., 'A Positive Approach to Taboo', *New Blackfriars*, Vol. 54 (1973), 634.

BROCKMANN, E., 'Maltese Memories', *Tifkiriet*, 2nd ed., London.

BUSUTTIL, V., *Holiday Customs in Malta*, Vol. XIV, 6th ed., Malta, 1948.

CACHIA, P., An Arabic's View of XIXc. Malta Shidyaq's 'al-Wasitah fi Ma'rifat Ahwal Malitah' in 'Maltese Folklore Review' Vol. 1, No. 3.

CARUANA, A.E., *Vocabolario della Lingua Maltese*, Malta, 1903.

CASSAR P., *A Medical History of Malta*, London, 1964.

–, The Meaning of the Maltese Countryside, Valletta.

–, 'The serpent of Aesculpaius, the Confraternity of SS Cosmas and Damian and the Bishop of Malta, a Medico-ecclesiastical Controversy of 1859', *The Saint Luke's Hospital Gazette*, Vol. IX(1974), 2.

CASSAR PULLICINO, J., *'Degli abiti, costumi, sponsali, matrimoni e funerali dei maltesi'* taken from manuscript no. 142, vol. 5, National Library of Malta, Conte G.A. Ciantar, in the appendix for vol. 1 of Malta Illustrata in 1770.

–, *Il-Folklore Malti* (2nd added edition), Malta, 1975.

–, 1575 – Social Aspects of an Apostolic Visit, Melita Historica, 1956, 40.

–, *Studies in Maltese Folklore*, Malta, 1976.

–, 'Lenten, Customs and Traditions in Malta', Sunday Times of Malta, 3 April 1955.

–, 'Pirates and Turks in Maltese Traditions,' Scientia Vol. XIV, 1948.

–, 'Antiche costumi nuziali maltesi', Malta Letteraria, Vol. III, Serie II, 22–24.

CASTAGNA, P.P., L-Istorja ta' Malta bil-Gżejjer Tagħha, 2nd ed. 1890, Vol. III, Appendix 97–118.

CHRISTOPHORO D'AVALOS, FELICE ANTONIO DE, *Discorso sopra la riunione definitiva di Malta alla Gran Brettagna*, Londra 1814.

CIANTAR, G.A., (Conte), Breve notizie d'alcune antiche usanze dei Maltesi, in Malta Illustrata (Abela Ciantar), 1772.

G. COCCHIARA, *Il diavolo nella tradizione popolare italiana*, Palermo, 1945.

CORSO, R., *Reviviscenze: studi di tradizioni popolari italiane*, Catania, 1927.

CREMONA, A. 'Maltese death, mourning and funeral customs' in *Maltese Folklore Review*, 1(1973), 4.

DOUGLAS, M. *Purity and Danger (A Comparative Study of Concepts of Pollution and Taboo)*, London, Routledge, 1966.

DUNDES A., *The Study of Folklore*, London, 1965.

ELLUL, E.J., *Uliedna Jistaqsu ... Inweġbuhom*, Malta, 1975.

EYSENCH, H.J., (ed.) *Encyclopaedia of Psychology*, Bath, 1972.

FERRAIRONI, F. P., *Le Streghe e l'Inquisizione, Superstizioni e realtà*, Roma, 1955.

FRAZER, J., *The Golden Bough, A Study in Magic and Religion* (Abridged edition), London, 1967

FREUD, S., *Totem and Taboo*, London, 1919.

–, *The Fear of dead in primitive religion*, London, 1933.

–, *Folk-Lore in the Old Testament: Studies in comparative Religion, legend and law*, London, 1929.

–, *Psyche's Task*, London, 1913.

GANADO, H., Rajt Malta Tinbidel, Vol. 1, Malta, 1974.

GOLDSTEIN, K.S., *A guide for field workers in folklore*, Hatboro, Pa., 1964.

HAMMOND, P.B. (ed.), *Culture and social anthropology*, New York, 1964.

HENNEN, J., *Sketches of the Medical Topography of the Mediterranean*, London, 1830.

JAHODA, G., *Psicologia della superstizione*, Italy, 1972.

KRAPPE, A.H., *The Science of Folk-lore*, London, 1930.

LACROIX, F.M., Malte et le Gozo, Paris, 1835–63.

MAIR, L., *Matrimonio: Un' analisi antropologica*, Il Mulino, 1976.

MALINOWSKI, B., *Sex, culture, and myth*, London, 1963.

–, *Magic, Science and Religion and other essays*, London, 1974.

MAPLE, E., *Superstitions and the Superstitious*, London, 1971.

MARINO, S.S., *Costumi e usanze dei contadini di Sicilia*, Palermo, 1968.

MIEGE, D., *Histoire de Malte*, Paris, 1840.

MITSHERCLICH, A., Society without the Father, London, 1969.

MITCHELL, G.D., A Dictionary of Sociology, London, 1968.

MORGENSTEIN, J., *Rites of Birth, Marriage, Death and Kindred Occasions among the Semites*, New York, 1973.

PEPPI, *Il-Mellieha*, April 1975.

PSAILA, L., *Il-Baħar Rasu Iebsa*, Malta, 1996.

PITRÈ, G., *Usi e Costumi, credenze e pregiudizi del popolo Siciliano*, Firenze, 1939.

ROGERS, R.S. (ed.), *Sex Education Rationale and Reaction*, London, 1974.

SATRIANI, R.L., *Credenze Popolari Calabresi*, Napoli, 1951.

SCHMIDT, Ph., *La Superstizione*, Milano,1961.

SCICLUNA, G., *Il-Mara li għexet*, Malta, 1975.

SINGER, J., *Taboos in Holy Scripture*, London, 1928.

STEINER, F., *Taboo*, Pelican Books, 1967.

ST. PRIEST, Chev., *Malte par un voyageur françois*, 1971.

WAAL, M. A., *Religion and Culture*, London, 1968.

WEBSTER, H., *Rest Days*, New York, 1916, republished, Detroit, 1968.

WESTERMARCK, E. *Ritual and Belief in Morocco*, London, 1926.

–, *Marriage Ceremonies in Morocco*, London, 1914.

–, *Wit and Wisdom in Morocco, A study of native proverbs*, London, 1930.

ZAMMIT A., 'Housing Concepts in Maltese Culture'– Dissertation study for the degree of Bachelor of Architecture (Honours) presented to the Royal University of Malta, June 1975.

ZAMMIT, G.A., *Il-Birgu fil-Ġimgħa ta' l-Għid - Drawwiet ta' l-imgħoddi*, Malta, 1973.

ZAMMIT, T., *Stejjer u Kitba Oħra*, edited by A. Cremona, Malta, 1961.

ZAMMIT-MAEMPEL, G., 'The Evil Eye and Protective Cattle Horns in Malta' *Folklore*, Vol. 79, Spring 1968.

–, 'Fossil Sharks' Teeth, A Medieval Safeguard against poisoning', in *Melita Historica*, Vol. VI, no. 4, 1975.

Articles in Newspapers

ABELA, J., 'Cospicua on Good Friday and Easter Sunday,' in *The Sunday Times of Malta*, 14 April 1976.

APAP, K., 'Id-Drawwiet tal-Għawdxin fl-ewwel tas-sena' *It-Torċa*, 1 January 1978.

–, 'Milied Għawdxi', *It-Torċa*, 18 December 1977.

–, 'F'Għawdex minn Ras ir-Randan sa l-Għid il-Kbir' *It-Torċa*, 8 January 1978.

ATTARD C., 'Wegħdi li saru u grazzji maqlugħa mill-Madonna tal-Grazzja' *It-Torċa*, 11 September 1977.

BORG, P. P., 'Ħaqq it-Torok tal-Ħabs', in *L-Orizzont*, 3 March 1976.

CORDINA, J., 'Tradizzjonijiet Maltin tal-Ġimgħa l-Kbira' in *Il-Ħajja*, 14 April 1976.

DIACONO, Ġ., 'Dehriet u Apparizzjonijiet' in *Il-Berqa* 6 January 1958 - 26 February 1958.

FENECH, D., 'L-Istorja tal-Festi Kmandati – Minn Mons. P. Pace sa Mons. Caruana' in *Il-Ħajja*, 12 January 1978.

GAUCI, A., 'Il-Kawkaw' in *The Sunday Times of Malta*, 12 December 1975.

–, 'The Tomb of the English Lady', in *The Sunday Times of Malta*, 11 December 1977.

LANFRANCO, G., 'Some local new year customs' in *The Times of Malta*, 23 December 1976.

M.A.C., 'Tifkiriet tal-Ġimgħa l-Kbira ta' l-1950' in *L-orizzont*, 13 April 1976.

MICALLEF, P., Kometa kbira fis-sema Malti, in *L-orizzont*, 14 February 1977.

STORACE, J.E., 'Storja u Folklore - Il-Balluta' in *Mixja*, October 1977.

VELLA APAP, N., 'Il-Ħares' in *Saghtar*, no. 38, Jan.Feb.1976.

–, 'Drawwiet fir-Rabat t'Għawdex - Id-Daqq tal-Qniepen waqt is-sajjetti' in *Saghtar* no.22. 1973, 23.

ZAHRA, W.R., 'Village Domestic Architecture' *The Sunday Times of Malta* Building and Architecture Supplement, 3 August 1975.

ŻURRIEQI, 'Santa Katarina matul is-Sekli', *In-Nazzjon Taghna*, 2 August 1977.

List of informants

The following informants were interviewed by the author during 1974–76.

Axiaq, M., 85, Żebbuġ, Gozo
Axisa, Ż., 80, Għaxaq
Attard, P., 90, Kirkop
Borg, Ġ., 75, Selmun
Borg, J., 12, Qormi
Borg, S., 50, Żabbar

Borg, W., 85, B'Kara
Bugeja, R., 70, Marsaxlokk
Bukaċċina (Il-), over 80, Nadur
Callus, M., 75, Kirkop
Camilleri, K., 75, Mġarr
Caruana, Ġ., 75, Marsaxlokk
Endrich, P., 73, Cospicua
Galea, Ġ., 80, Mġarr
Gauci, H., 45, B'Kara
Grech, Ġ., 70, Rabat
Mallia, T., over 80, Qormi
Mallia, W., over 70, B'Kara
Mifsud, Ż., over 70, Dingli
Muscat, M., 78, Mellieħa
Muscat, M., 50, Dingli
Muscat, S., 65, Mellieħa
Muscat, T., 82, Mġarr
Pace, A., 75, B'Kara
Sammut, K., 70, Dingli
Schembri, K., 8, B'Kara
Schembri, N., 70, Siġġiewi
Schiavone, M., 12, Qormi
Smith, A., 80, Valletta
Spiteri, P., 63, Tarxien
Zarb, A., 54, B'Kara